A HISTORY OF HORSEMANSHIP

A HISTORY
OF
HORSEMANSHIP

CHARLES CHENEVIX TRENCH

 LONGMAN

DEDICATION

To my Regiment,
Hodson's Horse, 1936–1947

LONGMAN GROUP LIMITED LONDON
Associated companies, branches and representatives
throughout the world

1970
© Charles Chenevix Trench

First published 1970
ISBN 0 582 10807 1

Printed in Great Britain by Jarrold & Sons Ltd, Norwich

Contents

ACKNOWLEDGEMENTS

A letter to *Horse and Hound* produced a troop of helpers, with many of whom I had a long and most interesting correspondence. I cannot name them all, but I must make special mention of Mr John Paget; Mr A. Adams, who gave me the run of his collection of historic books on equitation; Mr Tom Ryder, Mr Anthony Dent, Miss Wendy Butterfield and Miss M. Mutch, Sir John Russell, now British Ambassador in Madrid, found time to help me, as did my friend, Major Bill Enderby. Mr V. D. Browne dug deep into his boyhood memories of Boer horsemanship. My partner in this enterprise, Mr Maurice Michael, is entirely responsible for the collection and selection of illustrations. My colleague Major C. R. Burke, Chief Equitation Instructor at Millfield School, gave me the benefit of his great knowledge of modern riding. Mrs St George Saunders organized my research with her usual efficiency. To all these I am most grateful.

CHARLES CHENEVIX TRENCH

The publishers thanks are due to the directors of the following institutions for permission to reproduce articles in their possession

Alte Pinakothek, Munich
Ashmolean Museum, Oxford
Badischen Staatsgemäldesammlung, Munich
Bibliothèque Nationale, Paris
British Museum
Buffalo Bill Historical Center, Cody, Wyoming
Chapter Office, Westminster Abbey
Cleveland Museum of Art
Daigo-Ji Temple, Kyoto
Fogg Art Museum, Harvard University
Freer Gallery of Art, Smithsonian Institution
The Frick Collection, New York
Hamburger Kunsthalle
Heeresgeschichtliches Museum, Vienna
Hermitage Museum, Leningrad
India Office Library
The Irish Times, Dublin
Israel Department of Antiquities and Museums
Kaunovalst Istorinis Muziejus, Kaunas
Kungliga Biblioteket, Stockholm
Landesmuseum für Vorgeschichte, Halle
Museo Archeologico, Florence
Museo Archeologico Nazionale, Palermo
Museo Civico, Bologna
Musée de Besançon
Museo del Prado, Madrid
Muzeum Archeologiczne, Poznan
Museum für Indische Kunst, Staatliche
Museen Preussischer Kulturbesitz
Musée Guimet, Paris
Museum of Fine Arts, Boston
The National Gallery, London
Nationalmuseum, Stockholm
National Museum of Korea
National Palace and Central Museums, Taiwan
The Oriental Institute, University of Chicago
Palazzo Medici-Riccardi, Florence
The Palomino Horse Association, Mrs Edna Fagan
Państowe Muzeum Archeologiczne, Warsaw
Portuguese Information Office, London
Radio Times Hulton Picture Library
Staatliche Antikensammlungen, Munich
Staatliches Museum für Völkerkunde, Munich
Tokyo National Museum, Takeuchi Kimpli Collection
Tokyo National Museum
Topkapi Sarayi Müzesi, Istanbul
The University Museum, Philadelphia
Württembürgisches Landesmuseum, Stuttgart

and to the following photographers and private individuals:
Claude Arthaud, Paris
Charles Chenevix Trench
Baron Studios Ltd.
Ralph Brooks Esq., Ednam House Hotel, Kelso
Major C. R. Burke, R.H.A. now Chief Riding Instructor at Millfield School
Mr Werner Forman
Mr V. G. Gochneaur
Mr Gregory Lougher
Janet March-Penney
Milte & Co.
Desmond O'Neill Esq.
The Earl of Pembroke
Sport and General Press Agency Ltd.
Roger Wood Esq.

Thanks are due to the staffs of the Reading Room and many other departments of the British Museum, of the Swedish Institute, the London Library and the University Library Helsinki for their help and advice in collecting the illustrations.

1
The Ancient World

'After creating the heavens and the earth, the birds of the air and the fishes of the sea, God found it good to bestow on man a supreme mark of his favour: he created the horse. In the magnificent sequence of creation the last phase, that of perfection, was reserved for this beautiful creature. The horse was swifter than anything on the face of the earth; he could outrun the deer, leap higher than the goat, endure longer than the wolf. Man, encompassed by the elements which conspired to destroy him, by beasts faster and stronger than himself, would have been a slave, had not the horse made him king. In the Garden of Eden the horse was of no service to man, but the Fall of man revealed to the horse his noble mission.'

This excellent explanation, written in eighteenth-century France, of man's partnership with the horse, is not, alas, confirmed by the researches of the osteologist and the archaeologist. But the history they have unearthed is hardly less romantic and extraordinary; and certainly the horse has facilitated man's mastery over a hostile environment.

In their wild state horses inhabited only the great land mass of Europe and Asia north of the mountain range which runs almost unbroken from Mount Everest to Mont Blanc.

Rock-drawings, 2nd millennium B.C. *Right* Spain
Left Ladakh

Of the true horse, two types are known for certain, because they survived in the wild state until modern times. The central Asian wild horse, known as 'Przewalski's', was a stocky yellow-dun animal with dark points. A few wild specimens were captured in Mongolia between 1942 and 1945, and it is probable that some still survive there.

The European wild horse, known as the 'tarpan', a somewhat lighter, mouse-grey animal with a black dorsal stripe, survived until 1851 when the last herd was exterminated in the Ukraine because of the damage it did to crops and because of the wild stallions' partiality for domestic mares.

7

Both types are now being rebred for zoos. They can cross-breed with each other and with the domestic horse, and the progeny is fertile.

There is some evidence, not conclusive, from bones, teeth, and folk-legend, of two other types of wild horse. A white horse inhabiting the northern tundra of Europe and Asia, contemporary with the mammoth since their carcases have been found in the same ice, may have survived until modern times, since scientists searching for mammoth remains in the extreme north of Siberia heard native hunters tell of it as lately as 1926. The European forests certainly had a prehistoric wild horse which some people believe to be the ancestor of the heavy horses of Europe. That these existed is certain, but they may have been mere local varieties of Przewalski's and the tarpan.

Magdalenian cave-drawings (c. 10,000 B.C.) in the south of France strongly suggest a heavy horse, similar to the modern shire horse, quite distinct from the tarpan which is also there illustrated. But these drawings cannot be accepted as proving the co-existence of two different species of wild horses at the same time and place. Had they so existed, they would certainly have interbred, thus losing distinctive characteristics. So the differences between the horses in these prehistoric drawings can more plausibly be attributed to artistic licence and to the animal's different appearance in summer and winter coats.

We do not know how, when, or why man first domesticated the horse, thus establishing a biological symbiosis, or partnership from which both benefit, which prospers still. It was certainly later than the domestication of the dog in the late Palaeolithic Age (about 6750 B.C.), or cattle by Neolithic man before 4000 B.C., or of sheep and goats even earlier. We do, however, know where the horse was first domesticated and by whom – in the great steppes north of the mountain ranges, bordering upon the Black and Caspian Seas, by an ingenious, tough, aggressive people who spoke an Indo-European (Aryan) language.

They kept at this time no written records, but their neighbours south of the mountain ranges did. These knew vaguely of the horse as a creature of the mountains: two mentions of it have been found in clay tablets of the third millennium (3000–2000 B.C.). It is mentioned, in connection with chariots, rather more frequently in tablets written in the reign of Samsi-Adad, about 1800 B.C. But a letter written between 1750

Rock-drawings from Altamira. 2nd millennium B.C.

Altamira cave-drawing. Is the apparent nose-band intended
or a fault in the rock?

and 1700 B.C. refers to a large migration into Mesopotamia, bringing many horses
from the north. It is believed that this migration – eastward and westward, as well as
to the south – was caused by the desiccation of the Aryans' pastures and arable land;
certainly it was assisted by their monopoly of an invincible weapon of war – the
horse-drawn chariot. Against this, in open country, there was no effective counter but
other chariots: infantry would be as helpless as in the Western Desert against tanks.
Rapidly the chariot conquered the civilized world, reaching Egypt about 1580 B.C.,
Troy about the same time, Greece and India a generation later.

Even in the remote, barbaric hinterland of northern and western Europe, where
forest, mountain, and swamp precluded the use of chariots, the sudden increase of
horse-bones in connection with human settlements suggest that domesticated horses
arrived about 1700 B.C.

It has been argued that in Spain the domestication of a native wild horse,
ancestor of the Barb, proceeded independently. Evidence for this is scanty, being
based on a Palaeolithic cave-drawing of a horse with the Roman nose characteristic
of the Barb. Across its nose there is a mark which could be the noseband of a head-
collar; or it could be – just a mark. There are no other signs of domestication.

If domestication did take place independently in Spain, one would expect it to
have spread eastward across the Mediterranean, but there is no sign of it having done
so. The greatest modern authority, Professor F. E. Zeuner, thought that far more

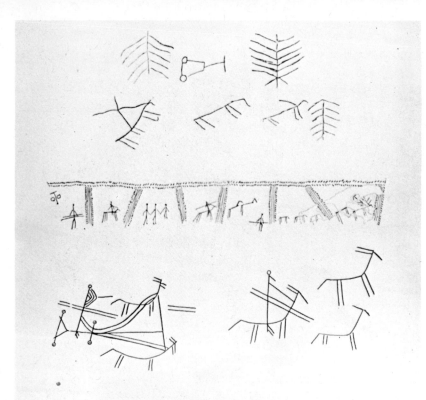

Rock-drawings
from the Hallstadt D
civilization

investigation of this point was needed before one could credit Spain as an independent centre of horse-domestication.

Since the use of chariots indicates a certain sophistication, an established practice of horsemastership, it is reasonable to suppose that the Aryans used the horse as a draught-animal well before 1800 B.C. Before that it must have been domesticated for other purposes. Where there is no evidence, one must resort to guesswork.

It can be assumed that man first viewed the wild horse simply as food. A swift animal in open country could be killed only by men and dogs in large-scale drives forcing herds into a swamp, over a cliff, perhaps into some artificial enclosure, where they could be slaughtered with ease. Pity for the young of wild animals seems to be a general human characteristic; so some of the foals would be spared, kept as pets, played with by the children, and allowed to run with the milch herds. No doubt the next step would be to milk the mares, which is easily done by hand and is practised by central Asian tribes today.

What was the next stage in domestication, riding or driving? It must be remembered that cattle, slower, more tractable and easier to train than horses, were being used as pack-animals and draught-animals even in the fifth millennium (5000–4000 B.C.), as is proved by plaques and cylinder-seals. It would, therefore, seem quite natural to use horses for draught work soon after their domestication began, probably in the third millennium. The desiccation of the steppes would enhance the value of the horse, faster, hardier, and needing less water than draught-cattle. The invention of the light spoked wheel, which made possible the light chariot, began that

Bronze sculpture
with south Arabian
inscription
2nd–3rd millennium B.C.

comradeship in war and hunting which for 4,000 years was to characterize the association between horse and man.

For war, for hunting, for ceremonial and general economic use, it is probable that driving preceded riding. But this does not, of course, mean that no one ever rode before the invention of chariots. A Sumerian plaque of the third millennium shows a man riding some sort of 'equine quadruped' but it need not have been a horse, for onagers were domesticated before horses. In the Pyrenees a very sketchy Neolithic cave-drawing, of about 2000 B.C., shows a rider, and tarpans are also shown in neighbouring cave-drawings. But here again the animal is not positively identifiable, and there is no supporting evidence of riding or even of horse-domestication in that area at that time. There is a curious cave-drawing from Djorat in the Sahara which shows a man crouching on the back of a galloping chariot-horse, holding a small round buckler. Perhaps in battle chariot-drivers employed slaves or other expendable persons as postilions.

Common sense, however, suggests that boys bringing in the milch herds in the evening would soon get the idea of being carried by a docile animal rather than walking several miles. They would find cattle, with a high-ridged back, very uncomfortable to ride, a fat mare much more pleasant. Nor would any form of bridle be necessary, as the mare would simply meander back home with the cows. Surely this must have been the true origin of riding. Perhaps the Centaur tradition grew from garbled travellers' tales of Scythians riding on horses in the distant lands beyond the Danube.

From the tomb of
Horenhab. 1600 B.C. The
rider is sitting right
back as if riding an
onager

Opposite
Hyksos bit from Tell
el-Ajjal. 18th century B.C.
Egyptian bit of
14th century B.C.

In central and western Europe carts did not appear before 1100 B.C., and the broken, forested country did not facilitate their use before the Romans opened it up with roads. But the domestication of the tarpan seems to have begun about 1700 B.C., in association with the invaders from the East using bronze battle-axes. It is, therefore, possible that there riding preceded driving. An objection to this theory is that no bits of that period have been discovered; but as bones show the domesticated tarpan to have been a small animal of 12 or 13 hands, a man could easily control him with a rope or rawhide halter, as did the American Indians.

Summing up, therefore, one can say that in its most primitive form riding may have come before driving. There is little or no positive evidence of this, but the Sumerian plaque and the various Neolithic cave-drawings that we know, mainly of the late third millennium, are not incompatible with it. But for war, hunting, or work, with which artists and scribes would be concerned more than with the antics of herd-boys, driving came first.

Archaeologists have discovered no earlier written record of horse-riding than a somewhat disparaging reference in the Mari records of the nineteenth century B.C. King Zimri-Lin advises his son: 'My lord should not ride upon a horse. Let my lord ride on a chariot or even on a mule, and let him know his royal status.' The mule seems to have been regarded as the more dignified mount, and a thousand years later Assyrian hunters were still catching onagers alive, presumably for mule-breeding. So in Ethiopia today a mule, with its smooth, quick-stepping paces and sure-footedness over the roughest ground, is regarded as the more appropriate mount for the aged, the infirm, the indolent, and the important; and one can imagine an Amharic gentleman

telling his son, 'My boy, you really can't go about on a horse. Go by Land Rover, or by mule if you like, but do not disgrace the family by travelling on horseback.'

In war, however, or in hunting, the speed and dash of the horse make him by far the better animal. The domesticated tarpan even, small, docile, and grass-fed, was better than the mule for galloping with a light chariot in and out of battle. But he had not the strength to carry a man, particularly an armoured man, fast and far. So the use of the riding-horse in war and in hunting had to await the development of a powerful charger and hunter, the work of many generations of selective breeding and, most important, of grain-feeding such as is only possible in fertile, civilized countries with grain to spare. There is, moreover, the problem of inventing a method by which a man riding bare-back can control a powerful, spirited animal. So the first pictures of men riding what are indubitably horses, and good horses at that, come from the tomb of Horenhab in fourteenth-century Egypt. (There exists a small statuette of an Egyptian riding a black horse which was supposed to date from 1580 B.C. The New York Metropolitan Museum has, however, withdrawn it from exhibition, implying that its authenticity is suspect.)

There is then a long gap in Near Eastern records of equitation. But a cave-drawing from Ladakh (the western end of the Tibetan plateau) dated about 1200 B.C. shows a mounted archer. The animal he is riding may be a kiang, the local variety of onager, or it may be a horse. If the latter, it may indicate the domestication and early use for hunting and war of Przewalski's horse. But too much should not be read into a single small cave-drawing of which even the date may be questionable.

Left
Painted horsemen of
Ti-m-Missaou in North
Africa. One is
controlling his horse
with a switch, using
neither bit nor bridle

Below
Horsemen of Liria
(Spain). 4th century B.C.

Parthian bronze
2nd century B.C.

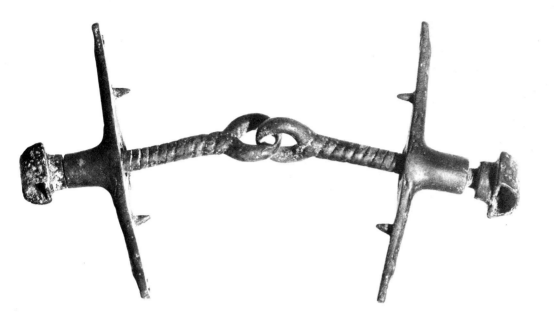

Above
Syrian bit.
4th century B.C.

Right
Mounted Amazon
riding long as
recommended by
Xenophon, but
not all Greeks
did so

Handle of an Egyptian lady's mirror

The first authentic reference to cavalry in the Assyrian Army is not until about 890 B.C. when the King of Nairi, south-west of Lake Van, was defeated in battle and made a vassal of the Assyrian Empire, bound by oath to provide a force of light cavalry. The Assyrians themselves are shown hunting and fighting on horseback during the subsequent reigns of Assurbanipal (885–860 B.C.) and Shalmaneser III (859–824 B.C.).

These crinkle-bearded, helmeted warriors seem neither relaxed, comfortable, nor proficient. Sitting far back, almost on the horses' croups like Egyptian fellahin on donkeys,* they appear somewhat apprehensive and ride like beginners, very 'short', with knees bent, gripping nervously with heel and calf. The archers each have a man riding beside him, leading his horse so as to leave his hands free for the bow. They are not horsemen.

The armoured cavalry of Tiglath-Pileser III (747–727 B.C.) look far more competent. They still sit rather far back: perhaps they have been 'left behind' by their horses' sudden forward impulsion. But they ride fairly 'long', gripping from knee to crutch, not with the lower part of the leg. These are horsemen, riding well-bred, light-weight horses of about 14·2 hands. It is not surprising that they scattered their enemies like chaff before the wind.

Those depicted are riding bare-back, but evidently this was not universal, for both before and after them Assyrian warriors are shown using fringed saddlecloths, secured by breastplate and crupper. One cannot see what was in their horses' mouths, but it must have been a sort of snaffle for their horses have no bend at the poll: they are extended, not collected. The bridle is held in position by browband and throat-lash. The cheekstrap is divided, like an inverted Y, the lower arms being attached one to each end of the oblong cheekpiece of the bit. (This form of bridle, with various types of bit, was general in the ancient world.)

The cavalry of Sennacherib (705–681 B.C.) who 'came down like a wolf on the fold,' sat on girthed, quilted saddlecloths, where the saddle is now. With conical helm, knee-length shirt of mail, spear, and straight sword, they resembled Norman knights at Hastings. Those of Assurbanipal, hunting lions or zestfully chasing bewildered,

* It will be noted that one of the riders in Horenhab's tomb has the same position, which can only be the adaptation to horse-riding of the seat which is most comfortable on a donkey. British officers in the early days of the occupation of the Sudan, riding out to dinner on donkeys, used the same seat.

Egyptian horses of 14th century B.C.

camel-mounted Bedouin, ride much as we do, without stirrups, today. They sit well down, with backs hollowed, eyes looking their own height, upright except when they lean forward to shoot. They grip from crutch to knee, and one's only criticism is that the lower part of the leg is slightly forward of the perpendicular, with toes pointing down.

Clearly the horse was no longer the small, docile, shaggy, grass-fed pony which had come over the mountains a thousand years before. Pedigrees, we know, were recorded, a proof of purposeful, scientific breeding. A bas-relief of an Assyrian cavalry camp in the ninth century (900–800 B.C.) shows horses being fed, presumably with grain, from mangers.

It is generally believed, though never proved, that the nomadic Hyksos introduced the horse to Egypt when they infiltrated in large numbers during the seventeenth century (1700–1600 B.C.). The Hyksos are usually identified with the Children of Israel. Whether or not the Israelites had ever been horsemen, they certainly were not by the seventh century B.C. Neighbours, enemies, and intermittent, unwilling subjects of Nineveh, their military history is of constant conflict between this hill-tribe and the horsemen inhabiting the plains on three sides of them. References in the Old Testament to this noble animal are scanty and not infrequently disparaging. 'Some put their trust in chariots and some in horses', but not so the Children of Israel. When David defeated the King of Zobah on the Euphrates, he captured 2,000 horses, 700 horsemen, and 20,000 foot: but the horses he caused to be hamstrung, reserving enough for only a hundred chariots. Absalom was plainly, and fatally, unable to control his mount, although it was, significantly, only a mule. The Israelites were, however, perfectly familiar with veterinary bills: 'The horseleach hath two daughters, crying, "Give! Give!"'

Job, indeed, paid a noble tribute to the war-horse. 'Hast thou given the horse strength? Hast thou clothed his neck with thunder? Canst thou make him afraid as a grasshopper? The glory of his nostrils is terrible. He paweth in the valley and rejoiceth in his strength: he goeth on to meet the armed men. He mocketh at fear and is not affrighted; neither turneth he back from the sword. The quiver rattleth against him, the glittering spear and the shield. He swalloweth the ground with fierceness and rage; neither believeth he that it is the sound of the trumpet. He saith among the trumpets, Ha, Ha; and he smelleth the battle afar off, the thunder of the captains and the shouting.' But this military paragon was most unlikely to have been an Israelite's steed: more probably it came with hostile intent across the desert from Assyria, the land of 'captains and rulers clothed most gorgeously, horsemen riding upon horses,

Horse-archers of Shalmaneser III still using the
back seat. 9th century B.C.

18

Cavalry of Tiglath-Pileser IV. 8th century B.C.
The riders are now riding well forward

all of them desirable young men' – and men, moreover, on whom certain daughters
of Israel doted, earning thereby the Prophet Ezekiel's disapprobation – an early
example of the familiar association of cavalry officers with fast horses and fast women.

During the sixth century B.C. military superiority passed to the Persian Empire,
where a larger, stronger horse had been bred for heavy cavalry. This may not have
stood much higher than the Assyrian horse, but was clearly up to more weight. Its
Roman nose and generally coarse appearance suggest an infusion of Przewalski blood
from central Asia, where the Persians would have been in touch with Turks, Huns,
and Mongols. In the sculptures, these horses are both over-bent and over the bit,
presumably by intent to make them more controllable but at the cost of impulsion
and speed. It is difficult to see how, with no form of curb, this could have been
achieved; for a snaffle of any kind, however severe, acting on the corners of a horse's
lips pulls his head up: it needs a curb to make him bend his head down. Perhaps the
Persians used a spiked noseband such as is now sometimes used in Spain, producing
there also horses which are often over-bent and over the bit: one can see on the front
of the noseband a projection which might be the stud of a spike. (Beware, when

buying a horse, of a sheepskin noseband: it may conceal a drawing-pin, placed there to encourage a collected head carriage.) This, indeed, seems likely, for the noseband, without cavesson or martingale, can really serve no other purpose. The throatlash is secured by a toggle, buckles not yet being invented. The divided cheekstrap is attached to the cheekpiece of the bit, which is carved at one end in the shape of a phallus, and at the other in the shape of a horse's hoof – a common convention, symbolic perhaps of a stallion's fertility. The mouthpiece of the bit is invisible. The bridle is tasselled and embellished with boar's tushes, the heavy forelock tied with ribbon, an elaboration which would be condemned in fox-hunting or Pony Club circles. Perhaps the Persians did not go very hard.

For centuries Arab horses have been esteemed for their speed, beauty, great hearts, fire, and gentleness. They are, indeed, the foundation of the English thorough-bred stock. Not unnaturally claims have been advanced that they and the Barb from North Africa, a somewhat similar animal but with a Roman nose instead of the Arab's dished profile, are a separate and superior race, descended neither from the tarpan nor from Przewalski's, but from a third root-stock. There is no archaeological or osteological evidence to support this. There are no prehistoric drawings of wild horses in Arabia, nor any indications of chariots or horsemen there prior to the Aryan invasions. The geographer, Strabo, writing during the lifetime of Our Lord, empha-sizes that there were then in Arabia no horses whatsoever. He was probably mis-informed: some must have been brought in from the north. But the Arab horse was of no economic importance and of no military repute for several more centuries.

In North Africa it was another story. Horses reached there some time in the middle of the second millennium: Saharan rock-drawings of horses and chariots suggest that they were well established by the thirteenth century, and Rameses III, invading Libya in 1175 B.C., brought back horses as loot. Probably the horse arrived

Assyrian huntsmen. 9th century B.C.

Assyrian mounted archer

via Egypt, though it may have been brought by the 'People of the Sea'. There is an Egyptian drawing of a horse being transported by boat.

The Garamantians, from whom may be descended the modern Touaregs, in the time of Strabo bred 100,000 horses a year, and long before this time had spread their conquests over the Sahara wherever the horsed chariot could go.

As riding replaced chariot-driving for sport and war, and horses were bred larger and stronger to carry armoured horsemen, control became more difficult. The ancient chariot harness pressed on the horse's windpipe, so checking him. Whereas a charioteer can lean back, feet braced against a footboard, and take a strong pull on the reins, a man riding without saddle or stirrups cannot. In considering ancient horsemanship we must always remember this; for though with a well-schooled horse one should not need to lean back and pull, most horses are not well schooled. Moreover, a charioteer could use both hands for controlling his horse: his passenger did the fighting. Far more attention, therefore, had to be paid to stopping and steering the riding-horse.

The Numidians, riding very small ponies, did it all without bridle or bit, simply by taps of a light stick, even in battle. Livy, usually an accurate historian, describes the Numidian light horse in Hannibal's army as contemptible in appearance, the ponies and men tiny and gaunt, the riders armed only with javelins. 'The ponies were without bridles, their ugly gait that of animals running with stiff necks and out-stretched heads.' They kept riding up to the Roman positions, then retiring, coming closer and closer as though their ponies were out of control. Then, suddenly, they spurred through the Roman outposts and ranged over the open country beyond, firing buildings and creating havoc in the Romans' rear.

Silius Italicus, writing about sixty years later, describes these tribesmen 'plying a light switch between their horses' ears, and the horse obeys, as docile as with a Gallic bit'.*

* That is to say, a curb-bit. See p. 33.

21

North African horsemen also seem to have used, according to Strabo, a single rein passing over the horse's poll, between the ears, and either attached to a nose-ring or muzzle, or knotted round the horse's lower jaw. All three methods are used today in the Sahara, but only for camels. They even used a sort of collar, similar to that used on the earliest chariot-horses, which stopped a horse by pressing on the carotid artery.

A vase-painting of the fourth century B.C., however, shows a Numidian riding quite a good-looking animal, and indubitably using bridle, reins, and bit. Perhaps those who travelled or served as mercenaries in foreign armies learned foreign methods: or perhaps their own style of equitation was adequate for small, docile, grass-fed ponies of the desert, but more positive methods of control were required for the grain-fed horses of the fertile areas of the maritime belt, from which is descended the Barb horse of modern times.

Early Egyptian chariot-drivers, those who pursued the Israelites into the Red Sea, used a dropped noseband so low that when the reins were pulled the noseband tightened across the nasal cartilage, making it difficult for the horse to breathe and thus impossible for it to bolt. This was not, however, very satisfactory, for one should be able to stop or slow down a horse without half-stifling him.

So there was developed, by the time of Horenhab (fourteenth century B.C.), a bit operating on the horse's mouth. These early bits were all forms of snaffle which in its most primitive state is simply a bar, held by the cheekstraps of the bridle across the horse's mouth and in contact with the corner of his lips. To each end of this bar is attached a rein which the rider can pull, and some kind of cheekpiece to stop the bit being pulled to one side through the mouth.

From very earliest days horsemen have elaborated on this simple device. The first elaboration was to replace the plain bar mouthpiece with a jointed one. This is more difficult for the horse to hold between his teeth or to get his tongue over, tricks

Attendants of Sennacherib. 7th century B.C.

Assyrian cavalry

which frustrate a bit's purpose; moreover, as the reins are pulled, not only does it press into the corners of the lips but, by a sort of nutcracker action, it squeezes the horse's face on each side. It is, nevertheless, a very mild bit, with which it is almost impossible to hurt a horse. The squeeze effect can be increased by furnishing the cheekpiece with spikes which stick into both cheeks when both reins are pulled, causing the horse to stop or slow down; and stick into one cheek when the opposite rein is pulled, causing him to turn. Such bits need not be cruel: the severity would depend on the length and sharpness of the spikes. They have been found in Egypt (fourteenth century B.C.), Scythia, Luristan, and India, so widespread as to suggest that the Aryans invented them before their dispersal. At the same time a bit from Olympia of the fifth century shows that the solid bar mouthpiece with plain cheek-pieces was still used, and it comes down to us as the half-moon snaffle, the mildest bit known.

To make the snaffle more severe, the Greeks and Persians of the sixth century onwards furnished the mouthpiece with sharp-edged discs and spiked rollers, making it, in heavy hands, an instrument of torture producing in the unfortunate animal's mouth flecks of bloody foam. More intelligently they sometimes fitted to the mouthpiece short lengths of chain or a smooth roller, to give the horse something to play with or, as Xenophon said, to 'pursue with his tongue', thus discouraging him from taking the bit between his teeth. Some modern snaffles, such as the chain-snaffle or breaking-snaffle, have a similar gadget, to keep the horse's mouth moist and so make the bit easier for him.

23

Neo-Babylonian. About 500 B.C.

There is no reason to suppose that Greeks were better horsemen than Assyrians, Persians, or Gauls: they may well have been worse. But we know more about Greek horsemanship because of the extensive literature which has survived from Heroic and Classical Greece, including a manual of equitation by a cavalry general, Xenophon, and fragments of an even earlier manual by Simon. There are no contemporary writings on equitation in other countries, though clay tablets from Assyria do give some instructions on the feeding and conditioning of chariot-horses brought in from grass.

In considering Greek horsemanship, four facts must be borne in mind. Their horses were unshod; their broken, rocky country, with steep hills and narrow valleys seamed with watercourses, puts a premium on collection rather than extension and free forward movement; they rode bare-back; and, riding bare-back on well-bred, spirited animals of about 15 hands, almost all stallions, they resorted to very severe, indeed cruel additions to their snaffle-bits to keep their horses under control.

Modern horsemen would not agree with Xenophon's views on the carriage of head and neck. 'The horse's neck should rise straight to the poll. . . . Thus the crest will be in front of the rider.' Although he added that the neck should be 'flexible at the bend', that is to say, should bend at the poll, most illustrations of Greek horses show far too high a head-carriage and virtually no bend at all, the horses poking their noses instead of (to use a non-technical expression) tucking in their chins.

Xenophon's theories must be considered in the light of modern ideas on 'balance' and 'collection'. An early and essential part of a horse's training is to get him balanced. In the words of the British Army's *Manual of Horsemanship, Equitation and*

Animal Transport, 'a horse is said to be balanced when his own weight and that of his rider is distributed over each leg in such proportion as to allow him to use himself with the maximum ease and efficiency at all paces. The head and neck form the governing factors in weight distribution, and it is by their position that the horse carries his centre of gravity forward or backward as his paces are extended or collected.'

Balance results from training and exercising over many months: it is only when a horse is properly balanced that he can be collected.

'A horse is said to be collected when his head is raised and bent at the poll, his lower jaw relaxed and his hocks brought well under him, so that he has the maximum control over his limbs and is in a position to respond instantly to the least indication of his rider.'

The curb is designed to make a horse bend his head at the poll. Without a curb, unless one resorts to the barbarity of the spiked noseband, this is very difficult, and requires more leg-action than seems possible for a bare-legged rider on a bare-backed horse. A snaffle, however severe, by acting on the corners of the horse's lips, raises his head but does not easily make him bend at the poll. So Greek pictures generally, not always, show the horse's head raised high and the hocks well under him, but little or no bend at the poll, because they did not use the curb-bit. With such a head-carriage the centre of gravity is well back, so that the horse cannot possibly achieve an extended gallop.

Furthermore, the Greeks nearly always rode stallions, which tend to carry their heads high as can be seen when one is showing off before a mare.

So this awkward head-carriage was the result of riding bare-back and without a curb-bit powerful and spirited stallions. In Xenophon's own words, 'a horse with this type of conformation would be least able to bolt even if he was very spirited. For it is not by flexing the neck but by stretching it out that horses endeavour to bolt.'

Xenophon used both 'rough' (or severe) and 'smooth' (or mild) bits, both essentially snaffles. The former, with or without the compressing action of the cheekpieces, was used generally for training a young horse: when sufficiently schooled, he graduated to a smooth bit. The severity of the rough bit, with its sharp discs and 'hedgehogs' made it necessary to ride with a loose rein. Any pull on the rein would make the horse fling up his head and perhaps rear. (There seems to have been no martingale.) The ancients had no notion of riding a horse into his bit.

Unfortunately, Xenophon gives no instructions on horse-breaking. (Odious expression! A young horse should be made, not broken.) We do not know how the Greeks set about this. As there is no mention of preliminary longeing or long-reining, the probability is that (like an Irish farmer I know) they simply put up on the unbacked colt 'a bold fellow, of no consequence', and let him get on with it.

Mounting a 15-hand horse bare-back is easy for the young and agile, but for those of riper years and stately build presents difficulties which must have been accentuated by heavy armour. To mount on the near side, wrote Xenophon, the rider should hold the mane with the left hand behind the horse's ears and with the right hand over his withers: then, pulling down with the left hand and pushing up with the right, vault on to the horse's back. The illustration on page 45 shows a rather corpulent boy attempting this feat without much success. Since the Greeks rode

Head of the horse on page opposite

generally without trousers, care must be taken in mounting, said Xenophon, lest one present an unseemly spectacle from behind.

If the rider carried a spear, he should hold this, instead of the mane, in his left hand, using it almost as a vaulting-pole to help himself up. Mounting-blocks were sometimes used by the elderly or the dignified, either made of stone or improvised by a kneeling slave: but the Greeks did not give the rider a leg-up as we do. Some horses were trained to crouch while being mounted (Persian horses, to kneel). I often ride a

26

Persian cavalry-horse. Clearly a much heavier,
coarser type than those used in Greece or Assyria

Spanish horse who has this considerate habit, straddling his legs so as to lower himself by several inches.

Xenophon rode 'long', with almost a straight leg. 'We do not recommend the seat as in a chair, but that which is like a man standing upright with his legs apart. For the thighs in this way have a better grip on the horse, and with the body erect one can with more force hurl the javelin and strike from horseback if necessary.'

Nevertheless, the straight-legged seat was by no means always used. Most

Etruscan horseman. 7th century B.C.

vase-paintings show Greek riders with the leg slightly bent, and in some the rider is actually sitting as though on a chair. The lower leg, he said, should hang loose, which must mean with the toe pointed down. (It was a long time before horsemen realized that raising the toe and lowering the heel strengthens the grip of the riding muscles between knee and crutch.) The body from the loins upward should be as supple as possible.

Xenophon's was to remain the orthodox seat for European horsemen until the twentieth century, and still the orthodox seat in the 'Western style'.

There were no saddles with trees: some of Xenophon's contemporaries used saddlecloths, but these were generally regarded as effete devices for soft-arsed Orientals. The Persians, remarks Xenophon severely, 'put more coverlets on their horses than on their beds, for they think of sitting softly rather than securely'. Most Greeks rode without trousers of any kind, only a few young dandies aped the Thracian fashion of breeches and boots. In a warm climate this was, oddly enough, not a great disadvantage. The bare human skin, provided it is hardened by practice, gives a good grip on the horse's sides, particularly when both are slightly sweaty. It was, after all, how Comanches and other Indians of the western plains rode, and they were

28

rated highly as horsemen. I have seen some remarkable Chinese pictures, unsuitable for these chaste pages, of ladies and gentlemen engaged in singularly ingenious amatory performances on bare-back horses. They could hardly have given their minds to these had they felt in imminent danger of sliding off.

Xenophon insisted on his men being trained and practised at riding across country. This meant negotiating small stone walls, eroded watercourses, and the banks of terraced hillside fields. He taught a young horse to jump by leading it across obstacles, while an assistant standing behind stimulated its courage with a whip. 'If he refuses, let someone hit him as hard as possible, and he will jump not only the distance required but far beyond it. And in future there will be no need to hit him, but if he just sees someone coming up behind him, he will jump. When he is used to jumping in this manner, one may mount and put him first of all at little jumps, and later at bigger ones too. When he is about to jump, strike him with the spur. In the same way teach him to jump up and down banks by striking him with the spur.' Xenophon rightly trained a horse to jump not off his forehand, but off his hocks, 'for if he does these things with his body collected, it will be far safer for both horse and rider than if he leaves his hind-legs behind him, whether in jumping over obstacles or on and off banks'. Sensibly, he did not disdain holding on to the mane rather than risk being 'left behind' and jabbing a horse's mouth. Oddly enough, Greeks never seem to have made up artificial jumps.

Nor did Greeks think of steeplechases, though they liked flat racing, wagering large sums on it. For training in cross-country riding Xenophon recommended hunting 'whenever suitable country and wild beasts exist'. He himself was an enthusiast on hound-work, and kept a pack of beagles which he hunted on foot. Vase-paintings, however, show fallow-deer and wild boar being speared by horsemen.

Boeotian horsemen – one is about to be thrown

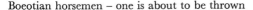

Greek horsemen of 6th century B.C.
Note the divided reins

He devised a sort of cross-country 'follow my leader', with one horseman chasing another, each armed with blunt javelins. His troopers, he said, when riding out from Athens to visit their farms, should always go across country, practising their horses in jumping and in riding at speed up, down, and across steep slopes.

One can hardly open his book on equitation without coming across some passage which might have been written yesterday. Horses, for instance, must be accustomed to leaving others and moving away alone. What cavalryman has not cursed the brute who objects to leaving the ranks? 'Never lose your temper in dealing with horses: this is the best of all precepts. . . . When a horse suspects some object and is unwilling to approach it, you must explain to him that it is not terrible, especially to a courageous horse, and if this fails, you must yourself touch the object that he thinks dangerous, and lead him up to it gently. But those who compel the horse with blows make him more frightened than ever. For horses think, whenever they receive any harsh treatment in such circumstances, that the suspected objects are responsible for that too.'

Xenophon's system of schooling a young horse was based on rewards and punishments. 'For men to instruct their fellow men in proper behaviour, the gods have granted the power of speech. But a horse can obviously learn nothing from mere words. But if when he behaves according to your wishes you show him some kindness in return, and when he is disobedient you punish him, in this way he will most easily learn to serve you as he ought.' For rewards there were rest, dismounting, soothing words, the relaxation of pressure on the bit: for punishments, whip, spur, and repetition of a botched movement.

The Greeks set a lot of store on making their horses 'splendid', 'brilliant', spectacular to ride on ceremonial parades or religious processions. They liked a horse to curvet, lift his head high and flex haughtily, like a stallion displaying himself before a mare. 'Indeed a curvetting horse is a thing so admirable that it captures the eyes of all beholders.' A high cadenced trot, with feet picked well up, free action, and high head-carriage should be the rider's aim – known in modern High School parlance as 'the passage'.

A cavalry commander, who wants to impress his fellow citizens, should indeed make all his troop display their horses proudly. 'The clatter of the hooves and the neighing and snorting of the horses will follow right at his back, so that not only he but all his followers will present a worthy appearance.'

Attic horseman

Dispatching a mounted
Greek soldier

Greek horses

Armoured
horseman of
Grimentum riding
very short.
About 550 B.C.

Below
North African horsemen
using switches

More to the point for active service, a cavalry leader on a campaign should be meticulously careful in matters of forage, water, quarters, and outpost duty. On the march he should rest the horses' backs and the men's legs by constant interchange of riding and leading.

Horses, Xenophon believed, should be taught always to canter or gallop with near-fore leading. It has been pointed out that this is most comfortable for a man carrying a spear in his right hand, and on Greek racecourses the circuit was always to the left. So to make a trotting horse canter, his head should be turned to the left and the aids given just as he was on the off-fore diagonal. Xenophon does not seem to have contemplated changing the leading leg at a canter or gallop, though he practised 'figures of eight'.

34

Xenophon is particularly good on riding a spirited horse. 'When you are mounted you must calm him for a longer time than an average horse, and in making him advance use the aids as gently as possible. . . . Sudden actions produce alarm. . . . Long, quiet rides settle a spirited horse down, but do not expect him to quieten by riding fast and far. Do not let him gallop at full speed, and never let him gallop alongside another horse. . . . Smooth bits are more suitable than rough; but if you do put a rough bit in his mouth, you must make it smooth by slackening the rein. . . . Upon the sound of a war-cry or of the trumpet you must neither let yourself appear alarmed to the horse, nor treat him in any way that may alarm him; you shall make him stand still, and if circumstances permit, you should actually bring him his morning or evening meal.'

As for a sluggish horse, Xenophon curtly advised the rider just to do the opposite of everything he would do with an animal of spirit.

We do not know how or when the horse reached Italy, but the style of Italian riding and bits suggest that it came from the Greeks, not the Gauls. The earliest record of Italian riding is a vase-painting of an Etruscan Army on the march in the seventh century B.C., about the time of Lars Porsena of Clusium. During the

Republic and Early Empire the Romans seem to have followed the Greek practice in equitation. But they were not great horsemen; their strength and pride lay in their heavy infantry of the legions, and the cavalry were mere auxiliaries, generally of barbarian subject peoples.

Nearly all horsemen of ancient times rode stallions. Horses must have been very scarce in rélation to the demand: Xenophon, during a personal financial crisis, sold a favourite horse for 1,000 drachmae, which was a brigadier's pay for a whole year: 300 drachmae would buy only a moderate animal. Mares were, therefore, very seldom ridden but were kept for breeding. The operation of gelding was all very well for slaves, but far too painful and dangerous for horses. Riding a stallion, particularly on active service, has many drawbacks: he may become quite unmanageable in the presence of a mare in season; he may bite and have to be led around in a muzzle; he will certainly fight other stallions, and neigh loudly on a secret night march just when silence is required. Nevertheless, in Xenophon's time and for hundreds of years afterwards, soldiers generally rode stallions.

Only the Scythians, Aryan barbarians living with great herds of horses on the plains north of the Danube, preferred mares and geldings in war for the rather recondite reason that stallions were always stopping to stale. The same could not be said of the Scythians who remained in the saddle while answering the minor calls of nature. This accomplishment, invaluable for fox-hunters, or at least for male fox-hunters, requires some co-operation by the horse and no little dexterity on the part of the horseman.

Bringing tribute. Persepolis.
6th century B.C.

Naked horsemen attacking deer.
6th century B.C.

With its steep, rocky hillsides, sparse grazing, and shortage of water during the campaigning season, the greater part of Greece is poor cavalry country, offering neither opportunity nor encouragement for the development of the mounted arm. Only in the plains of Thessaly and Macedonia could cavalry operate to advantage. With neither curb-bit, saddle, nor stirrups, shock-action was impossible. Xenophon makes this perfectly clear in a passage of his *Anabasis* written to encourage the Greek infantry to stand up to Persian horse. Ten thousand cavalry, he points out, are but ten thousand men, 'for no one ever perished in battle from being kicked or bitten by a horse. The foot-soldier can strike harder and with truer aim than the horseman, who is precariously poised on his steed and as much afraid of falling off as he is of the enemy.' The only advantage, said this cavalry general, of having a horse in battle is that one can take to flight with more celerity.

No doubt he would have written very differently had he been addressing his own troopers. But these used neither the couched lance nor the long sword, proper weapons for a charge. They were far too insecurely seated for shock-tactics. An extended gallop might carry them willy-nilly into the enemy ranks, with most unhappy consequences; the 'good, round trot' favoured by Cromwell in battle might have been almost as unsettling. So one can assume that they advanced at a slow canter, hurled javelins, their principal weapon, from fifteen or twenty yards and then wheeled round – a dangerous moment, this – and retreated.

37

It does not seem as though equitation developed much between Xenophon and Alexander. It is, therefore, extremely doubtful if Alexander's horsemen charged home in the proper sense of the word, though they might exploit an opportunity created by his tactical genius, outflanking an enemy or thrusting into a gap in the front of an over-extended phalanx. In pursuit, however, they came to their own. 'Men might drop and horses might founder', but Alexander after a victory pressed the pursuit until the enemy was utterly broken.

Despite the Greek inventive genius, the greatest development in horse-bitting was made not by them but by the Celts. Gauls invaded Asia Minor late in the third century B.C., and settled in the region which became known as Galatia. These barbarians, who were to be the backbone of the Roman cavalry, not only developed a remarkably modern-looking snaffle; but also, of far greater importance, invented the curb-bit.

The essence of the curb is a bar, thong, or chain which runs from one cheekpiece to the other fitting snugly into the horse's chin groove. The reins are attached to the bottom end of the cheekpieces, the cheekstraps to the top. When the reins are pulled, the curb-chain (or its ancient equivalent) acts as the fulcrum of a lever, so that the mouthpiece presses not upwards into the corners of the horse's lips, but downwards against the bars of his mouth, compelling him to bend his neck at the poll and so

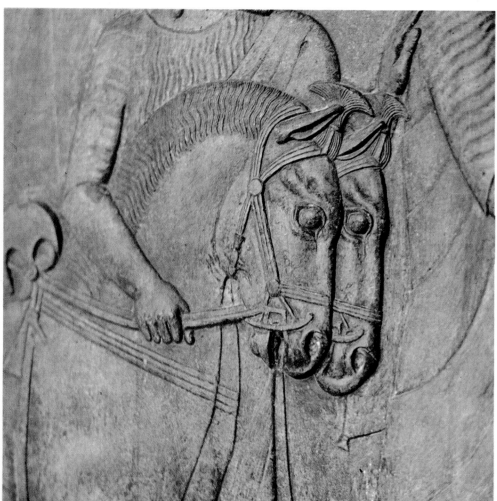

Persian horses.
Persepolis

Opposite
One of the
earliest
representations
of the stirrup.
4th-century A.D.
jug of the
Silla kingdom,
Korea

Clazomenian youth on
horseback. 6th century
B.C. The bridle is
decorated and has a
nose-band, throat-lash
and divided cheek-strap.
Bit with curved cheek-
pieces

Bokephalus
(oxhead)

Alexander the Great on
Bellerophon

Bellerophon rode
Pegasos!

Opposite
Head of Persian riding-
horse. 6th century B.C.
Massive head, Roman
nose different to finer
animal of Egypt, Greece,
and Assyria. Throat-lash
is fastened by toggle.
None of the other straps
looks capable of being
undone

40

The frog. Perhaps the
only thing about which
Xenophon was wrong

'tuck in his chin'. Spiked mouthpieces and other horrors are thus unnecessary (though they were still used): the horse is controlled not by brute force nor by pain, but by firm, gentle pressure applied at a mechanical advantage.

It is possible that the curb-bit was also used by Celtic Spaniards in the fourth century. Vase-paintings from Valencia show what seems to be a curb, but they are too small for one to be certain. They might show a thong tied round the lower jaw as is done in training young horses by Mexicans and gauchos today.

Thus at the beginning of the Christian era the civilized horseman, Greek or Persian, rode straight or almost straight-legged, straight-backed, on a stallion which was collected in that he had his hocks well under him, but was not bent at the poll. This collection was particularly necessary in the rocky terrain of Greece, and probably in the mountainous parts of Persia too, where control was more important than speed. But horsemen of the open plains such as the Assyrians and (as we shall see in the next chapter) Scythians rode in quite a different manner, with a loose rein, allowing free forward movement, their horses extended, not collected. The curb-bit was used only by its inventors, the Celtic barbarians. Three very important inventions – the horseshoe, the saddle-tree, and the stirrup – were about to be devised.

2

The Roman Empire and the Dark Ages

The first five centuries of the Christian era saw inventions and developments which transformed the art of equitation and, with it, the art of war. Unfortunately, they produced no Xenophon. Horsemen, then as now, tended to be inarticulate if not completely illiterate; so we have no direct evidence of their methods, but must infer what we can from statues, bas-reliefs, and archaeological remains.

The horseshoe seems to have been invented during the first century A.D. (See Chapter 11.) It enabled the horse to work all the year round in any part of the Empire. It did not, however, alter the style of riding.

For the first two centuries or so after Julius Caesar cavalry formed an unimportant part of the Roman Army. The legion was a wonderfully efficient and flexible infantry formation and found no difficulty in dealing with the trans-frontier tribes who were,

Horse 'portraits' from Roman North Africa

in the main, undisciplined, unorganized, unarmoured, and armed only with light javelins. The legion seemed to be the final solution to all problems of war, and its occasional defeats – by Herminius in Germany, by Parthian horse-archers at Carrhae – were thought to be isolated phenomena from which no lessons need be drawn. The legion needed, to be sure, some cavalry for reconnaissance, flank protection, and pursuit, but this was composed of *alae* ('wings') of auxiliary horsemen recruited from subject peoples and barbarians from the outer darkness.

Gradually, however, in the second and third centuries A.D., cavalry increased in numbers and importance. The barbarians became more formidable as more and more of them served in the Roman Army, learned Roman discipline and tactics, acquired armour and Roman-type weapons. In eastern Europe and Asia they were generally mounted, and having crossed the frontier, could pillage the provinces at will, avoiding battle with the slow-marching legions. Even in north-west Europe, where they had few horses and usually fought on foot, they were far more mobile than the legionaries. To round them up and bring them to battle, the Romans needed more cavalry.

A typical Roman frontier post, Newstead in the Scottish Lowlands, was garrisoned during the third and fourth centuries A.D. by a regiment of German cavalry,

The riding lesson
(*see page 25*)

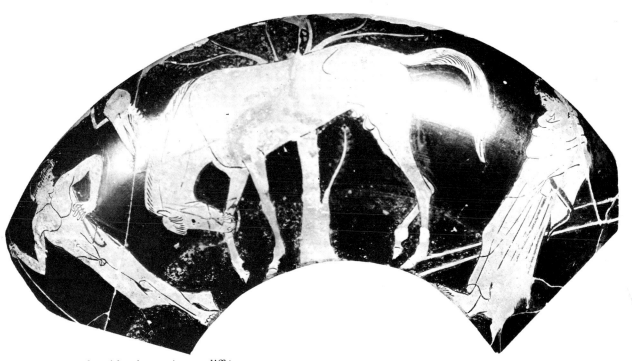

Two youths with a horse. A very different type
of animal to that on which the boy is being taught

Bringing tribute of horses to the Great Khan.
14th century A.D.

the Vocontian *ala*, composed of sixteen troops each of thirty men, and a headquarters troop. Archaeologists' diggings at Newstead disclose that the Vocontian *ala* was mounted for the most part on light well-bred ponies of about 12·2 hands; their baggage was carried by coarser, heavier ponies of the same height. There were also a few better animals, well-bred ponies between 14 and 15 hands, which might have been officers' chargers. They seem to have been kept in open horse-lines, probably protected by a wind-break, and were clearly too small for shock-action, but were used for skirmishing and patrols.

All cavalry stations had a cavalry parade-ground, presided over by *Campestres*, Gallic goddesses adopted as their special deities by the Roman cavalry. Some had also indoor riding-schools, thatched or roofed with tiles or shingles, for training in bad weather. Here troopers were practised in weapon-training with sword, javelin, and sometimes bow; and in equitation, including jumping over walls and ditches. For elementary training, wooden horses were used. They also practised skirmishing and mounted combat, either singly or troop against troop, protected by long shields and gilded, masked helmets. Perhaps this was the truth behind the legend of Arthurian tourneys.

The place where Roman cavalry was kept most busy was the Dacian frontier, constantly plagued by raids by the Scythians, perhaps the most horsey people who ever existed.

46

Our knowledge of the Scythians is curiously patchy, derived mainly from their Greek neighbours and from chiefs' tombs, for they had no writing. We do not even know their racial stock. Most pictures, bas-reliefs, and carvings show Scythians as bearded men with European features; but the skeletons in some Scythian tombs in their eastern grazing-grounds are of men of Mongol features, beardless but supplied with false beards of horsehair. Probably the Scythians came from that race of Aryans known as Iranian, but in the East interbred with Mongol Turks and Huns.

They may have had a few agricultural settlements, but were generally nomadic in habit, endlessly on the move, up and down the wide plains of the Crimea, Kuban, and Ukraine, seeking in summer grazing and water for their horse herds, camping in winter under the lee of a ridge where their precious horses could shelter from the bitter north winds. They wore, not the robes of the Greek and Roman worlds with which they fought and traded, but horsemen's clothes – woollen trousers and a warm hooded tunic.

They were very formidable in war, their principal weapon being a composite, double-curved bow made of horn. Being a horseman's weapon, it had to be short, but was very stiff and drawn to the ear. The maximum range of such a bow was probably about 500 yards; but shot from the saddle, its maximum *effective* range was probably about 100 yards. The Scythian's short sword, with a blade about two feet long, and his dagger, strapped to his leg, were hardly weapons for fighting on horseback, which indicates that Scythians relied on their bows for fighting, and did not charge home or fight hand to hand if they could help it.

They customarily beheaded their fallen foes and carried the trophies slung, like a fox's mask, from the saddle. Sometimes they found it more convenient to scalp a foe, making an incision all round the head above the ears and then, holding the hair, shaking out the skull. The scalps were hung from the bridle-rein, sewn into cloaks or used to cover the Scythians combined quiver and bow-case; while the skull, lined with gold (which was very common among these people) made a handsome goblet.

Somewhat savage in war, in peace these horse-people were lazy, humorous, pleasure loving, well fed.

The Scythians did not adopt the Gallic curb: their bit was a plain jointed snaffle, with long, straight cheekpieces. The saddlecloth was large, about six foot long, presumably, like the modern cavalry blanket, folded under the saddle during the march and used by the rider at night. Those found in tombs are made of felt, gorgeously embroidered and tasselled, but much used, obviously not kept just for show. The Greek, Roman, and Persian saddle consisted simply of a pad laid on the horse's back, secured by a girth and perhaps breastplate and crupper. The rider's weight was, therefore, distributed across the whole width of the horse's back, including the spine unless the horse's conformation was such that the spine was sunk

Mounted gladiators of Imperial Rome

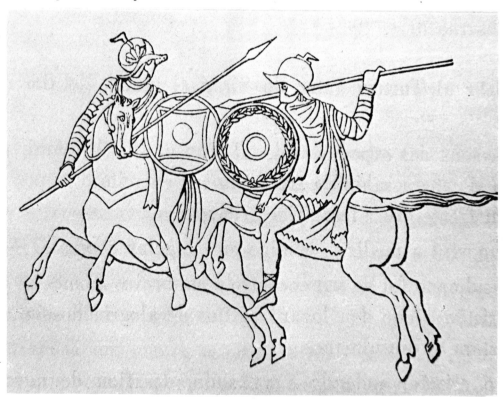

48

Saddle of leather and felt
from Pazyryk burial.
Altai 5th century B.C.

between the dorsal muscles. (This explains the excellence attributed by Xenophon and others to a 'hollow-backed' horse, for pressure on the spine produces first a rub, then a sore, then an abscess.) The Scythian saddle, however, was an improvement on this. It consisted of two cushions two foot long, well stuffed with deer's hair, resting on the saddlecloth, one on each side of the spine, joined by cross-straps. There was thus no pressure even on a prominent spine, and the rider's weight was borne by the dorsal muscles and ribs. This was a great advance in equitation. It meant that horses, even grass-fed ponies in poor condition or without hollow backs, could be ridden far longer without saddle-sores. It may well be the explanation for the Scythians' superior mobility.

Some authorities believe that these two cushions were attached to a high-arched wooden saddle-tree, which even more effectively takes the rider's weight off the spine and distributes it over a wider area than that on which he actually sits, making it less oppressive on the horse. I have myself seen no convincing evidence of this; if the Scythians developed or adopted from their neighbours a saddle-tree, it must have

been very late in their history. Since it is impossible for a horse-archer, both hands occupied with bow and arrow, to ride collected, the Scythian must have adopted naturally the nomad's extended style, allowing his horse to gallop freely over the wide, grassy plains. This is confirmed by such carvings as we have of Scythian hunting.

Roaming over wide plains teeming with game, the Scythians were dedicated hunters. On their sturdy ponies they rode after wild boar, hares, wapiti, even tigers, and shot them at point-blank range. They seem not to have used nets or traps, but to have relied on hard galloping and straight shooting.

Herodotus tells a tale which, if not Gospel-truth, at least illustrates both the Scythians' tactics, and their passion for the chase. Darius of Persia, deciding to discipline these unruly neighbours, led a vast host into their country. But the Scythians, more mobile than the heavily armoured Persian cataphracts with their coats of mail for men and horses too, simply refused battle, withdrawing before him (while picking off his outposts and harassing his patrols) and leading him further and further away from his base, into those limitless steppes.

Sometimes the armies were quite close, but still the Great King could not get to grips with his elusive enemy. 'Thou strange man,' called Darius, exasperated, on one such occasion, 'why dost thou keep flying before me?'

50

'This is my way, Persian,' replied the Scythian King. 'In return for calling thyself my lord, I say, "Go weep!"'

Week after week the fruitless chase continued until one day, when the leaders were exchanging insults, a hare got up between the armies. Immediately, with a rare sense of priorities, the Scythians sped whooping and holla'ing after it.

'Truly,' observed Darius, 'these men do utterly despise us.' He gave up the campaign and rode for home.

These Scythian tactics were admirable for raids and irregular war: by them the Scythians could avoid defeat, but they could hardly, against well-trained troops, win victory.

The eastern neighbours of the Scythians, probably also of Iranian stock, were a group of tribes known to Classical authors as the Sarmatians, not to be confused with

Ethiopian St George

Opposite
Horses and groom

Flavius Bassus of the
Noric Cavalry Squadron,
Cologne, using a Gallic
curb-bit. 3rd century A.D.

Bronze bit from Poland
made in the days of
Roman influence

Thracian warrior and captive from the golden
treasure of Letnitsa. 4th–3rd century B.C.

Riding pillion in medieval England

Opposite
In medieval times doctors of both men and horses had frequent recourse to blood-letting in order to cure their patients. Certain parts of the horse, however, are governed by certain stars and blood may only be let from those parts at the correct, propitious moment. These moments are listed in *Libro de la Merescalcaria de li cavali*, written in Greek by Misere Bonifacio, a physician of Cantabria, about the time of Charles I of Naples (13th century). This chart is taken from a later transcription of perhaps the 17th century

Sauromatians, an earlier, semi-legendary tribe of matriarchal culture, whose women could not marry until they had killed a man in battle, which was, perhaps, the factual basis for the legend of the Amazons. These, too, were nomadic horse-people, with a culture very similar to that of the Scythians from whom, however, they differed in one vital respect: they were not light mounted archers, but heavy cavalry; and though they used the bow, they relied mainly on a lance so long and heavy that the Greeks called it a 'barge-pole'. They wore, like the knights of the Bayeux Tapestry, conical helms and long coats of armour; even their horses were sometimes armoured. Unlikely as it sounds, there is contemporary evidence that their armour was at one time made of scales sliced from horses' hooves, sewn on to leather tunics: later this gave place to iron scale armour and then to chain-mail. Heavily armoured, carrying a lance which obviously could not be thrown or thrust overhead, javelin-fashion, but must be held with both hands or couched under the arm, the Sarmatians clearly employed – perhaps they were the first cavalry in history to employ – shock-action.

54

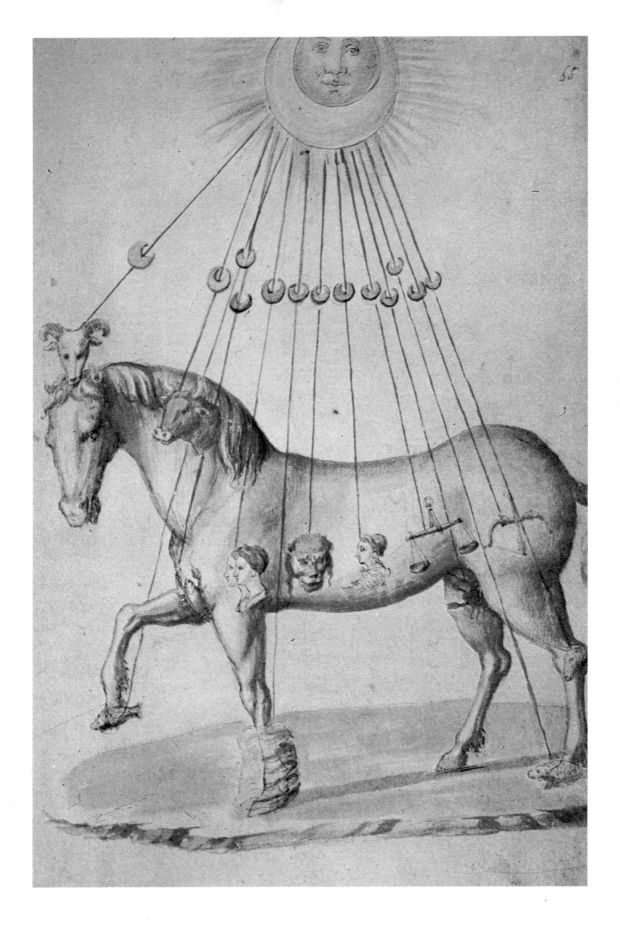

Scythian hobbling his horse. Chertomlyk Vase
4th century B.C.

Silver vase from Solokha tumulus. Scythian
4th century B.C.

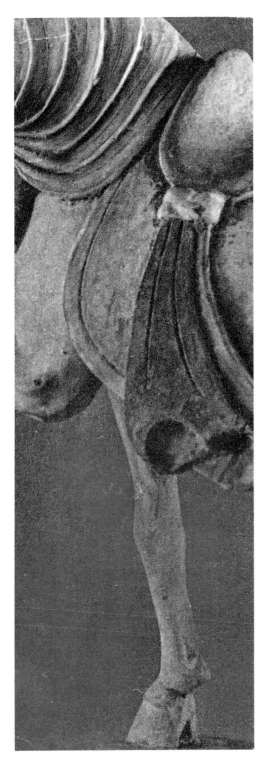

Chinese saddles.
Han dynasty

57

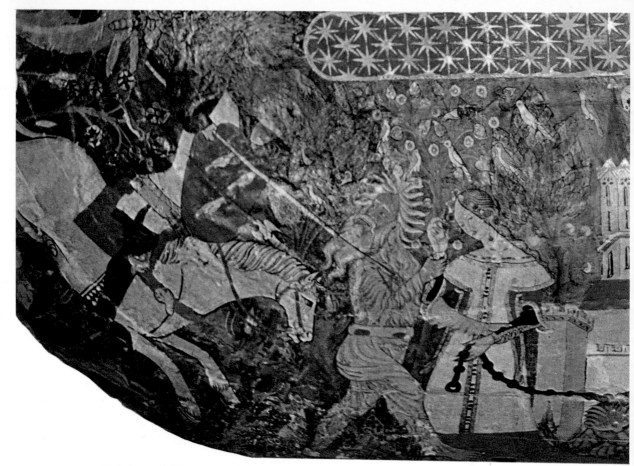

Christian and Moor at war in Spain

It is impossible to charge home with couched lance unless one is sitting securely in a saddle with a high cantle. Stirrups can, perhaps, be dispensed with in a charge where horse, rider, and lance are not required for hand-to-hand fighting in a mêlée but simply make up a single missile, directed straight at the enemy, to overthrow him by weight and impetus. But a saddle, with a proper saddle-tree shaped into a high cantle behind the rider, is necessary: without it, he will simply be forced, by the terrific shock of impact, back over his horse's croup and tail. The Sarmatians must have used a saddle with a solid wooden tree and high cantle; and, sure enough, contemporary, eyewitness illustrations of these vigorous barbarians show just such a saddle.

Curiously enough, in some paintings Sarmatian warriors are shown riding side-saddle. This I cannot explain. Perhaps they are about to slip off their horses and fight on foot, a method favoured by the German tribes who, according to Julius Caesar, 'frequently jump off their horses and fight on foot, and they train their horses to remain where they stand, and if need arises they betake themselves to their horses with all speed'.

We know nothing about Sarmatian horses, but it seems that, armoured themselves and carrying armoured men in a charge, they must have been a good deal bigger than the ordinary Scythian pony. Living alongside the Persians, the Sarmatians probably obtained good horses from them.

The nomadic horsemen of the Eurasian steppes were in a state of constant movement, generally in a westerly direction. The Huns or Mongols pushed the Sarmatians, the Sarmatians, originally established between the Caspian and the Black Seas, pushed the Scythians westward from about 200 B.C. until about A.D. 200 when the Sarmatians were pressing on the Roman frontier posts along the Danube, and the Scythians were either absorbed by their conquerors, or confined to two small enclaves in the Crimea and the Dobrudja. Then came a southward movement of Germanic tribes, Visigoths and Ostrogoths, who, under Mongol pressure and unable to make headway against the firm Roman frontier of the Rhine, moved south towards the Danube. The Sarmatians – now generally known, from the name of their strongest clan, as Allans – were in their turn absorbed or accepted as junior partners of the Goths. The Goths brought with them, or adopted from the Allans, the tactics of heavy

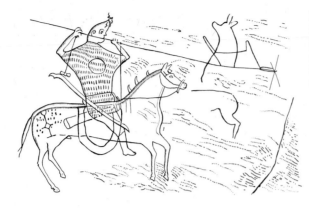

Rock-drawing from
Preslav of Sarmatian
lancers and the seat that
eventually developed
into the straight-legged
seat of western Europe

cavalry, mailed horsemen charging home with couched lances. Indeed, they went further than the Allans, in discarding the bow altogether. Almost certainly they used a saddle with a high cantle, but not stirrups.

It is interesting to find, in the opposite side of the Empire, another tribe being employed as cavalry *foederati*. This was the mysterious people known to archaeologists as the 'X Group', whose tombs and burial-mounds litter the Nile Valley in rich profusion in Nubia, about the present Egyptian-Sudanese frontier. They were probably a Negroid race, in a fairly advanced stage of civilization greatly enriched by commercial and cultural contacts, through Egypt, with the Mediterranean. But no one knows whence they came, from the Kharga Oasis to the west, down the Nile Valley or even from Ethiopia.

Known to the Romans as the Nobades, they seem to have been raiding into Egypt during the fourth century, and then to have been employed by the Imperial authorities to protect the frontier against raids by the fierce tribesmen of the Eastern Desert, ancestors of the Bisharin and Hadendowa. A mid fifth-century drawing on baked clay shows their king at war, mailed, riding a light Arab-type pony.

Iron bit used
in 5th century A.D.,
Poland

Opposite
Rock-drawings
of Sarmatian from
Kara-lovo

To us there are three things of great interest about the Nobades. They used a long lance underhand, like the Sarmatians, not overhand, like all other African people. As one might expect from this, they used a saddle-tree. Many have been found in fourth- and fifth-century tombs, made of wood, silver mounted, high in the pommel and cantle like Arab saddles today. There are no stirrups.

Finally, they used a unique type of bit. It was a sort of ring-bit, but jointed exactly like a jointed snaffle. Curved pieces encircled the horse's lower jaw, terminating in arms about six inches long. These were joined at the ends by three rings, to the middle one of which both reins were attached. When the reins hung loose, the arms were two inches or so apart, and the bit exerted no pressure on the jaw; but when the reins were tightened, the ring clamped on the jaw. They must, of course, have ridden on a loose rein, and used the indirect or neck rein; the direct rein would not be possible with that bit. It was made either of iron or, like some Mexican bits, of silver.

In the latter half of the fourth century A.D. the Goths came under increasing pressure from the Huns and sought refuge south of the Danube, as clients of the Empire. There were quarrels between the Imperial authorities and these warlike refugees, culminating in an attack by a large Roman Army, commanded by the Emperor Valens himself, on a Gothic fortified camp near Adrianople. While the Romans were assaulting the wagon laager, they were suddenly charged, in flank and rear, by thousands of Gothic horsemen who had been out on a foraging raid. It was a slaughter. The auxiliary horse prudently decamped and the steadfast legions, pressed inwards and jammed so close that they could not use their weapons, were almost exterminated. With long lance and sword, the Goths slew and slew, until the Emperor Valens himself and over 40,000 Romans had been killed. It was one of the decisive battles of the world, and the start of a thousand years' ascendancy in Europe of heavy cavalry.

Meanwhile, like some terrible visitation on civilized man, there emerged from the mists and snow-blizzards of Mongolia, the Huns, under their chieftain Attila, 'the scourge of God'. According to legend, the witches of Scythia were, for foul and deadly practices, driven from society. In the wilderness they copulated with evil spirits, and

One of the illustrations to the *Mahabharata* by a
Mughal artist. A.D. 1598

the Huns were the offspring of this execrable conjunction. Squat, bow-legged, beardless, with long unkempt hair, flat noses, small black eyes, and shrill voices, their
appearance seemed to confirm their demonic ancestry. Like the Scythians, they almost
lived on horseback: 'their indolence refused to cultivate the earth, and their restless
spirit disdained the confines of a sedentary life'. In less picturesome terms, they were
nomads, inhabiting a vast country too barren to support a way of life based on
agriculture.

In war, so long as there was grazing for their innumerable horses, a Hun horde
was extraordinarily mobile. They carried no bulky corn, but subsisted on meat on
the hoof, horse-meat dried or smoked, and on mares' milk.

'Their ample leisure, instead of being devoted to the soft enjoyments of love and
harmony, was usefully spent on the violent and sanguinary exercise of the chase.' They
indulged in hunting on a huge scale, forming circles of forty or fifty miles wide of
horse-archers who gradually converged on the centre, driving every living thing
before them to a final holocaust of slaughter. 'They acquired the habit of directing
their eye and their steps to a remote object; of suspending or accelerating their pace
according to the motion of the troops on their right and left; and of watching and

Opposite
Detail from *Conversion of*
St Hubert. 15th century

repeating the signals of their leaders. Their leaders studied, in this practical school, the most important lesson of the military art; the prompt and accurate judgement of ground, of distance, and of time.' Unquestionably they rode shaggy ponies extended, not collected.

Above all, they invented the stirrup.

From earlier times there are isolated examples of objects which could, with some stretch of the imagination, be construed as stirrups. The Assyrian King Shalmaneser III (859–824 B.C.) is shown riding with something under his foot which may possibly be a plank-like support. The Chertomlyk vase of the fourth century B.C. shows a Scythian horse with, hanging from the saddle, an object which might possibly have served as a sort of stirrup, but could equally well be just a loose strap or rope.

On the basis of this and of remains found last century in Scythian tombs, a Russian, W. W. Arendt, has reconstructed a putative Scythian saddle with stirrups attached not to the saddle but to the girth. On the whole one must treat this with some scepticism. If such a useful discovery as stirrups was made in the third century B.C., why did it not spread?

The first undoubted evidence of the stirrup is in the biography of a Chinese officer who flourished in A.D. 477. He says it was invented by the Huns. A fifth- or sixth-century A.D. Korean jug in the shape of a rider and his mount shows that stirrups were used there at the time. Thereafter its use spread rapidly eastward into China, westward across Siberia and the steppes into Europe, and in the next two centuries mentions and illustrations of the stirrup are innumerable. Of particular interest is the bas-relief from the tomb of the Emperor T'ai Tsung A.D. 627–49, for it shows in detail a central Asian nomad extracting an arrow from the chest of a horse which carries a solid-treed saddle indubitably fitted with stirrups.

It is surprising that horsemen took 1,500 years to think up something so simple. One is reluctantly driven to the distasteful conclusion that we are not really a very bright set of people.

The Huns, inventors of the stirrup, worshipped Opona as goddess of horses and horsemanship

The god Mithra hunting. Wall-painting of B.C./A.D.

The stirrup was perhaps mankind's most important technical invention since the bit. Without it, mounting a large or restive horse is difficult and even hazardous for a small or inactive rider. The Persian King Cambyses actually met his death 'leaping on to his horse: the tip of his scabbard fell away and the naked blade was driven into his thigh'. The elderly, the corpulent, or the dignified horseman had to resort to a mounting-block, or the back of a kneeling slave. But a stirrup made mounting easy, even for those of riper years.

Stirrups also made it possible to ride further and faster. A horse gallops better if the rider stands in his stirrups than if he sits down in the saddle. Grain-fed horses in hard condition, and riders who are very fit, can cover long distances at a canter or slow gallop; but in general, for covering long distances at a fair speed without exhausting horse or rider, it is best alternately to walk and trot – provided one has stirrups.* Without stirrups, as every Pony Club member knows, trotting for any length of time is far from pleasant, either for oneself or one's mount. Stirrups, therefore, greatly increased the mobility of horsemen.

* This view is a personal one based on Indian cavalry experience. It is fiercely disputed by many experts who prefer the slow canter or the amble.

Equally important was their tactical effect. Consider first the implication of stirrups for the mounted archer. An arrow shot by a horseman has a shorter range, since he cannot lay his body to the bow, and less accuracy, since he is shooting from an unstable platform, than an arrow shot by a foot-archer. To compensate for these disadvantages, the horseman must exploit his great advantage, mobility: he must keep on the move for, stationary, he is a sitting duck to the man with the longer ranged, more accurate weapon. In what direction should he move while shooting? Not, clearly, towards the enemy. Doing so, he is an easy target: his range and the elevation at which he must discharge his arrows is constantly changing, making his shooting very inaccurate; and before he has shot off more than two or three arrows at an effective range, he will be at dangerously close quarters. Obviously, his best tactic is to canter or gallop parallel to the enemy's front, shooting into the enemy a stream of arrows all more or less at the same range, while providing them with a very difficult moving target. He shoots, so to speak, over his port beam, and if the enemy, goaded by these attentions, sally out to drive him off, he swings away and continues shooting, 'the Parthian shot', over his port quarter or directly astern. To do this efficiently he must twist his body round to the left, which is difficult if he has to sit down in the saddle preserving a precarious balance without stirrups, but easy enough if he stands in his stirrups. Polo-players can hit with far more force and accuracy standing in the stirrups than sitting.down in the saddle, and a sovereign cure of mishitting is to shorten one's leathers. No doubt the same principles apply to mounted archery, so the archers of central Asia rode very short and stood in their stirrups to shoot. They could not, of course, collect their ponies.

For heavy cavalry the stirrup was of even greater importance. To fight in a mêlée a man must be able to put the weight of his body behind the blow, either hacking down at the enemy, cutting or thrusting to right or left. This is quite impossible without stirrups, just as it would be impossible to play fast polo without them.

Stirrups gave no sustained advantage to the Huns over their neighbours, who very soon copied them; but they dramatically increased the advantage of cavalry, either mounted archers or armoured knights, over infantry.

For several centuries the Huns had plagued the Chinese Empire, so much so that in the third century B.C. the Chinese armies had actually adopted Hun weapons, tactics, and dress, discarding the dignified robe of civilized man and wearing instead the trousers and hooded tunic of the nomad. From Persia they imported 'heavenly

After a wall-painting in a catacomb at Kerch.
Those on the right are (presumably) Sarmatians,
some apparently riding side-saddle

stallions', and in 111 B.C. introduced alfalfa to feed them. The hot, damp lowlands of China were inimicable to horses, who flourished on the dry limestone steppes and sparse grazing of the north and west; so there in the seventh century the Tang Emperors established vast stud farms, catering for 300,000 horses at seven acres to a horse.

To obtain good Ferghana horses, the Son of Heaven sent an expedition right across Asia, accompanied by two horse-trainers to select, handle, and ride them. These rough-riders were given the rank – no doubt acting and unpaid – of military governors. At a tremendous cost in treasure and human life, the expedition returned more or less victorious, with a score or two of the best horses and some inferior ones. The Son of Heaven thought these well worth the cost.

The Chinese taught their horses the gait we call 'ambling', which is still very popular all over the East, being extremely comfortable for riders of riper years, ample dignity, and embonpoint. Unfortunately, it is very hard on the horse. An ambling horse is taught, by joining the legs of each side with a cord, to move both near legs, then both off legs, together – in contrast with trotting, a natural pace in which diagonal legs move together, which is not so comfortable for the rider but far better for the horse, because (as Horace Hayes explained) the horse's equilibrium is maintained better by a diagonal than by a lateral pace. One is not surprised to learn from the tomb of the statesman Ch'ao Ts'o that 'Chinese horses cannot vie with [the nomad's] horses in climbing rocky heights or fording mountain torrents, nor our horsemen with theirs, in galloping over steep paths or shooting arrows while in rapid motion'.

In the perpetual war between the Celestial Empire and the Huns, the advantage lay now with one side, now with the other. Sometimes the uncouth horse-people were able to impose humiliating terms on the most civilized nation on earth, such as an annual tribute of the most elegant, gently nurtured virgins sacrificed to their hard life and rude embraces; at other times the Chinese armies drove back the nomads pressing upon their frontiers thereby setting off among the pastoral tribes a chain reaction which reached even to the Rhine.

We have from the Papal Ambassador to the Great Khan a detailed description of Mongol horsemen. Although it was written in 1246, these people had probably not changed much in the intervening centuries, and the description described pretty closely the nomadic horsemen of the Dark Ages.

Each man carried on campaign two or three stiff bows, and three quivers full of arrows. A few also bore scimitars and lances, but the bow was their main weapon. The arrows were two foot, one palm, and two fingers long, with heads triangular in section, kept needle sharp by files which each man kept in his quiver. Their helms were of leather, with a crown. Some wore iron scale armour, but most were protected only by cuirasses of overlapping leather bands, stiffened with bitumen. Their shaggy ponies wore leather bardings and iron frontlets on the forehead. Their horses seem to have been mainly grass-fed, which is not conducive to great speed or endurance; but mobility was achieved by each man leading one, two, or three remounts, riding them in turn, and by the fact that they were not hampered by slow-moving supply trains. To cross a river, they tied up their clothes and saddles in leather groundsheets, making waterproof bags which were towed across tied to the horses' tails, while the riders swam at the heads. Their invasions were a thing of horror, incredibly, wantonly destructive as they slew and pillaged. They even had the deplorable habit of boiling down their captives to produce an incendiary fat.

Towards the middle of the sixth century, one tribe of Huns, quarrelling with the rest, was driven headlong out of Mongolia and, turning its back on the Great Wall, set its face towards the Danube. Known as Avars or Exiles, these horse-people eventually settled in what is now Hungary, where they plagued the Eastern Roman Empire as once they had plagued the Empire of China. Their stirrups were copied by their Allan and German neighbours, by the Persians whose borders they had passed *en route*, and were even carried by Viking pirates and traders to northern Europe, where they have been found in graves in Sweden.

The Eastern Roman, or Byzantine, Emperors were quick to adopt the stirrup, both for their own Herulian and Massagetic Hun mercenaries (horse-archers from the shores of the Caspian) and for the Gothic, Thracian, and Lombard troopers in their heavy cavalry. To counter Avar raids, the great Byzantine general Belisarius (500–565) devised, and the Emperor Maurice Tiberius (or his ghost-writer) laid down in his military manual *Strategicon*, a new system of tactics based on the all-purpose cavalryman, combining the advantages of the light horse-archer and the heavy armoured lancer.

The Byzantine trooper as trained and equipped by Belisarius wore a rounded iron helm, a thigh-length mail shirt, breeches, and long rawhide boots fitted with prick-spurs. He sat on a large, well-stuffed saddle, fitted with stirrups which Belisarius introduced to the Byzantine Army. He carried an extraordinary variety of

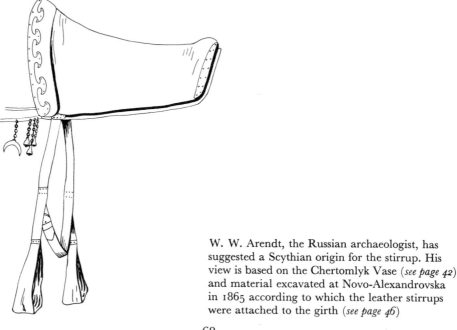

W. W. Arendt, the Russian archaeologist, has suggested a Scythian origin for the stirrup. His view is based on the Chertomlyk Vase (*see page 42*) and material excavated at Novo-Alexandrovska in 1865 according to which the leather stirrups were attached to the girth (*see page 46*)

Reiterstein from Hornhausen.
7th century A.D.

weapons: a lance; a broadsword; half a dozen heavy, feathered darts carried on the back of his shield; a very stiff bow which could drive an arrow through mail; and a quiver of arrows. For shock-action the Byzantines needed horses which were far larger and better bred than central Asian ponies, and correspondingly difficult to manage: but since the bow needed two hands, these big horses had often to be controlled without reins and bit, by knee- and thigh-pressure. Robert Graves, drawing from Byzantine sources, describes how a trooper strung his bow. 'The right hand reaches behind for the bow, pulls it forward, rests the strung end on the right foot and bends the bow by pressing it downwards. The left hand, which has meanwhile snatched an arrow from the quiver, unties the loop of the bow-string and slips it over the catch; then down comes the left hand to the centre of the bow, transferring the arrow to the right hand – and in a moment the bow is in action.' To do this at a gallop clearly required a very high standard of equitation, good hands, and an independent seat. Anyway, the Byzantine trooper, the all-purpose cavalryman produced by Belisarius, held the frontier of civilization more or less intact for 500 years.

69

The principal enemies of the Empire, from the seventh century onwards, were the Arabs. The horse, as has already been argued, was not indigenous to Arabia: indeed the Arabs became horsemen centuries after their neighbours. But by the fourth century A.D. there were enough horses in Arabia for Arabs to be enlisted in the light cavalry of the Empire. They fought naked, bare-back on small ponies: there is a description of a Goth being killed in single combat by an Arab mercenary: 'the hairy, naked savage, applying his lips to the wound, expressed a horrid delight while he sucked the blood of his vanquished enemy'.

But by the time of the Prophet Mohammed, the late sixth century, Arab horsemanship was much more sophisticated. As the old Saharan proverb goes:

> Horses for a quarrel,
> Camels for the Desert,
> And oxen for poverty.

So for war the Arab took to the horse, the steed of soldiers, instead of the camel, mount of brigands, and the Arab horse, fed on the dry grass of the limestone deserts

Central Asian horseman removing
an arrow from his horse

A tatemono showing
what may perhaps be a
very early form of stirrup.
Haniva, Japan.
3rd–4th century A.D.

and on barley grown in oases, was a very fine animal indeed, a prime factor in the
great Arab conquests. The idea prevalent in the West that the five famous strains of
pure-blooded Arab horse are descended from the five mares on which the Prophet
and his successors fled from Mecca to Medina does not seem to be familiar to the
Arabs themselves; but it was the Arab mare which carried Islam from the Indies to
Spain, and across the Pyrenees to the Moslems' providential defeat in 732 by Charles
Martel and his mailed Franks at Poitiers.

3

Middle Ages

For most people in Britain the Middle Ages begin, as crisply as the new act of a play, in 1066. Historians may cavil at this over-simplification, but in a history of equitation it will serve better than any other date; for we have in the Bayeux Tapestry a whole series of pictures showing how the Norman knights at Hastings rode and fought. No doubt men had ridden and fought in this manner for many years before 1066, but we have little record of it.

At this time the word 'knight' (*chevalier, ritter*) meant no more than a cavalryman. There was as yet no ceremony of knighthood, no lore of heraldry, and very little concept of chivalry. The knight wore a conical iron helm, with a nasal to protect his face; a mail coif under the helm to protect his neck; and a hauberk, rather like a night-shirt, calf-length, with half-sleeves, slit at the back and front to facilitate riding. Very few had mail leggings. The hauberk itself was either of linked chain-mail, or of overlapping metal scales sewn on to leather. Under the armour he wore a padded leather or cloth gambeson and cap, to guard against bruising and prevent the mail chaffing or being driven by a heavy blow into his skin. On his heels he wore fairly short prick-spurs, like those of the Romans. His wooden shield was long and kite-shaped, held by the left hand near the top, or broad end: it covered most of his chest, half his stomach, and his left thigh.

These details are given to remove some common misconceptions. What did the knight's armour weigh? No early medieval hauberks now exist, but Indian mail shirts of the eighteenth century weigh about twenty-five to thirty pounds. Hauberks at Hastings can hardly have weighed less: the Bayeux Tapestry shows three servants carrying two hauberks, slung on poles thrust through the sleeves, between them; but there is no reason why they should have weighed more. Surviving saddles of the Late Middle Ages weigh about forty pounds; eleventh-century saddles probably weighed less because they did not have to carry so much. Men in those days were smaller than they are now, averaging perhaps ten stone. Add a few pounds for lance, sword, and shield, and one comes to the conclusion that in the eleventh, twelfth, and thirteenth centuries, that is to say before the development of plate-armour, the knight's charger carried about sixteen stone.

In 1914 a British cavalry horse carried between seventeen and a half and eighteen stone, assuming that the rider himself weighed eleven. German and French cavalry horses carried more. One therefore concludes that, until plate-armour came into fashion, the medieval charger need have been no larger or heavier than the cavalry horse of the twentieth century, which averaged about 15·2 hands in height and a thousand pounds in weight. This view is supported by all contemporary illustrations, from the Bayeux Tapestry onwards. The horses resemble light- or medium-weight

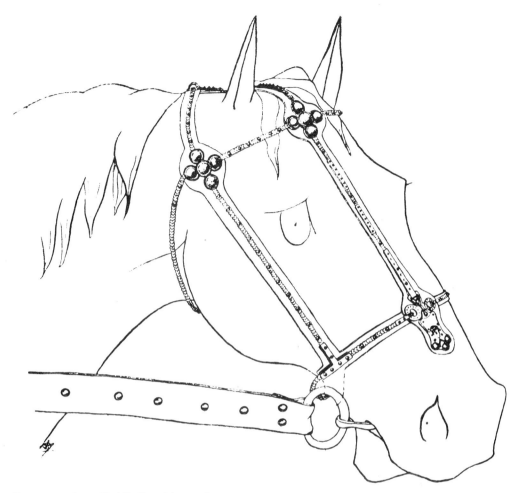

Reconstruction of bridle found in a 4th-century
A.D. grave at Szwajcaria, Poland

hunters, not massive cart-horses – they gallop into action, which a cart-horse could hardly do; and if they are suddenly stopped, or killed, they turn head over heels, which proves that they were going at a good speed. Richard Cœur de Lion's favourite horses on the Third Crusade were a Cypriot horse and a Turcoman, both fairly light breeds. Evidence that Edward I, for instance, encouraged the breeding and importation of 'Great Horses' does not affect the issue, for there is not the slightest evidence that the 'Great Horse' of the twelfth and thirteenth centuries was anything like the 'Great Horse' of Tudor times. The evidence is, indeed, all to the contrary.

For war they rode stallions, schooled as carefully as Metropolitan Police horses to crowds, banners, arrows, noise, and blows; one could not ride any old horse 'in press

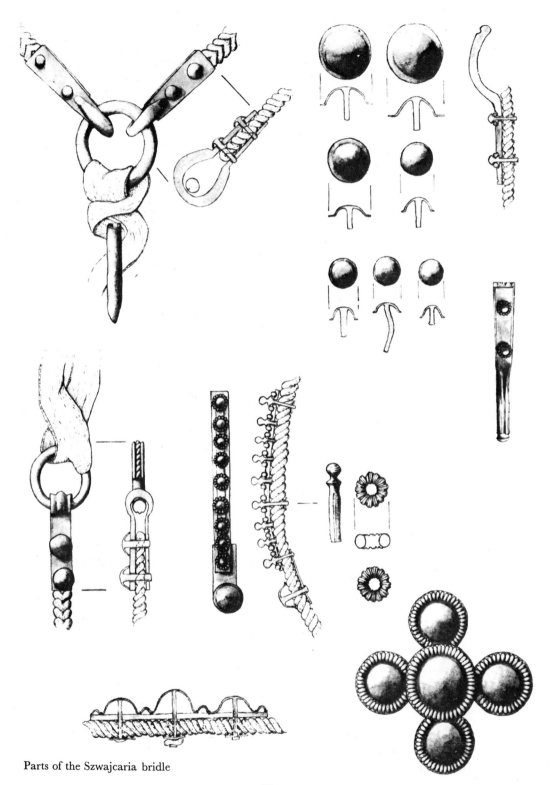

Parts of the Szwajcaria bridle

74

Reconstruction of an
11th century Polish
saddle and the stirrup
that was found with it

of knights'. It was considered a remarkable feat when Richard Cœur de Lion, plunging on foot through the surf in an opposed landing on the Cyprus shore, grabbed a common hack on the beach and, vaulting upon it 'with the aid of his lance placed behind the saddle', riding with cords for stirrups, spurred furiously after the caitiff Emperor Isaak, shouting, 'My Lord and Emperor, I challenge you to single combat!' But this base fellow, as though he were deaf, positively ignored the opportunity to distinguish himself against the most formidable warrior of the day, and fled swiftly away.

There was evidently a distinction between chargers or destriers, hacks or palfreys, and race- or running-horses (*equites cursores*). The last are specifically mentioned as having been imported into England in the twelfth century and, indeed, in earlier times. King Richard had two such racehorses, Favell and Lyard, described as being swifter than dromedaries or destriers: he declared, no doubt with some exaggeration, that he would not part with one for a thousand pounds.

Probably these running-horses were used by the King's messengers, and for hunting, of which the Norman and Angevin Kings were extravagantly fond. There do not seem in Europe to have been any organised races in the Early Middle Ages, though impromptu races were run at Smithfield horse sales, no doubt so that prospective buyers could get some idea of comparative speeds. 'A shout is immediately raised and the common horses are ordered to get out of the way. Three jockeys, or perhaps two as the match is made, prepare themselves for the contest; such as, being used to ride, know how to manage their horses with judgement; the point is to prevent a rival from getting before them. The horses, on their part, are not without emulation; they tremble and are impatient and are continually in motion. At last, the signal given, they strike, devour the course, hurrying along with unremitting speed. The jockeys, inspired with the thoughts of applause and the hopes of victory, clap spurs to their willing horses, brandish their whips, and cheer them on with their cries.'

No doubt the jockeys were light-weights, perhaps boys. We do not know whether they rode straight-legged like the knights, but pictures of fifteenth-century boy jockeys show them riding with something like the modern forward seat.

The nobles of France, England, and indeed all Europe had a passion for hunting red- and fallow-deer, wild boar and wolf. A Venetian Ambassador (surely no sportsman) complained that the Court of France, and therefore its Government, 'are only in one place so long as the game lasts. . . . Anyone who wants to talk to the King must get a horse and go to the forest.' There was considered to be a sort of moral virtue in hunting, still discernible in hunting circles today. As Count Gaston de Foix wrote in 1387, 'I never saw a man that loved the work and pleasure of hound and hawks that had not many good qualities in him . . . whether he be a great lord or a little one, a poor man or a rich one.' His contemporary, the Duke of York, the greatest English authority on hunting, thought that 'men are better when riding, more just understanding, and more alert and more at ease and more undertaking, and better knowing of all countries and all passages. In short and long all good customs and manners come thereof, and the health of man and of his soul.'

The knight rode not merely 'long', but straight-legged, feet well forward, toes pointing down. With legs braced against the stirrup-irons, buttocks pressed hard back against the cantle, he was locked in position in moments of stress or emergency. This seat, which prevailed in Europe for many centuries and is only just going out of fashion in 'Western' riding, seems so strange to riders brought up to the 'balanced seat' that it requires some explanation.

It was clearly not inherited from the Greek and Roman horseman who rode without stirrups; although they rode 'long', their legs hung at a natural angle and were slightly bent at the knee, not straight with the feet thrust forward. Nor can it be explained by the difficulty of bending the leg in armour: most Norman knights at Hastings wore no leg-armour, and when leg-armour became common during the twelfth century, it consisted only of laced mail leggings with felt knee-caps. The explanation must lie elsewhere.

Part of the explanation, of course, lies in the fact that the stirrup-leathers were then attached to the saddle as far forward as possible and thus well in front of the rider's centre of gravity, and this meant that he had to sit with his legs sticking out forward. In the Early Middle Ages mailed cavalry dominated the battle-field. Without good missile weapons the best infantry could not withstand horsemen, as was proved by the defeat of Harold's Housecarles at Hastings and of the Varangian Guard, the Byzantine Empire's English and Viking mercenaries, by Norman knights at Dyrrachium. The short hand-bow was too weak, the early cross-bow too scarce and too long in loading, to affect the issue. The charge and subsequent mêlée, against either infantry or other cavalry, was all that mattered. In a headlong charge a horseman is most likely to be thrown either forward if his horse props or is brought to a sudden halt by impact with the enemy, or backward by a thrust from his enemy's lance. Being flung forward was probably the most dangerous, because he could be badly injured by the high pommel of his saddle. We regard the forward slope of the thighs as the best safeguard against 'going out of the front window': within reason, the shorter one rides, the greater the resistance to being thrown or pulled forward (unless, of course, the leathers are so short that one is riding purely by balance, with no grip at all). Clearly the knight thought his best safeguard against being flung forward was to ride with a stiff leg, feet thrust well forward, so that his stirrups and legs absorbed the shock and kept him braced back against the cantle, and this may have been the reason why his stirrup-leathers were attached so far forward. The other danger, that of being thrust back off the saddle, is prevented by the high cantle. It is not an emergency which ever occurs in modern equitation, but it seems that a man riding long could withstand a powerful thrust better than a man riding short.

The knight's seat was, therefore, well devised for a special purpose. The surprising thing is that it lasted so long after that purpose had disappeared.

His left or bridle hand held also, at the point of balance, his long, kite-shaped shield. This meant that the reins were held almost shoulder-high. In that position, he could not pull strongly on the reins to stop his horse, so he used a very severe curb-bit. The high bridle hand, loose rein, and severe curb still survives in Western riding, which is derived from the medieval style. Naturally he could not ride the horse into such a bit, so the reins are left hanging loose down the horse's neck. When hunting, or otherwise riding without a shield, he held his left hand in the normal position, just over the horse's withers; but he still rode with a severe curb-bit and a loose rein.

A curious feature of the Bayeux Tapestry is that many knights are shown using their spears javelin-fashion, throwing or thrusting overhand with them, as Greeks and Romans had done before the invention of saddle-tree and stirrups. This practice does not seem to have lasted into the twelfth century. Perhaps these knights' horses had propped or lost their impetus up the steep slope of Senlac Hill; perhaps they themselves feared to close with the shield-wall and the terrible Danish axes of the Housecarles; or perhaps they were just old-fashioned. In a mêlée, or if one's horse is standing still or moving slowly, there is something to be said for the overhand spear: hog-hunters in eastern India always preferred it to the method used elsewhere. But

A Swedish king
out hunting

charging at a gallop, the lance-point strikes with far more force and accuracy if held couched under the horseman's arm. An Arab cavalier of the twelfth century explained that 'he who is on the point of striking with his lance should hold it under his arm, close to his side, and should let his horse run and effect the required thrust; for if he should move his hand or stretch out his arm while holding the lance, then his thrust would have no effect whatsoever and would result in no harm'.

At the end of the eleventh century the Frankish knights of western Europe met for the first time – if one excludes occasional mercenaries and travellers – the horse-archers of central Asia. The Seljuk Turks, emerging like Huns and Mongols from the mysterious lands north of the Oxus, had overrun the Moslem world as far as Egypt, captured Jerusalem from the comparatively tolerant and highly civilized Saracens, and were pressing hard upon the Byzantine Empire in Asia Minor. The object of the First Crusade was to capture the Holy Places and, in doing so, to take pressure off the Empire. (This secondary object became rather confused, but that is another story.)

The Crusaders had no inkling of what they were up against, and in their first battle, at Dorylaeum, were utterly confounded by an enemy who scampered away before a charge, would not come to grips, but rode round the sullen Frankish masses pouring in a hail of arrows which, though they seldom penetrated the knight's mail, cruelly galled the horses. More by good luck than management, just as the main army was in despair and the Turks were closing in for the *coup de grace*, a detachment of several hundred knights from the Rhineland, led by Godfrey de Bouillon, emerged from the hills behind the enemy, charged home unexpectedly, and won a resounding victory.

The Moslem cavalier sat in his padded, quilted saddle with something like the modern 'balanced seat' – that is to say, with bent knees, his lower leg slightly behind the vertical and his stirrup under his centre of gravity. This is shown more accurately in Persian pictures than by Frankish artists, who generally fail to differentiate between the equitation, weapons, and tactics of West and East. He rode short so as

Normans in 1061

79

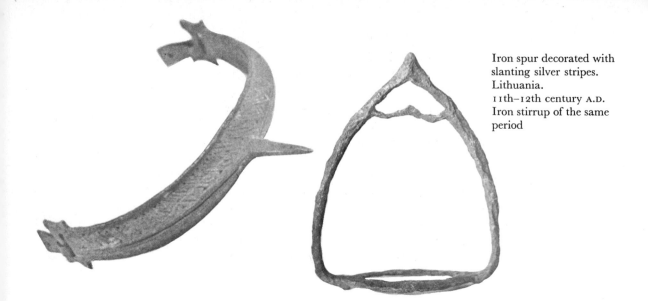

Iron spur decorated with slanting silver stripes. Lithuania.
11th–12th century A.D.
Iron stirrup of the same period

to use his bow more effectively, but the balanced seat may have made Moslem armies more mobile than Christian armies, as being less tiring for the horse. That they were more mobile is indisputable; that it was in part attributable to a better seat is mere surmise. When it comes to a charge, however, the Moslems, be they Turkish horse-archers or Saracen knights armed, like Franks, with lance, mace, and sword were generally overthrown. Admittedly they were smaller, lighter men, riding 14-hand Arab ponies; but undoubtedly they rode too short for shock-action, and the terrific impact of a head-on collision simply bowled them over. It was for this, after all, that the knight's straight-legged seat was developed; while the Moslems rode short so as to stand in their stirrups, as we can see in numerous Persian pictures, to shoot or slash with curved scimitars. Perhaps, too (though I am advancing a theory with no evidence to support it) the Western curb-bit made the Franks' horses more handy in a mêlée than the snaffle-bitted Arab ponies.

We can find some interesting comments on Eastern horsemanship in the writings of Sir Bertrandon de la Brocquière, Councillor and First Esquire Carver to the Duke of Burgundy, an intrepid knight who, after making the pilgrimage to Jerusalem, travelled back to Christendom overland, disguised as a Moslem. This was in 1432; but I do not think the art of horsemanship, either in Europe or Asia, changed much between the twelfth and the fifteenth centuries. 'Their saddles are commonly very rich, but hollow, having pommels before and behind, with short stirrup-leathers and wide stirrups. . . . They sit as in an arm-chair, deep-sunk in them, their knees very high and with short stirrups, a position in which they cannot support the smallest blow from a lance without being unhorsed.' He himself at first found this seat even more uncomfortable than sitting cross-legged, Moslem fashion, on the ground: 'I suffered so much that, when I dismounted, I could not remount without assistance, so sore were my hams; but after a little time this manner seemed even more convenient than ours.'

'We Europeans prefer a stone-horse (i.e. a stallion) of a good breed, but the

Moors esteem only mares. In that country a great man is not ashamed to ride a mare, with the foal running after the dam. I have seen some exceedingly beautiful. . . . They never allow them to get fat.' Elsewhere, however, he mentions geldings being ridden, as well as mares, though the latter were thought better rides. 'They have wide nostrils, gallop well, and are excellent, costing little on the road.' They 'only walk and gallop, and when purchased, those that have the best walk are preferred, as in Europe those who trot the best'. He does not mention amblers, though these were certainly valued, by idle and comfort-loving travellers, in Europe and Asia. 'They gallop well for a long time.' Ordinarily Eastern ponies walked on a journey, but galloped in war. 'They choose no horses but such as walk fast and galloped for a long time, while we select only those that trot well and at ease. . . . This is the reason why they cannot wear such complete armour as the French.' At night they 'cover their horses with felt or other stuffs, and I have seen such coverings very handsome'.

By the end of the eleventh century the Arab horse was well established as a breed – a smallish, lively, intelligent animal, very sound in the legs and feet, docile and hardy. We regard the Arab horse as rather slow, but he is slow only compared to the thoroughbred, and certainly faster than the Crusaders' horses. The light-armed Turks, wrote John of Joinville, a knight who took part in St Louis's Crusade, 'when put to flight by a greater force, fled away with the utmost agility, for they have not their equals for agility throughout the world. If they see their pursuers stop, it is their custom to turn back, like the fly which, if you drive it away, will go, but when you cease, will return. . . . So likewise the Turks, if you desist from pursuit, they will attack you, and if you attack them, they will fly away.' The Franks' difficulties were increased by the fact that they all rode stallions, while the Turks and Saracens rode mares, so Crusader horses sometimes went over to the enemy.

Oldest known example of
mounted soldier with
fire-arm. About 1470

81

The Franks captured first Antioch, then Jerusalem, which they held for about eighty years. They learned that victory against mounted archers depended on close co-operation between mailed knights and cross-bowmen. The cross-bowmen, with their longer ranged missiles, could keep the mounted archers at a respectful distance; and when opportunity came for a charge, the knights seldom failed to smash five or six times their number. They learned that in a tropical country water, grazing, and the administration of an army are as important as the bravery of the knights: men-at-arms and squires had to take considerable risks to cut grass for the Army's horses in the face of an active and enterprising enemy. When they forgot these precautions, when the knights allowed themselves to be separated from the cross-bowmen or drawn into waterless country until their horses were exhausted, they were beaten.

'From the Isle de Graye, when sharks cruise below the castle walls and the skyline is Arabia, to the Amanus Range in the north, where camels cross into Turkey stepping fastidiously through the snow', stretched the Latin Kingdom of Jerusalem, familiarly known as Outremer. The arid deserts and steep, rocky hills were uncongenial to horses bred in the lush pastures of France and Flanders. Moreover, the voyage of many weeks from the south of France or even from northern Europe, the horses cooped up without exercise in small, storm-tossed ships, killed off many at sea: those that survived landed in very poor condition, but often had to be flung into battle almost at once, without time to rest and acclimatize.

So conditions in Outremer demanded horsemastership of a high order, and probably the best horsemasters, because they had strict rules, continuity, complete dedication, and long experience of the East, were the fighting monks of the military

Not all medieval women rode side-saddle

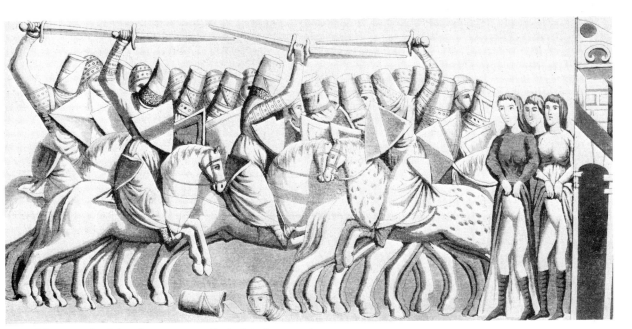

The rewards of the victor were not limited to the accoutrements of the vanquished, but included carnal prizes here illustrated as being (sometimes) on display. From *Breviaire d'Amour*

Orders, the Knights of the Temple and of the Hospital of St John, and the Teutonic Knights. These, wrote St Bernard, 'never dress gaily and wash but seldom. Shaggy by reason of their uncombed hair, they are begrimed with dust and swarthy from the weight of their armour and the heat of the sun. They do their utmost to possess strong and swift horses, but their mounts are not garnished with ornaments or decked with trappings, for they think of battle and victory, not of pomp and show. Such hath God chosen for his own, who vigorously and faithfully guard the Holy Sepulchre, all armed with the sword and most learned in the art of war.'

Horses were the property not of individual brethren but of the Order. In each convent or castle the Marshal allocated horses on the scale of three chargers and a hack to each knight, one charger and a hack to each sergeant. The Marshals also allocated mules, pack-horses, and jades for the mechanical task of drawing water from wells. They did their best to match horse and rider, but this was not always easy. 'If any brother,' say the Rules of the Templars, 'has a horse that is restive, or pulls, or rears up, or shits,* he must show it to the Marshal; and if he sees it, the Marshal should not make him keep it, but change the horse if there is good reason. And if the Marshal does not want to change it, the brother may put up with the inconvenience if he wishes, but need not mount the horse. The Marshal cannot make him mount it, by any order, unless he does so voluntarily.'

Brethren were forbidden to gallop their horses at full speed without permission.

---

* I cannot quite see why this should be a vice, but the medieval French, often obscure, is here quite clear.

The joust

On a march they usually walked their horses or ambled, keeping silence if marching at night. There was strict march discipline. If any brother left the column for any purpose, he must go downwind, so as not to incommode the others with dust. Watering, feeding, and resting horses all had to be controlled and made subject to tactical requirements. Brethren might not leave the line of march to water their horses, but could water in peacetime, without permission, at any stream *en route*. In war they could only water if the Standard-bearer did so. On reconnaissance or outpost duty brethren might not unsaddle their horses, take out the bits, nor feed their horses without permission.

On active service, a brother who wanted to try out his horse to see if the saddle was properly adjusted could leave the ranks without permission only if he left his shield and lance behind; if he took shield and lance, he must obtain permission. Otherwise it was strictly forbidden to break ranks and prick forward alone: the Templars wanted no individual displays of gallantry, and offenders who broke the rules to distinguish themselves by single combat were punished by being sent back to camp on foot, carrying their gear. The only acceptable excuse was to save a Christian in imminent danger of death at the hands of a Turk: then and then only, if in his conscience he believed he could rescue his comrade, a brother might prick out on his own, without permission.

Top Polish bridle.
11th century A.D.
Bottom Bronze mounting
of the saddle opposite

So strict was discipline in matters of horsemastership that in moving off in the morning no brother might saddle up before he received the order (though he might tack up his horse with light articles such as a picketing-rope and a water-bottle). On the march he required a superior officer's permission even to shorten his stirrup-leathers, or tighten his girth. In any alarm in camp, only those near the alarm could ride out with shield and lance: other brethren must await orders, even if the alarm was caused by a lion or beast of prey. No horse was to be sold unless it was too old or unfit for the brethren's use, and then only by orders of the Capitulary Bailiff. None could be given away, or even lent, without permission of the Master. Nor could saddlery be sent out of the Kingdom. Capitulary Bailiffs in Europe organized 'passage' of remounts to Syria. The King of Jerusalem bore the cost of replacing horses lost in battle, an important point since they were more vulnerable than knights to Turkish arrows. (Joinville, at the Battle of Mansura, was wounded by five arrows, his horse by fifteen. Surprisingly neither were put out of action: perhaps the arrows were fired from a long range and did not penetrate.) The cost of replacing horses, however, might not matter so much as the sheer difficulty of finding replacements. This the enemy appreciated, and in one of Richard's skirmishes against Saladin, when a party of Turks were surprised and surrounded, the Turks 'performed the horrible act of cutting the sinews of [their] horses to prevent them being used by Christians'. Deliberately killing or maiming horses was far more reprehensible than butchering prisoners.

No doubt the Franks rode Arab ponies, but these were not really up to weight and they preferred, when they could get them, horses imported from Spain, or Turcoman

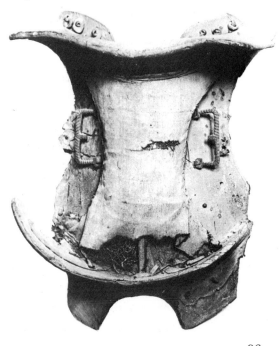

Henry V's saddle
in Westminster Abbey

Seal of Birger Jarl. Sweden

horses from the north. Certainly they never rode anything like the ponderous cart-horses which popular history attributes to them.

Joinville draws a vivid picture of Count Peter of Brittany retreating slowly, along a narrow lane, from Mansura. 'He had been wounded in the face by a sword-cut, so that the blood was running down to his mouth. He was mounted on a strong, stocky cob. He had thrown the reins down on the saddle-bow and was holding the saddle with both hands, so that the men behind, who were pressing him hard, might not force him to quicken his pace. It was easy to see that he thought little of them, for he was spitting the blood out of his mouth and repeating, "God's head! Look at them! Did you ever see such a rabble?"'

Their strategy, essentially defensive and dictated by a desperate shortage of manpower and a long, open frontier, was based on a network of mutually supporting castles, some of colossal size and strength, stupendous feats of engineering. One would like to know how they kept their precious horses fit through long sieges: Krak of the Knights, for instance, where the storerooms held five years' supplies for the garrison, was beleaguered on twelve occasions; Belvoir held out for eighteen months. Presumably they organized some sort of manège within the castle walls.

The Franks who settled in Syria had a lot of contact with their Moslem neighbours. In times of war they fought savagely, thought nothing (on both sides) of mutilating or beheading prisoners who were not worth a ransom and reverted to their ancestors' barbaric practice of riding home from battle with their defeated enemies' reeking heads hanging from the saddle-bow. During long truces they exchanged visits and presents; litigated in one another's courts, apparently confident

87

of a fair hearing; shared crops and hunting-grounds. Some of these dealings are recorded by Usama ibn Munquidh, a twelfth-century Syrian gentleman whose Castle of Shayzar was on the Frankish border.

In one battle a knight charged the Moslem Army alone, performed prodigies of valour and, when his horse was killed, fought his way back on foot. A few months later a Frank arrived at Shayzar with a letter from Tancred, the Norman Lord of Antioch. 'This is a revered knight of the Franks who has completed the holy pilgrimage and is on his way back to his country. He has asked me to introduce him to you so that he may see your cavaliers. . . . Treat him well.' 'The knight,' wrote Usama, 'was a young man, handsome in looks and well dressed; but his body bore traces of numerous cuts. His face showed the mark of a sword-blow which had cut him from the middle of his head to the fore part of his face.' It was the knight who had made the solitary charge, and Usama pointed the moral, 'holding aloof no more retards fate than adventure hasten it'.

After one battle Tancred begged an Arab magnate for a horse which he had particularly admired in the fighting. 'It was dispatched, mounted by a Kurd named Hasanun, one of our valiant cavaliers, young, good-looking and thin, in order to hold races with other horses in the presence of Tancred. Hasanun ran a race and his

Like all sports in which men compete it was important that women be among the spectators of the medieval tournament

horse outran all the horses which were in the race. He was brought before Tancred, and the knights began to inspect his arms and wonder at his thin physique and youth, recognizing in him a valiant cavalier. Tancred bestowed a robe of honour on him'.

It is interesting to read of Usama deliberately putting his mare at a wall, clearing it, and then jumping back to take a Frank by surprise. Jumping a horse was obviously a novelty to the Franks, and the only record we have of one doing so is when King Richard jumped clean over a huge boar which charged him at such close quarters that there was no other way of escape.

There must have been a keen pleasure in worsting the other side in a horse-deal. Usama's brother had a famous mare, swift and bold, which he gave to a Frank – after, *bien entendu*, it had become 'slow of gait' – as part of the rent of a Moslem village which the Frank owned. After a year the mare died and the Frank, evidently an optimist, claimed a refund of its price. 'We told him, "Thou hast bought it and used it and it died in thy possession. What right hast thou to demand its price?" He replied, "Ye must have given it something to drink, of which it would die after a year." His ignorance and low intelligence amazed us.' It seems more likely that the knight was just trying it on.

One of the famous legends of the Third Crusade is that Saladin, or his brother sent Richard a fine charger. But Richard, who knew a thing or two, ordered a groom whom he thought expendable to mount the animal, which immediately bolted back to the Saracen camp. Saladin was then so ashamed of the trick, or of its failure, that he sent another horse, without the homing instinct.

Hunting was a passion for Franks and Moslems alike, and in times of truce they often hunted together. Small game – bastard, francolin, duck, hares and gazelles – were hunted with hawk and hound; big game – lion, leopard, and wild boar – were ridden down and speared or shot on horseback, an exacting test of equitation in rough, hilly country.

Lions were very common, and man-eaters not unknown. Usama tells of a knight being pulled off his riding-mule on a journey, dragged into the forest and devoured. An English knight on the Third Crusade, Hugh de Neville, slew one with his sword. A party of Norwegian knights on St Louis's Crusade devised a novel and ingenious method of lion-hunting. They galloped after a lion, shot an arrow into him and then, when he angrily pursued them, dropped an old cloak for him to savage. While he was tearing at this, they attacked again, and so on until the lion was killed. Usama, perhaps, would not have considered this quite sporting, for he killed lions face to face, on horseback, with his lance, many of them without help. 'A lion fears man and flees from him . . . except when wounded. But once it is wounded, then it becomes the real lion it is. That is the time when it is to be feared.' Leopards were even more formidable, because of their extreme cunning and agility. One leopard took up residence in a church tower, and when the local seigneur, Sir Adam, rode to church in full armour to rid the parish of this disrespectful pest, the leopard jumped through a

An Anatolian nomad grazing his horse

捉 Pa
里 Li
荒 Fêng

Mongolian nomad
of the 14th century A.D.

window on to him, broke his back, and escaped. The Moslems honoured this animal
as 'the leopard who fights in the Holy War'.

Franks learned from Arabs the use of the cheetah, carried pillion behind an
attendant, for hunting gazelle. One, in his ignorance, tamed a leopard in mistake
for a cheetah and tried to sell it to Usama who was 'amazed at its tractability and
conduct with the Frank'.

It must not be supposed that all Moslems were thrusters like Usama. His near-
contemporary, Kai Kaus ibn Iskander, a Persian prince, gave his son advice on
horsemanship which was cool and markedly unheroic, reminiscent of Lord Chester-
field's advice to his son.

'When you set out to ride, never mount a horse that is too small – however
handsome a man may be, he appears insignificant on a little horse, whereas although
a man may be insignificant in stature, he appears to great advantage on a big horse.
Also, except on a journey, do not ride an ambling horse, because while riding an
ambling horse a man holds himself in a bad posture. In a town, therefore, and in your
own precincts, ride a spirited and high-stepping horse, so that because of the horse's
mettle you are prevented from being careless of your own person. Always hold
yourself erect if you do not want to display an ugly posture in the saddle.

'When hunting, do not urge your horse recklessly forward; to gallop rashly ahead
is to act like a child or an immature youth. Do not go in chase of ferocious beasts;

there is no benefit to be obtained, and nothing is got from it except risk to one's life. . . . Let your attendants charge ahead – except when there are great princes present, and then it may be permissible with a view to acquiring a reputation and bringing oneself to their notice. . . .'

Although they discuss in detail the points of a horse which a purchaser should recognize, neither Usama, Bertrandon de la Brocquière, nor Kai Kaus mention the lucky marks and whorls of hair to which Eastern horsemen attach such significance. A fourteenth-century Hindu manual of horsemanship, however, devotes many pages to this engrossing subject, 'because if good whorls are found in inauspicious places, they cannot bring good luck to their masters'. Particularly auspicious is a whorl in the centre of the forehead, which brings 'immense wealth, fame, and happiness' to the fortunate owner. Horses so endowed 'are not very passionate. In their appearance they look grand and beautiful, and they like war and hunting. . . . Their neighs are pleasing to the ears. They desire to be ridden by Maharajahs, Ministers, and nobles.'

But numerous are the inauspicious marks and faults in conformation of which a buyer should beware. The author of *Asva-Sastra* lists no less than 117, including such distressing but comparatively rare faults as blue teeth, spotted testicles, hairy penis, effeminacy, horns on the head, more than four legs, body odour, and a tendency to roam about at night. To choose a horse in fourteenth-century India must have been a lengthy process – simplified, however, by lumping together all types of unsoundness in the leg and foot under one heading: 'They should not be lame.'

Lack of manpower proved, eventually, the downfall of the Crusaders. Hundreds of thousands of Franks were prepared to make the pilgrimage to Jerusalem, fight a battle or two, and return home; but occasional influxes of enthusiastic visitors did not compensate for a permanent shortage of settlers. In 1291, 290 years after the First Crusaders captured Jerusalem, the last Knight Templar embarked at Chastel Pelerin and the great adventure was over.

The Franks who made their homes in Outremer adopted many things from the Moslems – clothes, food, an Oriental way of life. But they never learned anything from Turkish and Saracen horsemanship. It never occurred to them that the bent-legged, almost balanced, seat could have had anything to do with their enemies' superior mobility.

It is, however, just possible that they learned something from the Byzantines. In Cyprus in the early twelfth century there was a riding-master of extraordinary ability, Nicephorus Magistros, in the employ of the Byzantine ruler of the island. A hundred and fifty years later, in the employ of the Lusignan Kings of the Island – Crusaders – we hear of a famous 'horse-tamer' Nicephorus tou Kalia. It was not usual for Franks to employ Greeks, especially in responsible work to do with horses. Can there be any connection between these two Greeks? Can a riding-school have been established in Cyprus which kept alive the horsemanship of Xenophon? This has been suggested, though, frankly, there is a very weak foundation of fact to support this romantic concept.

But at the far end of the Mediterranean Spanish and Portuguese cavaliers, in contact for centuries with those accomplished horsemen, the Moors, learned a lot from them. In the south they took to riding in the Moorish style, *à la gineta*, with short stirrup-leathers. They developed a lightly armed cavalry who skirmished with javelins. Their knights, mounted on handy Andalusian horses, fought with lances against savage bulls. Militarily their tactics were not very effective against the professionalism of English long-bowmen and dismounted knights, but they were, in all probability, far better horsemen than the men of France, Germany, and England.

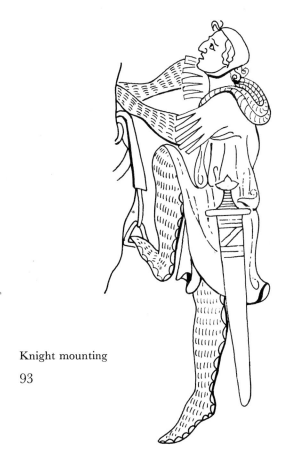

Knight mounting

93

Kara Kitan

黒契丹

The nomads of Kara Kitan obviously had a close relationship with their horse. Indeed, like the early Lithuanians, they may have thought more of them than of their wives

War, as a regular occupation for a gentleman, had many disadvantages. It was, of course, necessary from time to time to go to war in the service of one's liege lord or of God; but added to the perils of death, wounds, or broken bones by enemy action, then was the even more disagreeable danger of death by dysentery or scurvy; one might have to sleep on the cold, stony ground in biting winds or snow; in Outremer war certainly involved long, thirsty marches, baking in one's mail under a blazing sun. There was, to be sure, excitement and renown to be won in war. 'Seneschal,' called the good Count of Soissons to Joinville, holding the bridge against heavy odds near Mansura, 'let these dogs howl; by God's bonnet, you and I shall yet talk in ladies' chambers of this day's work.' But just as much renown could be won, at far less inconvenience, in tournaments.

These were, at first, simply battles arranged on some trumpery pretext at some suitable rendezvous between parties of knights roughly equal in numbers. From these bloody conflicts, fought with ordinary sharpened weapons over a wide stretch of countryside, there developed the tournament conducted according to a complex code of rules. In tournaments a knight could enjoy all the excitement, danger, and glory of war, with none of the dirt, flies, disease, discomfort. After the fight he could soak in a warm bath his bruised, bloody limbs, put on something loose, eat a good dinner, and retire, appropriately accompanied, to a soft, warm bed. In war he might win fame and, with luck, fortune; in tournaments he could win these and much more also. For central to the idea of the tournament was the chivalric ideal of courtly love. A knight selected some lady, beautiful, accomplished, and preferably married to a husband of rank slightly higher than his own. In her honour, perhaps wearing her token, he fought and, if he fought well enough, he expected to receive his reward. There was a direct conflict between the Christian ideal of monogamy and the chivalric ideal of courtly love, that is to say of polite, aristocratic adultery. It was considered among those who bore arms downright disgraceful, absolute treachery,

94

for a lady to refuse her favours for a knight who had fought in her honour – especially if he had at the same time beggared himself by the most grotesque extravagance, pouring out his money on armour, liveries for his attendants, fancy-dress for his squires, feasts, and all the costly trappings of a tournament. This other aspect of the tournament is well indicated in a number of poems and chansons and indeed in Arthurian romance, no less than in a thirteenth-century miniature showing the lady spectators of a tournament lifting their skirts to display the prize of victory.

It was up to the lady, whether she wanted to or not, to dispose temporarily of her husband and make arrangements for the assignation. Even if, as in the epic poem of Moriz von Kraun, she found on arrival at the rendezvous that her gallant, exhausted by his exertions, was snoring in her bed, she was still expected to go through with it. The brave deserved the fair, though she might, in the eyes of the Church, belong to someone else. English readers will, however, be gratified to learn that knights of the Island Race had the reputation of being neither addicted to nor adept at courtly love. In England a tournament was regarded rather as serious training for war and an occasion for fresh air and exercise. The French were the real experts, in both the tournament and its sequel.

The ordinary knight was an amateur performer prepared always to have a go. There was, besides, a class of tournament professionals, generally landless younger sons. A knight errant who planned his itinerary carefully could reckon on performing every two or three weeks during the summer season (in winter travel was too difficult), and making a good living from the ransoms, horses, and armour of those whom he defeated. For an ordinary knight to pit himself against one of these *chevaliers tournayeur* was about as hopeless as an amateur boxer taking on Joe Louis. For such professionals the customary gestures of extravagance and generosity to the vanquished were generally made with an eye to the main chance.

Gradually during the thirteenth century tournaments ceased to be miniature battles with no holds barred, and became organized spectacles, subject to accepted conventions and fought often with blunted weapons. To kill a man in a tournament was considered wrong – or, at least, very, very unfortunate. For killing a horse there was no excuse. The knight's object became the less sanguinary one of knocking off their horses as many opponents as possible and, in the process, breaking as many of one's own lances as possible; for obviously the more lances a knight broke, the greater must have been the impetuosity of his charge.

From a team event, tournaments gradually changed into displays of single combat, fought according to rules which might, for instance, limit the fight to three runs with blunted lances, three strokes with sword or axe dismounted, and three with the dagger. They required, of course, a high standard of horsemanship. Not only had a knight to keep his seat against the terrific shock, with both horses at full gallop, of a lance-point on his helmet or shield; but he must be able to prevent his own horse running out, aim his own lance accurately, to hit his opponent fair and square in an 'attaint', and at all costs to avoid giving a foul blow below the belt. He was not allowed to tie himself to the saddle; and to leave one's helm loose, so that it was knocked off without one being dislodged from the saddle, was not particularly *buen vu*.

95

There was an element of snobbery in tournaments. They were a gentleman's occupation, just as the subsequent adultery was a gentleman's diversion – not really for the bourgeoisie. But sometimes the lower orders aped their betters. There is a thirteenth-century picture of a gay party of courtesans riding to a tournament impudently dressed as knights.

Tournaments were generally viewed with disapprobation by the Church, because they distracted knights from the Crusades; and by the State, because they cost money and valuable lives, and served sometimes as foci for rebellion. Popes and Kings might fulminate against them, but were quite powerless to stop them.

Monkish artists pointed the moral by painting demons hovering over a tournament or riding pillion behind knights thus sinfully employed. There are many relevant and improving stories on the subject. One knight was so imprudent as to engage in a tournament without his armour. He was, deservedly, slain, and his ghost rode round the country on a spectral black horse until a serf dared to withdraw the lance-point from his heart and display it as a ghastly warning.

In the last quarter of the twelfth century horses began to be protected by bardings of leather or padded cloth, embellished with their owners' arms and resembling modern horse-rugs but reaching nearly to the ground and covering head and neck as well as body. They probably gave quite good protection against arrows, but must have greatly slowed down and hampered a horse. They could hardly have been used in a tropical country, but by that time the Crusaders were confined to a few coastal strongholds.

The late thirteenth century was rich in military invention. Besides the minor invention of bardings for cavalry-horses, it saw a revival of light cavalry. These, armed with javelins, had always been employed, on both sides, in the long wars between Christian and Moslem in Spain: Polish and Hungarian horsemen were

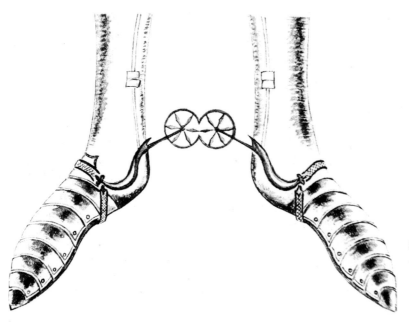

Sir John Lysle's spurs.
A.D. 1407

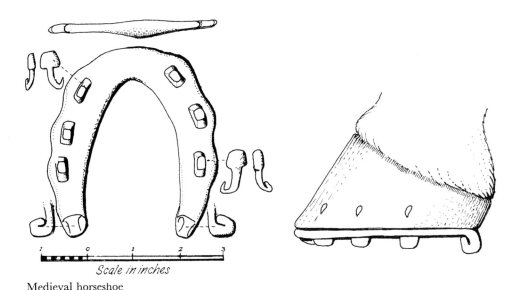

Scale in inches

Medieval horseshoe

lightly armed by Western standards. But in north-west Europe light horse had
hardly been seen since Roman times. However, the Wardens of the Scottish border
were plagued by lightly armed raiders, mounted on ponies, carrying little more than
a bag of oatmeal at their saddle-bows. Neither knights nor infantry could catch them
on the Northumbrian moors, so the English in their turn employed light horse,
clad only in leather jerkins and armed with sword and spear, called 'hobilars'. Their
use spread, for reconnaissance and foraging.

Far more important, indeed of paramount military and social importance, was
the development, at the same time, of the long-bow. Originally a Welsh invention,
this was wonderfully exploited by the English who used it first, with devastating
effect, against Scottish spearmen. Europe remained in happy ignorance of this
terrible weapon, almost until the Battle of Crécy, in 1346. The long-bow was far
more accurate, powerful, and long-ranged than older types of short-bows, and with
it a man could shoot half a dozen shafts while the cross-bowman could shoot only
one. The narrow head, triangular in section, easily penetrated mail. Except in the
hands of a superb marksman (and superb marksmen were rare) it was not so much a
precision weapon as a weapon of mass-destruction. The arrow hail, directed by
under-officers on to this part of the battle-field or that, could create at any range up to
300 yards a beaten zone in which no cavalry could survive. Hundreds of cloth-
yard shafts, falling steeply from the sky, transfixed men and slaughtered horses,
driving the surviving animals mad and unmanageable with pain and fear, so that
they threw their riders and trampled them underfoot.

The immediate, obvious answer to a better missile weapon is always heavier
armour, so in the fourteenth and fifteenth centuries plate-armour gradually replaced
mail. Plate would deflect an arrow, unless it penetrated a joint or made a ninety-
degree impact at fairly close range; but this did not help the horses, who were

97

exposed to the merciless arrow hail unless they too were armoured in plate. So by the mid fifteenth century the knight's charger carried a ten-stone man, some eight stone of arms and armour, a heavier saddle, and the horse's own armour, nearly thirty stone in all. This did require an enormous weight-carrier which, even with the largest and sharpest spurs, could barely be legged into a trot.

In this tactical use of the long-bow the English showed themselves, not for the first time in their history, masters of the defence, but not very enterprising in attack. Most of the knights and men-at-arms dismounted, leaving only a small mounted reserve. The led horses were held by squires and pages in the rear, and the fighting men formed up in something like the Saxon or Danish shield-wall, but with salients or 'harrows' of archers to take in the flank any enemy who ventured a frontal attack. The co-ordination of hobilars, archers (who were often mounted for the march but dismounted to fight), armoured infantry, and a mounted reserve require a military expertise well beyond the ordinary king or baron; so a class of professional officer grew up, of which the prototype was the famous Sir John Chandos.

For most of the Hundred Years War it seemed as though there was no answer to the English defence; but eventually the French discovered the answer – not to attack it, at least not frontally, but to outflank, harass, and finally, as cannon became a significant weapon, to break it up by gun-fire.

But the long-bow and later the musket, and the phalanx of swiftly moving Swiss pikemen or Spanish infantry, relegated cavalry to a secondary role on the European battle-field. Only in the little wars of Italy did they survive, because there was no good infantry, and the battles were fought by exotically clad mercenaries, often foreigners, whose motto might have been, 'He who fights and runs away will draw his pay another day.'

The story of Absalom
depicted on a Norwegian
painted casket

The horses of 15th-century Italy being ridden with
a high degree of collection well before
Grisone's day

Meanwhile, the tournament continued to flourish, but lost all touch with military reality and became simply a magnificent spectator-sport. The greatest danger was of a head-on clash between two galloping horses, or smashed knees as they passed too close to one another. The first was lessened by great pads of straw bound to the horses' chests; but even then there could be nasty accidents such as when the sharp spike on one horse's headpiece pierced the nostril of another, who reared up, fell back, and crushed his rider. So the 'tilt' was devised, to keep the horses apart. At first this was simply a rope stretched the length of the arena. Each knight galloped down his own side of the rope so as to pass his opponent left-hand-to-left-hand. Later the rope was replaced by a stout wooden barrier, so there was no chance of a collision and there could be no hand-to-hand fighting. Knight's armour, horse's armour, and the Great Horse itself became so ponderous that antagonists advanced on one another at a very slow canter or an earth-shaking trot.

The object of the exercise was still to break one's lance or to topple one's opponent off his horse. But now, to facilitate these objects, the lance had either a long, slender, softwood shaft, or one of enormous thickness, several inches in diameter, and far too heavy to be of any use in battle. In the latter case the saddle's pommel rose to a great iron shield, covering the rider's body; iron leg-guards were built into the saddle; and the cantle was removed altogether so that a rider could roll over backwards. As a final precaution, the knight let go of his lance at the moment of impact.

Discarding his shield, a knight could do much more with his reins, so collection became possible in the tilt-yard. With the need to steer, stop, and turn the ponderous 'Great Horse' for another carrière, it became not only possible but necessary.

With the decay of the idea of chivalry every precaution was taken to make the tournament as innocuous as possible. It no longer seemed reasonable to risk one's life, or another's, by fighting just for fun, and gentlemen began to take an interest in equitation as distinct from war and tournament.

4

The Revival of Scientific Equitation

No manuals of medieval ecclesiastical building have survived. Yet the men of the Middle Ages contrived to build tolerably good cathedrals, churches, and abbeys, beautiful, functional, and still in use.

We should not, therefore, assume from the absence of manuals on equitation that medieval horsemanship was a hit-or-miss sort of affair in which slow, lumbering creatures were constrained by brute force and cruel bits into some sort of compliance with their riders' crude wishes. Men who dealt with horses in the fourteenth century were far less likely to be literary minded than men who dealt with cathedrals, and there may well have been an orally based science of horsemanship, of which we have an occasional clue such as medieval pictures of horses being, apparently, taught the High School airs.

As the heavily armoured, mounted knight was relegated from the battle-field to the chivalric romances, and the tournament, no longer practical war-training, became simply a gorgeous spectator-sport hardly more dangerous than the Folies Bergère, so the carousel became fashionable. This was a sort of pageant in which gentlemen in fancy-dress tilted at rings, or at the quintain, took part in stately musical rides and performed various feats of horsemanship not in combat but in display, parade, or procession.

In the sixteenth century, there was a spate of books on equitation by authors who were stimulated by the revival of Classical learning and elated by the discovery that scientific equitation had its roots as far back as Xenophon. Probably they did no more than standardize and describe in writing an art or science which was already well established.

Xenophon had aimed at producing both a useful horse for active service, and a splendid parade-horse with a noble head-carriage and a high-stepping, cadenced trot, on which a commander could display himself to advantage at the head of his troops. Sixteenth-century experts paid lip-service to the practical value in a mêlée of these High School exercises. The curvet, for instance, in which the horse raises his forehand in a half-rear while maintaining a lively cadenced pace behind, all without advancing, or while turning on the forehand or moving laterally, was claimed to be 'very necessary, and especially in a horse of service, to make him keep his head always towards an enemy in fighting hand to hand'. Turning on the haunches, the *volte*, was 'of all other turns the most beautiful, most gallant, and most assured and strong, both for man and horse, it is most in use in service, especially in that manner of fight which our English soldiers term fighting at the croup'. By a rapid half-*pirouette* a horseman could clear a space among a crowd of enemy foot-soldiers. The object of the *capriole* was, presumably, to unman an enemy infantryman sneaking up from behind. But

The drunken
Babur riding
through his camp
after celebrations
in A.D. 1519. Note
the nosebags and
rugs on the horses
beside the well

Abu'l Mihjan meeting Sa'd Ibn Wakkas on the
road to Medina. From a Kashmiri miniature
of about A.D. 1686

all this was, of course, nonsense. The long-bow and fire-arm had long ago made
mounted attacks unprofitable, save those executed with speed and surprise on a
breaking enemy; while in a mêlée no one has time for antics. Moreover, as an English
writer, Thomas Blundeville, remarked, who wants a horse which, spurred forward in
battle, 'falls a-hopping and dancing up and down in one place?' The object of the
manège was art for art's sake, to practise a very difficult and, to its practitioners,
satisfying form of equitation: and why not? It also served the useful purpose of
displaying great men in a glamorous and heroic role, curvetting and caracoling
about, before lesser mortals. One's only regret is that the practice has not survived.
How much more impressive our politicians and pace-setters would look prancing
along on a great horse, in an elegant series of *levades* varied by an occasional *capriole*,
than scurrying past in a large car.

The principles of the manège, as of modern cross-country riding, were first
systemized and reduced to writing in Italy where the first of many riding-
schools was started by Federico Grisone in Naples, and soon became a centre of
fashionable equine culture frequented by the young gentlemen from Italy, France,
Germany, Spain, and even England, a country where scientific equitation has never
had a great following. Henry VII, pawky and parsimonious, had prepared his horses

for State occasions by twenty-fours' starvation, to induce a state of docility suitable for a royal rider who was no horseman. But Henry VIII took to equitation with characteristic zeal and extravagance, introducing to Hampton Court a riding-master, Robert Alexander, 'sometime Grisone's scholar'. 'The most honourable exercise', Sir Thomas Elyot assured King Henry in 1531 – significantly before the publication of Grisone's book – 'and that becometh the estate of every noble person is to ride surely and cleanly on a great horse.'

The methods of Grisone as set out in 1550 in his *Gli Ordini di Cavalcare*, and of his pupil and successor, Pignatelli, soon spread all over western Europe. For those whose command of sixteenth-century Italian is incomplete, they can be studied in books written by several English plagiarists.

The first thing that strikes one in reading these books is that the emphasis was not on suppling a horse or winning his confidence, but on breaking his resistance by 'correction' and then rewarding him either by 'cherishing' or, more often, simply by a cessation of punishment. This, for instance, is how, according to Grisone and Blundeville, a young horse should be backed.

Charger of Duarte da Gama being landed at Nagasaki

Schooling horses in 16th-century Japan

'The horse being thus saddled and bridled, cause him to be brought forth to some block, whereas if he will not stand still while you take his back, then let him that bringeth him make much of him, and sometimes threaten him with his voice, and thrust him with his hand on the right side toward the block, whereupon you shall stand, continually cherishing him with your hand, to the intent that he may suffer you to get up. But if he be so forward and so stubborn, as he will not come nigh the block, then all to rate him with a terrible voice, and beat him yourself with a good stick upon the head, between the ears, not leaving him until you have made him come to the block, whether he will or not.' Alternatively, he could be taken out to a heavy ploughed field and flogged round on a lungeing-rein until the devil of disobedience had been exorcized. Just the way to make a horse look forward to the next lesson! Grisone's methods with nervous youngsters had, at least, the virtue of simplicity: 'In breaking in young horses, put them into a circular pit; be very severe with those that are sensitive and of high courage: beat them between the ears with a stick.'

The saddle was a padded affair, with a high pommel and cantle, sloped sharply like the medieval or the modern Western saddle, from front to rear. The pommel formed a distinct horn: as this was not needed for roping, its only purpose must have been to give the rider something to hold in moments of crisis – far better than hanging

105

The Hunt
by Paolo Uccello. 15th century

on by the reins. The rider's thigh was wedged between pads fore and aft. The only horse which the manège expert rode, known as the 'great' (or, more incongruously, the 'pleasure') horse was the huge, ponderous creature bred to carry thirty stone of knight and armour. To make this vast creature handle as lightly as a polo pony, it was necessary, above all things, to get him back on his haunches and to carry his head 'like a fighting ram' in what we should call a grossly 'overbent' posture. To this object all early schooling was directed, and for this, too, the bit was designed.

The bit, always a curb, might be either 'open' (with a port) or 'closed' (without a port); it might have either a solid or a broken mouthpiece. The open bit with a broken mouthpiece was suitable for a hard-mouthed horse, because the port stopped him lifting, with his tongue, the bit off the bars of his mouth, and the broken mouth-piece produced, when the reins were pulled, a sort of nutcracker effect on the sides of the horse's mouth. The 'arm' or cheekpieces were as much as fifteen inches long, producing terrific leverage to bend the thickest and most inflexible neck; but the power of the bit would depend on two variable factors – the tightness of the curb-chain and the rider's hands. The cannons of the mouthpiece were generally smooth

106

and of large diameter, so comparatively innocuous in their pressure on the bars of the mouth. Dangling 'keys' were sometimes attached to the port as in modern breaking-bits, to give the horse something to play with and keep his mouth moist. To some bits was attached a thin 'flying trench' which seems to have been a sort of bridoon, operated independently of the curb by its own pair of reins. Reinforced by sundry spikes, the sixteenth-century bit could be an instrument of torture; without the spikes it was an instrument of power, but not necessarily painful to the horse unless the rider had rough hands.

It was not used with a young horse, for which there were various devices which acted with more or less severity on the horse's nose. Blundeville noted that 'our riders in England use a chain not much unlike in effect unto the cavesson, but yet in my judgement not so meet for a young horse, for that it straineth the tender gristle of his nose too sore'. Almost as severe was a musrole, a sort of noseband made of twisted iron which should 'lie upon the centre of his nose neither so low as to crush the tender gristle of his nostrils, nor so high that it may by the correction be any blemish to the horse's face'. But Grisone himself, 'for fear of marring the mouth', used

W. Browne's method of
teaching the artificial
pace of the amble.
16th century

a plain leather cavesson. Even this could be misused, as was shown by the way 'the
silly horses be tormented and mangled therewith about their noses, so as the skin and
flesh is worn to the bones; and where it should lie flat by nature *come un muttone* (as
Grisone said) like to the nose of a sheep, they by their violence make it arise in the
middle like to the beak of a hawk'. The proper way, however, to use a cavesson on a
young horse was to 'use it so gently as he may not only be content to wear it, but also
to be quietly led thereby. Neither must you use any other kind of bridle than this, or
any other saddle for fear of hurting his back than a soft pad of straw, until your horse
can trot clean, keep the ring, stop and turn roundly on both hands.'

When that stage in a horse's training was reached, the reins attached to the
cavesson were first supplemented, then replaced by 'false reins' attached either to the
'flying trencher' or bridoon, or to the top rings in the arms of the bit, as though it
were a Pelham. Finally the false reins were first supplemented, then replaced, by
reins attached to the ends of the arms of the bit. It is noteworthy that, however tough
their method in other respects, sixteenth-century horsemen were careful never to
spoil a horse's mouth. Even the fearful spikes attached to Grisone's cruellest bit took
effect on the sides of a horse's face, not on the corners of his lips nor on the bars of
his mouth.

There were seven 'helps' or aids in the manège: voice, tongue, rod or wand,
bridle, calves of the leg, stirrups, and spurs. Voice, rod, bridle, calves, stirrups, and
spurs were also used as 'corrections', as was 'treading the ring'. 'You help a horse to
the intent that he may not err; but you correct him for that he hath already erred.'

Great importance was attached to the voice. 'The voice is that which any horse

feareth most, and is needful in all disorders.' According to the tone and words used, it could be a correction, a help, or a cherishing. 'For if you would correct him for any shrewd toy, or obstinacy, you must all to rate him with a terrible voice, saying, "Ah, traitor, ah traitor, turn here, stop there," and such like. But if you would help him at any time, then you must use a more mild and more cheerful voice, as when you would run him, to say, "Hey, hey," or "Now, now." Likewise if you would have him go back, you must say to him with a loud voice, "Back, boy, back I say." Also if you would have him advance at the stop, you must say cheerfully, "Hup, hup." Likewise to make him light behind you must say, "*Derrière, derrière*", or use such terms as you shall think good. But if you would cherish your horse, or coy him for doing well, then your voice must be most mild of all, as when you say, "Holla holla", or "So boy, so boy" or use such cloying words.' The sound of the tongue clicked against the palate, was also a very necessary help in stopping and turning, as was a sudden parting of the lips pronouncing as it were the word *Powgh*. (It seems that in the sixteenth century horses were more gifted, intellectually and linguistically, than they are now. I cannot see any horse of mine reacting intelligently to the command '*derrière*'. But Shakespeare's England could boast a calculating horse called Marocco, an equine paragon who, in the presence of large audiences, would restore a glove to its owner whose name had been whispered in its ear, or indicate the number of pence in a silver coin. Unfortunately, this talented quadruped was taken by his owner to exhibit his powers in Rome, where both were found to be diabolically inspired and were burnt at the stake.)

'The rod or wand serveth to correct disordering of the head, or to drive shrewd

15th-century horse-dealers displaying the paces
of an Arab stallion

The Horse Drummer

Below
M. Pluvinel assisting
Louis XIII to mount

Gustavus-Adolphus at the Battle of Stuhm mounted on what appears to be an Arab

toys out of his mind.' Held in the right hand, upright like a sword at the 'carry', it had many uses besides the obvious one of mild chastisement. Tapping the horse's outer shoulder or holding the point of the rod alongside the horse's outer eye were aids in turning or circling. Tapping his forelegs made the horse rein back or raise his forehand in a *levade*. Tapping his croup in different places was the signal for raising his quarters in the *croupade* or *ballotade*, or lashing out in the *capriole*. (The same result was sometimes obtained, less kindly, by tapping his sheath with the tip of the wand, an aid which is even now sometimes used by horse-copers who do not boast of it.) The noise of the wand shaken or swished through the air indicates to the trained horse that he must increase his pace; and scratching his neck or crest with the butt of the rod was a form of 'cherishing' or making much of him.

Some description has already been given of the sixteenth-century bit. A young horse should be bitted with a plain cannon, mildest of mouthpieces, which might with advantage be anointed with honey and salt 'to make him more delight in it and to be always champing thereon'. Sterner measures could be taken with an older horse. For instance, one who had developed a one-sided mouth, so that he was difficult to turn in one direction, could be corrected by fitting sharp pricks, like cocks' spurs, to the cheekpieces or curb-chain hook on the opposite side. Grisone warned his pupils that cruel bits could ruin a horse's mouth, and recommended them to abstain from such, 'seeking rather to bring your horse to have a good mouth, while he is young, by riding him with a gentle bit, and bearing a temperate hand. . . . For, assure yourself, it is art and good order of riding which maketh the good mouth, and not the bit.' When one sees some of the engines which Grisone and his pupil, Pignatelli, devised, one wonders what he meant by 'cruel bits'.

The reins were held, generally in the left hand, exactly as they are now, divided by the little finger, and turned over between thumb and forefinger, with bent wrist, finger-nails towards the rider. Their use was mainly, it seems, in stopping the horse: in circling or turning him reliance was placed on the rider's legs and wand, rather than on the inside rein. There is no evidence of the indirect or neck rein being used. Any exaggerated movement of the bridle hand was deprecated as bad style.

Leg-aids were, in order of severity, squeezing the horse with one's calves; tapping him on the outer shoulder with the stirrup-iron; a delicate pricking with the spurs and the powerful use of sharp spurs in punishment. The use of the legs to turn a horse, not merely to make him increase his pace, was one of the most important developments in horsemanship during the 1,800 years which separated Xenophon and Grisone. It may be connected with the fact that the early medieval knight, carrying in his bridle hand a great heavy shield, could not use the reins with any delicacy for steering; so he equipped himself with long sharp spurs and used his legs.

In turning on the forehand, or circling with the horse's head pointing towards the centre of the ring, his hind-legs making a track outside that of the forelegs, lateral

The Capriole. Painted by Baron d'Eisenberg. 18th century

aids were used: that is to say, legs, wand, and rein all on the same, the inner side. But in turning him on his haunches, or circling him so that his hind-legs followed exactly in the tracks made by the forelegs, diagonal aids were used – inner rein, outer leg, and wand. This follows the modern practice, though turning on the forehand is not now generally practised except in teaching a hunter to open a gate.

'Treading the ring' is classed as a correction, though it might be better included among the aids. In order to make a horse move straight forward and backward, halt in his tracks, and be 'just' in his turns and circles, he was schooled along narrow paths, carefully measured and trodden-down, in a ploughed field. Naturally he preferred to keep to the smooth, trodden paths than to plunge fetlock-deep into the mud. Much thought and ingenuity was devoted to devising the best size and pattern of rings for different manège exercises. Rings could also be made between walls of furze bush. Treading the rings at a trot or gallop, round and round, again and again, as in a prison treadmill, was useful in making a horse forget his 'shrewd toys', and an indispensable correction for such deplorable faults as jumping without order, flinging with his heels, being too hasty or furious, running away, or pissing always when handled.

Finally, much use was made of footmen, suitably armed, who could assist the rider by rating, beating, or physically shoving an obstinate or uncomprehending horse into compliance with his master's wishes.

In general 'the voice correcteth without disorder, and maketh the horse afraid

Duke of Newcastle (*left*) schooling horse and
rider in the capriole

Caprioles à Droite.

An old woodcut
supposed to depict the
famous Federico Grisone

without putting him in despair, whereas the cudgel many times maketh him desperate and faint-hearted'. Nevertheless, desperate remedies might have to be taken
'when the rider lacketh art, and knoweth not the order of riding, how to get the
mastery of his horse'.

Of all forms of equine vice the most infuriating is nappiness, a plain, mulish
refusal – for no apparent reason – to move forward, varied by backing rapidly into
a ditch, tractor, or some similarly unsympathetic object. One legs the brute until
both are in a muck sweat, turns him round and round till both are giddy, wallops
him and swears at him – all to no effect: there is some foul fiend ahead and he will *not*
go forward to meet it. Fortunately, the vice is rare, and man's invention will always
overcome the obstinacy of brute beast. Blundeville recommended 'a whelp or some
other loud-crying and biting beast', or even an iron bar armed with prickles,
suspended from the horse's tail and drawn up by the rider, whenever the horse proved
recalcitrant, by means of a cord passing between the hind-legs. If this failed, 'let a
footman stand behind you with a shrewd cat tied at one end of a long pole with her
belly upwards, so as she may have her mouth and claws at liberty. And when your
horse both stay or go backwards, let him thrust the cat between his legs so as she may
scratch and bite him, sometime by the thighs, sometime by the rump and often times
by the stones.'

But such vigorous remedies were not without drawbacks. When the King had

117

trouble with an old, restive horse turning nappy, Master Vincentio Respini, a Neopolitan expert, prescribed a live hedgehog 'tied straight by the foot' under the culprit's tail. It worked. The vice was corrected, but 'in such sort that he had much ado to prevent the contrary vice of running away'.

Blundeville considered, however, that 'to correct a restive horse by tying a cord with a riding knot unto the horse's stones, holding the same and straining it when need did require, is more hurtful than profitable, not to be used but in some extremity'. The application of fire to the tender portions of a horse's anatomy, another common aid, was deprecated by progressive horsemen.

Many a Pony Club member has suffered his pony's insistence, half-way through a bog or midden, of stopping to lie down and roll. A footman with a syringe full of water can help in curing this vice, by squirting water in the horse's eyes 'whenever he offereth to lie down'. Unfortunately, a footman with a syringe full of water is seldom in attendance in the hunting-field or at Pony Club rallies.

If your pony is addicted to lying down when crossing a stream, you may 'cause a servant to ride him into some river or water, not over-deep, and appoint three other footmen with cudgels in their hands to follow him hard at the heels into the water, to the intent that when the horse beginneth to lie down, they may be ready to leap upon him, and with the help of the rider to force him to duck his head down

Part of the collection of studies of Haute École.
Painted by Baron Reis d'Eisenberg for the
Earl of Pembroke

Opposite
The capriole again. Also by Baron Reis d'Eisenberg

119

under the water so that the water may enter into his ears, not suffering him to lift his head again of a good while together, but make him by main force keep it still under, continually beating him all the while with their cudgels and rating him with loud and terrible voices'. When the horse eventually emerges from the water, let everyone stand clear, 'lest there be disorder'. 'If these corrections do not work, truly the fault is in the footmen, lacking perhaps such terrible voices, cruel looks and gestures as should serve the purpose.'

The summit of achievement in the manège was an exact and polished performance of the 'airs above the ground', but for these feats preliminary exercises were necessary to get the horse off his forehand, his centre of gravity back, and his hocks well under him. Halting a horse while going down a slope was helpful in this. The young horse was very early taught to 'yerk', that is to say, to kick out with both hind-legs, as a preliminary to the *capriole*: first make him 'advance', then beat and spur him (not letting him move forward), not 'leaving to molest him in such sort until you see that he beginneth to gather up his rump and to lift his hinder legs'; then cherish him, and he will soon get the message. Molesting him in his stable was also efficacious in making him yerk.

Mounting, first stage

Another preliminary exercise was the 'advance', in which a horse raised and lowered his forehand in a series of controlled half-rears without, in fact, moving forward. To teach this the rider halted him at a trot, and then, without letting him go forward, legged him, clicked his tongue, and shook the rod in his hand; 'which at the first will peradventure but move in your horse a stammering or amazement, but be you careless, go on trying and you will succeed'.

Finally, as the climax of his training, the horse was taught to 'bound aloft' in the *corvetti* and the *capriole*.* 'The *corvetti* is a certain continual prancing up and down still in one place, like a bear at a stake, and sometimes sidling to and fro.' In the *capriole* he bounded aloft while at the same time yerking out behind. Both were taught from the 'advance', the aids of the rod, the spur, and the word 'hup' being freely used.

Then and only then could a horse 'be ridden in best show before a Prince', which was, perhaps, the object of the exercise.

In any study of history one tends automatically to label men, literature, buildings,

* It is significant of the prestige of Italian horsemanship in the sixteenth century that English writers used all the Italian manège terms. Later, the French equivalents were to become universal.

Arjuna trying to free his horse which became stuck while
rubbing against a rock. A painting by a Mughal artist in
an A.D. 1598 MS.

and politics by their century, forgetting that the end of a century is not, except in
our imagination, a hard-and-fast line limiting men's lives and cultures. But in the
science or art of equitation one can surely see a clear distinction between the sixteenth
and the seventeenth centuries' views. Antoine de Pluvinel, who in the early seventeenth century ran in Paris a young noblemen's finishing school with an emphasis on
equitation, and the Duke of Newcastle who, in exile during the Commonwealth,
ran a riding-school in Paris and Brussels in mid-century, were more patient in their
methods, more thoughtful; they really studied the physique and mental attributes of
the horse and adapted their training methods to the individual animal; they never
used – or, at least, never recommended – cudgels, cats, hedgehogs, or punitive bits
in training horses. They were, in short, more sensible, more scientific, and more
humane than Grisone, Pignatelli, and their sixteenth-century English plagiarists.

Pluvinel, a soldier and a diplomat as well as a riding-master, wrote a classic on
equitation which was published in 1623 under the title *Manège du Roy*, and re-
published five years later as *L'instruction du Roy en l'exercice de monter à cheval*. The

frontispiece of his book indicates his approach to the subject. It shows on one side of the page a Herculean figure labelled *Robur*. Despite his impressive muscular development, he experiences difficulty in controlling a thoroughly upset, rearing horse which he is trying to lead by means of a watering-bridle. On the other side is an elegant young lady, *Scientia*, undraped to her delicious navel, leading a docile, obedient stallion by a scientifically designed curb-bit, while in the other hand she holds a book which she is diligently studying.

The book itself is in the form of a dialogue between a respectful but authoritative Monsieur de Pluvinel and his extraordinarily zealous, perceptive, and intelligent pupil, the young King Louis XII. Courtiers occasionally intervene with remarks designed to bring out their royal master's genius.

'I wish to learn,' says the latter, 'not only what is necessary as a King, but what is needed to obtain perfection in these exercises.'

Note the forward seat of Rembrandt's Polish horseman

Mounting, second stage

Monsieur Pluvinel finds him a pupil after his own heart, capable of becoming not merely a 'bon homme de cheval', but a 'bel homme de cheval'. Very early he points out that 'the horse must find pleasure in the manège, or the rider can do nothing gracefully'. No horse can be described as 'schooled' until he is perfectly obedient to hand and spur.

'How,' asks the King, 'can one treat a horse who disobeys?'

'It is far better to teach by kindness than by strictness. . . . If a horse refuses to obey, a good horseman finds out what prevents him. . . . He should be whipped only if he disobeys through laziness. 'Il faute être avare des coups, et prodigue des caresses.'

The great thing was to study the individual horse. 'Some are so stupid, cowardly, and weak that they are capable only of walking along a road two leagues a day. They are better for a cart than a manège, and so unworthy of being presented to Your Majesty that we will not talk of them before you. Others are strong, but cowardly and one must use intelligence to improve them.' It might answer to shut such a horse up in a dark stable for a month or six weeks, meanwhile stuffing him with as much corn as he could eat. 'This will animate him, which is what is wanted.'

124

Firmly in the saddle

Pluvinel added to Grisone's aids the *chambrière* and the *poinçon*. The former was a short-handled whip with a broad (and therefore innocuous) lash, used by an assistant on foot to stimulate the action of the horse's hind-legs; the latter a short wooden handle with an iron point at one end which, applied to the horse's croup made him kick up his heels. He also invented 'the pillars'.

These were the key to Pluvinel's methods, and are still used in High School training today. A single pillar was used instead of the ring. A young horse was tied to it by a rope, of varying length, attached to the cavesson; and then, with or without a rider, made round it, at various paces, the turns and circles of the High School.

Tied by the cavesson ropes between two pillars, and appropriately stimulated behind by the *chambrière*, a horse could be taught the *piaffe*, a high-stepping, cadenced trot in one spot, without moving forward, as though 'marking time'. Further stimulated, but still unable to move forward, tapped a little on the chest or forelegs, he could only go upwards, raising his forehand in a series of *levades*. If, while his forehand was raised, the *poinçon* were applied to his croup, he would then raise his quarters so that all four legs were off the ground – either in the *croupade* with his hind-legs tucked under his belly; or in the *ballotade* with his hind-legs drawn up below his quarters; or

125

Troopers of Skinner's Horse

in the most difficult *capriole*, the goat-leap, when he kicked out behind with the soles of his feet turned up to the sky. Between the pillars a horse could be practised with or without a rider. Soon the *poinçon* and *chambrière* would be unnecessary; the former replaced by a touch on the croup with the butt or tip of the whip, the latter by a squeeze of the leg or a light pricking with the spur.

The most severe aid was the strong use of sharp spurs. The whip was used less to punish than to tap as a signal or, held alongside a horse's face, as a guide. Swished through the air, it told the horse to get a move on.

Another way of raising a horse's forehand, without the pillar was to move towards him, while he was doing a *piaffe*, a stout pole, held between two footmen about eighteen inches off the ground. As it reached his knees, the horse was almost certain to perform a *levade* to evade it.

Throughout his training, Pluvinel's two guiding principles were individual treatment of each horse, and the application of force not cruelly, but with irresistible mechanical advantage.

Much the same principles were followed by the Duke of Newcastle, a patrician of ineffable conceit and reckless courage, whose procrastination and military incompetence was largely responsible for the Royalists losing the vital Battle of Marston Moor. He consoled himself during his subsequent exile by the scientific study of equitation and by running a riding academy, first in Paris and then in Brussels, which was a rendezvous for the *jeunesse dorée* of Europe.

He counselled above all things patience, not trying to teach a young horse too much too quickly. 'A boy is a long time before he knows his alphabet, longer before he had learned to spell, and perhaps several years before he can read distinctly; and yet there are some people who, as soon as they get on a young horse, entirely undressed and untaught, fancy that by beating and spurring they will make him a dressed horse in one morning only. I would fain ask such stupid people whether by beating a boy they could teach him to read without first showing him the alphabet? Sure, they would beat him to death, before they would make him read.'

His methods in dealing with difficult horses were the very antithesis of Grisone's and Blundeville's. 'I have not yet seen that force and passion prevail upon a horse; for the horse having less understanding than his rider, his passion is so much the stronger, which makes him always get the better of his rider and shows that violent

An Anatolian nomad plaiting his horse's tail.
14th century

Cavalry at exercise from *Militärkunst zu Pferde*

methods will not do. So if he backs, pull him back: if he pushes forward, push him: if he insists on turning to the right, keep him turning that way until he sickens of it.'

Newcastle backed a young horse after it had been handled in the stable for two or three winters, and led for a few days beside a quiet old Dobbin. It could then be mounted quite easily, without recourse to 'ploughs and morasses'.

We have from the Duke of Newcastle the best description of the seventeenth-century seat on a horse. It does not differ essentially from that taught by Pluvinel and the Italian masters, but is described in more detail.

'Before a horseman mounts, he ought first to take care that his horse's furniture is in order, which is done without prying into every minute circumstance to show himself an affected connoisseur in the art. . . . He ought to sit upright upon the twist, and not upon the buttocks. . . . When he is thus placed upon his twist in the middle of the saddle, he ought to advance as much as he can towards the pommel, leaving a handsbreadth between his backside and the arch of the saddle, holding his legs perpendicular as when he stands upon the ground, and his knees and thighs turned inwards towards the saddle, keeping as close as if they were glued to the saddle. . . . He ought to fix himself firm upon his stirrup, with his heels a little lower than the toes, so that the end of his toes may pass about half an inch beyond the stirrup, or somewhat more. He should keep his hams stiff, having his legs neither too near nor too far distant from his horse. . . . He ought to hold the reins in his left hand. . . . his arm bent and close to the body in an easy posture. . . . The bridle hand ought to be held three inches above the pommel and two inches beyond it. . . . He should have a slender switch in his right hand, not too long like a fishing-rod, nor too short like a bodkin. . . . The rider's breast ought to be in some measure advanced, his countenance pleasant and gay, but without a laugh.'

128

To the normal aids he added the rider's body, the proper positioning of which was a great help in the various figures of the manège. The leg-aids he divided into the thigh, the calf, and a gentle pinching with the spurs: a more forceful use of the spurs was a correction or punishment, not an aid. It was, indeed, the only proper correction: 'it is neither the switch, the *chambrière*, the calf of the leg, nor gentle treatment which will conquer a vicious jade; you might as well give him rose-water and sugar'.

The *poinçon* he used in teaching a young horse the airs above the ground, but as soon as possible the switch replaced it. The switch was a most useful aid. Its mere noise would animate a horse; at a touch on the outside of the hock, he would draw up

ymer Pen.   G.Bickham de se

Insultare solo, et gressus glomerare superbos.

A Polish cavalryman, again riding short

his hind-legs in the *croupade*; a touch on the middle of the croup was the signal for the *ballotade*; at the end of the croup, for the *capriole*. But one should not rely too much on it; on serious occasions the right hand might be carrying a sword.

Pluvinel seems to have done all his schooling inside a manège, but the Duke maintained that 'he who does not always ride in the same place, and who has neither pillar nor wall, finds his horse the most obedient to the heel'. As to bits, 'the rule chiefly to be observed is, to put as little iron in your horse's mouth as you possibly can'. Nor did he approve of work between the pillars. 'The method of two pillars is worth nothing; for it puts a horse so off his bars and his curb, and so upon the cavesson, that he will not go without the pillars.'

'Our only aim is to put a horse well upon his haunches.' For this purpose he used, in early stages of training, a single pillar, to which the horse was tied very short and 'animated' with the *chambrière* (which, it must be emphasized, had a wide, flat lash which could not hurt a horse). In this position, a horse 'cannot easily rise, so puts himself short on his haunches', as a preliminary to the curvet. Generally, however, the horse was not tied to the pillar; it was simply a guide, marking the centre of his circle. Newcastle was strongly opposed to too much reliance on the pillar, the longe attached to the pillar, and the *chambrière*.

Like his predecessors, he used lateral aids for turning on his forehand or circling

In the 16th century you could ride out to shoot
duck

with hind-legs following a wider circle than forelegs; but diagonal aids for the
terre-à-terre (turning on his haunches) or circling with hind-legs following in the track
of forelegs. But he made more use of the weight of his body, leaning, for instance,
slightly out and forward for the *terre-à-terre*, and back to halt, so that the horse 'puts
himself on his haunches'.

It is not quite clear whether Pluvinel, riding a trained horse, with the reins in
one hand, had used the direct or the indirect rein. I think it was the latter: in his
instruction for turning to the left he says, 'Carry your bridle hand over to that side
and help with your right spur.' But it is perfectly clear that the Duke of Newcastle,
even when riding a fully schooled horse and holding both reins in his left hand, still
did not use the indirect rein: he turned a horse by the inner rein and (according to
whether the turn was on the forehand or the haunches) the inner or outer leg, helped
by the switch tapped against the neck or held close to the horse's inner or outer eye.
Here, for instance, are his instructions on making a *volte* or large circle with hind-legs
following in the tracks of forelegs. 'Whether a horse walks, trots, or gallops in large
circles, the rider's hand ought to be a little without the *volte*, that is to say, outside the
horse's centre-line as he circles, that he may work the inside rein. . . . When he goes
to the right, the nails of the rider's hand ought to be turned upwards, the little finger
towards the left shoulder; and to the left, turned upwards towards the right shoulder.'

131

Angles for rider and mount

In other words, the rider tightens the inside rein by moving his bridle hand towards the other, outer side, 'helping always with the contrary leg'.

The invention of which Newcastle was most proud was a running- or 'bearing-rein' attached to the cavesson. One end of this rein was tied to the horn on the pommel; it then passed under the 'fore-bolster' of the saddle, through the ring on the side of the cavesson, back to the rider's hand. They gave the rider, in pulling on this rein, a two to one mechanical advantage which would be increased if the rein passed not through the nearest cavesson-ring, but round the horse's nose, through a ring on the far side, and back round the nose to the rider's hand. No horse could resist this 'bearing-rein': he must yield to it, bending his head towards the inside of the circle 'though he be stiff-necked as a bull'.

Newcastle maintained that this bearing-rein 'bends a horse from nose to tail', so suppling him especially in the shoulders. One would have thought, however, that so far from suppling a horse, it unduly constricted him. He also maintained that it made a horse strike off with the inner leg at a canter or gallop. This also is questionable: the modern practice is, in the early stages of training, to turn a horse's head out-wards, away from the desired leading leg, in order, so to speak, to free it; and, by placing the horse's and rider's weight all outwards, to bring to the ground the outer hind-leg or leg of impulsion. Only at a later stage of training, when a horse strikes

132

off correctly and changes legs freely, is the head turned towards the desired leading leg, to indicate that he should strike off on or change to it.

His Grace would have been astonished to learn that he had not written the last word on horsemanship. In one of the illustrations to his *A General System of Horsemanship in all its Branches*, published in 1666 when he and the King enjoyed their own again, he is shown mounted on Pegasus, performing a polished *capriole* among the clouds, while the Olympic Gods above and a circle of admiring horses below applaud with equal fervour. But although most of his doctrine was, for the specialized requirements of the manège on 'pleasure horses', very sensible, his teaching did not really catch on or wrest from the French the leadership in this art. Perhaps this was because of the patent fallacies in his excessive reliance on a running-rein.

The true heir of Pluvinel and the prophet of the modern High School equitation was the great riding-master François Robichon de la Guerinière who in 1751 produced his book *École de Cavalerie*.

Of his methods it is not necessary in this chapter to write at length because, as Alois Podhajsky, the greatest modern dressage rider, says, they are applied unaltered in the Spanish Riding School today.

I shall note here only his instructions on the use of the bridle hand in turning a horse, since they set out for the first time, with clarity, the principle of turning by the indirect or neck rein, and are in direct contradiction to the Duke of Newcastle. 'In turning to the right, in carrying your hand to that side, have your nails upwards so that the outside, which is the left rein, the one which must act, can operate more promptly' [afin que la rène de dehors, qui est la rène gauche, laquelle doit fair action, puisse agir plus promptement]. He goes on to say that in the manège only one should, holding both reins in one hand, have the inside rein a little shorter than the

The recommended seat

Attaching weights to
make a horse pick its
feet up

outside to make a horse turn his head gracefully; but riding in the open, hunting or on active service, the reins should be held at equal length, and the horse turned by the outer or indirect rein.

Without, at this point, going further into the details of the modern High School, we may note in the eighteenth century a completely modern approach to manège riding. Richard Berenger, strongly influenced by de la Guerinière's teaching, in 1771 describes the seat and the position of the bridle hand almost in the words used by Newcastle: these had not changed over the centuries since Grisone. What had changed was the mental attitude of the rider to his horse. 'The knowledge of the different characters and the different nature of horses, together with the vices and imperfections, as well as the exact proportions of the parts of the horse's body, is the foundation on which is built the theory of our art.'

'Disobedience in horses is more frequently owing to want of skill in the horseman, than proceeding from any natural imperfection in the horse. In effect, three things may give rise to it: ignorance, a bad temper, and an incapacity in the animal to do what is required of him. If a horse is ignorant of what you expect him to do, and press him, he will rebel; nothing is more common. Teach him then, and he will know; a frequent repetition of the lessons will convert this knowledge into a habit, and you will reduce him to the most exact obedience.

'If he refuses to obey, this fault may arise either from a bad temper, dullness, or from too much malice and impatience; it often is the effect of the two first vices, sometimes the result of all. In either or all these instances, recourse must be had to rigour, but it must be used with caution; for we must not forget that the hopes of recompense have as great an influence over the understanding of the animal, as the fear of punishment.

'It behoves then every horseman, who would be perfect in his art, to know from whence the different sorts of defences and rebellions in horses proceed.

'For horses that are addicted to lie down in the water, you must provide yourself with two little leaden balls, and tie them to a piece of pack-thread, and in the moment when he is lying down, you must drop these into his ears; and if he rises instantly, or forbears to lie down, draw them back.' There is in this advice a note reminiscent of the White Knight's ingenuity, but it is a world apart from Blunde-ville's stout footmen belabouring a terrified horse with cudgels.

Horses in the seventeenth and eighteenth centuries were not, of course, reserved exclusively for the manège which was a rich man's pastime and an exercise of which few horses were physically capable. Far more were used for travel, hunting, racing, and war. This produced a conflict of opinion and, indeed, an exchange of hot words and acid observations such as is not unknown in equestrian circles and in the correspondence columns of equestrian magazines even in our enlightened day. Some who would call themselves practical horsemen considered the pleasure horse, grotesquely overbent, probably over the bit too, and totally deficient in impulsion, quite unsuitable for any fast work. The Duke of Newcastle put in a nutshell their arguments, and at somewhat greater length his own retort.

Long-reining is still practised. Note the weights
on the horse's feet

'Some wag will ask, what is a horse good for that will do nothing but dance and play tricks? If these gentlemen will retrench everything that serves them either for curiosity or pleasure, and admit nothing but what is useful, they must make a hollow tree their house, and clothe themselves with fig-leaves, feed upon acorns and drink nothing but water. . . . I presume those great wits (*the sneering gentlemen*) will give Kings, Princes, and Persons of Quality leave to love pleasure horses, as being an exercise that is very noble, and that makes them appear most graceful when they show themselves to their subjects, or at the head of an army to animate it.'

He, and most horsemen regarded 'pleasure horses' and 'hunting-horses' as entirely different animals, almost different species.

Gervase Markham, a country gentleman devoted to hunting, shooting, fishing, gardening, and all 'country contentments', saw both points of view. Of course for racing and a long day following hounds something lighter, faster – and cheaper – than a great horse was needed; for service too, now that fire-power dominated the battle-field. 'As hitherto I have showed my experience in training and bringing to perfection great horses, meet either for service in the wars or for the pleasure of princes, so here I will disclose (since not anyone else hath undertaken the like treatise) my knowledge in the dieting and ordering of those horses which we term hunting horses, because the pleasure we enjoy by them in the following of hounds, an art in every way equal with the former and as necessary in some kinds of service in the war (especially desperate exploits to be done suddenly, or upon occurrents or discoveries, or any other kind of service wherein either the toughness or the swiftness of a horse is to be tried) as the former.'

But he could see a connection between the manège and hunting, and the value of dressage in training any horse, and his observations on this have a remarkably modern note, anticipating those of Colonel Podhajsky. 'Yet what horse is perfect upon his bit and can well perform all the lessons mentioned in a former chapter, must of force be perfect upon his snaffle, and if his master so please, be after made into a hunting-horse; where, contrariwise, if a horse be from the beginning trained to a continual loose kind of gallop, as hunting-horses are, he will ask great art and labour

A 16th-century
Muscovite horseman
riding short in the
Eastern fashion

The young King of France has a lesson in
Haute École

to set upon a bit and be made proud and gallant. I will therefore make them not two
arts but one, making the latter an appendix to the former.'

The hunting of red- and fallow-deer was a craze for all Englishmen whose position allowed it – and, indeed, for many others. Henry VIII was passionately addicted
to it, pounding after hounds, pouring with sweat, wearing out three or four horses
in a day. Fond also of the manège, and a noted man-at-arms (though an extraordinarily incompetent commander), he had a personal interest in weight-carriers and to
improve the breed in England ordered the castration of undersized stallions and a
slaughter of all horses under 13 hands. Elizabeth too rode to hounds, and went well
even in her seventies: 'every second day she is on horseback, and continues the sport

138

Another lesson, using the pillar

long'. A passion for hunting was about the only redeeming feature in that singularly unattractive character, James I. He insisted on his sons being taught to hunt 'with running hounds, which is the most honourable and noble sort [of sport]; for it is a thievish form of hunting to shoot with guns and bows, and greyhound hunting is not so martial a game'.

Charles I was an accomplished manège rider, with a knack for ruling difficult animals with a lighter hand than that with which he tried to rule England.

In stricter Puritan eyes hunting bore, perhaps, a faint aura of recusancy and ungodliness, but riding to hounds and horsemanship were Cromwell's only diversions, and foreign potentates or Parliamentary delegations just had to wait if the

The exercise of skills
involved in the use of
weapons on horseback
was as much of a sport in
the 17th and 18th
centuries as field sports
have been in the 19th
and 20th centuries

Taking the head with a
lance . . .

. . . and with a pistol

Lord Protector was engaged in the hunting-field or the manège. Captains of English
ships sailing the Mediterranean were well aware that the sure way to official favour
was to bring home a good Arab or Barb stallion. Old broken Royalist huntsmen and
hawkers could be sure of sympathy and help from Oliver Cromwell.

Stag- or buck-hunting was for the privileged few: the usual quarry of country
gentlemen and yeomen was the hare, who ran slower than the stag and in a much
smaller circle, but whose cunning tried hounds to the utmost. Hare-hunting was the
prime diversion of those interested in hound-work.

The fox was generally regarded as vermin. In the Earl of Strafford's trial, one of
his bitterest enemies urged that he should not be regarded as a stag or a hare and
given law, but as a fox to be 'snared by any means and knocked on the head without
pity!' So the Commons, unable to prove him guilty of any offence, simply voted that
his head be cut off.

Any form of riding to hounds could be enlivened by side-bets, a matter to which
Gervase Markham gives a good deal of attention. Wagers were made not only on a
horse's performance with hounds, but also on the 'wild-goose chase', a sort of follow-
my-leader cross-country race.

Hunting was criticized as being too hard on horses: 'this extreme chasing and
riding of them maketh them lame and unsound'. Gervase Markham indignantly refuted
this. 'That there be some unsound, and many hunting-horses lame, I deny not; yet
for every such one lame horse, I will find twenty more lame that never knew what

hunting meant. . . . Hunting horses are never lamed through their immoderate riding or labour, if they have a good keeper, but now and then through greediness of sport. . . . Whereas on the contrary part who is so simple that he knoweth not, if a horse be kept in a stable and want exercise, his hooves will straiten, his sinews dry up, and he prove lame incurable.' Great Horses were as subject to lameness 'as any hunting-horse whatever'.

Proper exercise and feeding made hunting-horses 'long-winded, tough, hard, and stout, insomuch that a poor nag of six or seven pound price, well trained and dieted, will not only tire but kill outright a courser worth a hundred pounds, if he be ill and foul fed. . . . Moreover, the cry of the dogs is as pleasant to the horse as it is to the man, and addeth to him both a courage to run and a willingness to continue his labour.'

The great thing was to have a horse *fit* for hunting, not to hunt him off grass or in soft condition. This was done by a progressive course of properly regulated exercise and feeding. The basis of his food was oats; 'horsebread' made of beans, wheat, and rye – anticipating, perhaps, modern horse-nuts; and coarse but sweet hay. So trained and fed over several weeks, a horse could follow hounds a whole day and lead a wild-goose chase at the end of it, 'ridden while he is able to set one foot before another . . . till he be in that extremity that some suppose he cannot live an hour, yet within two or three hours afterwards be so fresh and courageous as if he had never been laboured'.

The wild-goose chase, if a large wager was at stake, involved a certain management,

Throwing the javelin . . .

not to say gamesmanship, on the part of the owner. 'If you find your horse of little speed yet wonderful true and tough, then make your match to follow the dogs so long as you can, as until 3 or 4 of the clock, that in that space you may with much correct riding . . . so toil the horse that runs against you that when you come to run the wild-goose chase, you may have as much speed as he. . . . If you find your horse to be wonderful arrand swift, yet not so tough as he will endure to toil out a day's work with extremity, then I would advise you not to make your match to hunt the hare after the dogs, but rather to run train scents* made with a cat . . . choosing such kind of earth as you know your horse may show his speed upon. . . . Seeing that your speed fails, then loiter after and keep your horse as fresh as you can, that coming to the wild-goose chase, taking the leading, see if with slips and turns you can foil him that rides against you. . . . The wild-goose chase being started, in which the hindermost horse is bound to follow the foremost, and you having the leading, hold a hard hand on your horse, and make him gallop softly at great ease . . . suffer him to come so near to you that his horse's head may well-nigh touch your horse's buttocks, which when you see, clap your left spur in your horse's side and wheel him suddenly half about on your right hand, and then take him up again till such time as he come to you again.'

* A drag.

. . . and using the sword

It is a pity that Gervase Markham gives no clue as to how men rode to hounds, save that it was apparently on a snaffle. We can only presume that they used the same straight-legged seat as in the manège.

It is natural for horsemen to race against one another, and during the sixteenth century races – obviously quite informal affairs but enlivened, no doubt, by betting – increased in popularity so much that Puritan writers felt obliged to condemn them though conceding that they 'yielded good exercise'. Racing seems to have been even more popular among 'rank riding Scots', and it is possible that James I gave it the stamp of royal approval. Cromwell, no doubt with some reluctance, suppressed it as ungodly while continuing the Stuarts' practice of importing Arab and Barb horses. As is generally known, it was in the reign of Charles II that racing at Newmarket became established as the sport of kings and people too, with professional jockeys riding against such talented amateurs as the Duke of Monmouth and even, on occasion, His Majesty himself. Naturally race-riders had no use whatever for collection, and joined hunting-folk in deriding it.

The orthodox cavalry tactic when Markham wrote was to trot to within some fifteen yards of the enemy and there halt. The front rank then fired one pistol; returned it to the holster, drew and fired another; and wheeled round to reload while the second rank did likewise. (This is the origin of the 'counter-march' in cavalry bands' drill.) The sword was seldom used except in pursuit or against such

143

A 13th-century Japanese horse and rider

second-class enemies as the Irish. These tactics were almost identical with those of Xenophon, whose cavalry advanced slowly to within a few yards of the enemy, hurled their javelins and wheeled away. For such stately evolutions the manège horse would be eminently suitable, though very few cavalrymen could afford one.

Prince Rupert revived the older practice of charging home, sword in hand, at the gallop, but relying for safety on speed, not armour. He probably had to do so, for in his ranks there were too few pistols and too many undisciplined young men riding hunters. We may be quite sure that few, if any, great horses took part in his wild charges.

The Ironsides struck a mean between these two methods of attack, firing a volley from their pistols and then closing, at a 'good round trot', to fight it out sword to sword. In the subsequent mêlée a manège horse might, perhaps, be useful if the rider had time for the finer points of equitation; but there cannot have been many in Cromwell's 'lovely company'.

Nor was there any need for a horse now to carry thirty stone. Horse-armour was no longer in use, and the cavalry trooper's armour was reduced to 'breast, back, and pot', that is to say, cuirass and helmet, weighing only about twenty-five pounds. Sir Arthur Hazelrigg, who raised a regiment for Parliament, managed to equip them in antique sets of complete plate-armour. Not only did they suffer the humiliation of being dubbed, by both sides, 'Hazelrigg's Lobsters', but they almost expired of heat in the first summer of the war. (The armour, however, served Sir Arthur himself well, for it defied all the assaults made on it in the pursuit after a skirmish when the Lobsters were worsted. This provided the occasion for one of Charles I's rare jokes: 'If Sir Arthur had been victualled as well as fortified, he might have stood a siege.')

So by the time of the English Civil War the day of the great horse in war was over. We know that the New Model Army and the cavalry of the Restoration was mounted on medium-weight horses of 15 to 15·2 hands, the dragoons on 'good, squat dragoon cobs'. Geldings were preferred to stallions, though the latter were still sometimes ridden in the ranks.

For travel the hobby, a horse trained to amble, was highly esteemed. As Gervase Markham put it, 'this ambling motion in his smooth stealing away, as it were with a soft and tender touching of the ground, carries his burden gently and without shaking'. Horses had to be taught to amble, in heavy plough with trammels linking near-fore to near-hind, off-fore to off-hind, so that the legs on each side move forward together. But English nobles, like Kai Kaus of Ispahan, found the amble inelegant and undignified before an audience. The Earls of Northumberland kept in their stables 'great gambading horses' which on long journeys were led, not ridden 'by the way'. They were mounted only on approaching a town, when His Lordship passaged, piaffed, and curvetted through the streets to the admiration of the populace.

The popularity of the amble for long-distance travel may have been due to the fact that seventeenth-century horsemen in western Europe did not rise to the trot: they bumped, despite the more sensible example of Asiatic riders. But in the eighteenth century the roads greatly improved and coach-horses could pound along at a long-striding, bone-shaking trot which postilions, bumping up and down in the saddle, found so uncomfortable that they started rising or, as it was called on the Continent, 'posting' to the trot.

Let us now examine a rival school of sixteenth- and seventeenth-century horse-manship. The North African horsemen of pre-Christian times, as we have seen, used no bridle, controlling their ponies with light switches. But at the beginning of the Christian era Strabo describes Numidian horsemen as using a single rein, passing between the horse's ears and attached to the noseband or muzzle. It sounds as though he were describing, not quite accurately, the camel-halter, *hakma*, adapted to the horse. In so far as their horse-culture has survived the discovery of oil, the Cadillac, and other marvels of modern science, the Syrian Arab and the Moor still train a young horse on the *hakma*, which acts not on the horse's mouth but on his nose, and finish him on a ring-bit. This ring-bit travelled with Arabs or Moors to Spain, and was known in western Europe as the *mors à genette*. Now the modern Californian horseman, whose horse-culture is purely Spanish, also makes a young horse on the hackamore, and finishes him either on the ring-bit ('Chileno') or more commonly on a spade-bit, which may be a development of the ring-bit and has much the same action. (Either in rough hands can be an instrument of torture, but so can many of the bits used in Europe. They are not cruel if used by first-class horsemen on horses which have been trained by the hackamore to answer to the very lightest touch of the rein.)

Californian horsemanship is discussed in detail in a later chapter. Suffice it now to say that similarities in techniques and in nomenclature (for instance *hakma*, *jaquima*, hackamore: *gineta* and Zenata, a Moorish tribe) support the theory that *gineta* horsemanship was learned from the Arabs and Moors; carried across the Atlantic by the *conquistadores*; and now, thanks to the rodeo and western competitions, has reached its full flowering in California.

Before stirrups were invented, everyone rode more or less long. Nor, when introduced to the stirrup, did either the Iberians or the Moors at first alter their seat. But Moslems from the Maghrib and from Turkestan would meet and mix on the pilgrimage to Mecca; so during the Middle Ages the Moors adopted the seat of the steppes, riding short and even on occasion rising in their stirrups to gallop. So did Christian *gineta* horsemen, riding (as Blundeville put it) 'short, in the Turkey fashion'. Neither Moors nor Christians, however, adopted the snaffle-bit and the extended head-carriage of the steppes: their horses were highly collected on the ring-bit. The reason for this may be that the early warriors of the Prophet, emerging from their deserts on camels, learned their horsemanship from the Persians, who (as bas-reliefs show) believed emphatically on collection. But this is no more than a fascinating speculation.

So, to summarize the undisputed facts, by the fifteenth century the Spanish *gineta* horseman rode short and collected his horse by a very light hand on a very severe ring-bit. It is probable that his horse received its early schooling – perhaps from a slave or a Morisco (convert) – on a *jaquima*, which developed elsewhere in the Peninsula into a cruel toothed noseband, the *cerreta*.

Anyway, as we know from a fifteenth-century King of Aragon, it was a style eminently suitable for light horse skirmishing and for the *jerid*, a furious pursuit game, similar to Gervase Markham's wild-goose chase. It was also adopted by dashing young gentlemen who diverted themselves by bowling over savage bulls with the *garrocha*, a blunt bull-pike, and then dismounting and slaying them with a stabbing-spear – a sport requiring far more horsemanship and hardihood than tilting and stag-hunting.

La gineta prevailed in the south of the Peninsula. In the north, Italian and French influence were stronger and until the present century most men rode in orthodox west European style, *à la brida*, with straight leg and curb-bit. For chivalry was international: just as in Islam the Haj must have encouraged a certain standardization of horse-culture, so in Christendom would the knights' pilgrimage to the shrine of their patron-saint, James of Compostela. It was the highest praise to say a gentleman could 'ride well in both saddles', i.e. *à la gineta* and *à la brida*.

In Naples, a possession of Aragon, the Spanish and Portuguese sport of mounted bull-fighting became so popular and perilous that in 1558 the Pope banned it. So *la gineta* must have been perfectly familiar to Grisone and other Neapolitan masters. But to make the bulky Great Horse perform like a handy Andalusian of 15·2 hands was far from easy. Attributing the horse's failure to a subhuman malice, to his 'shrewd toils', they whipped the offending Adam out of him and daunted the brute by horrific curbs, by the toothed noseband or *cerreta* instead of the gentle hackamore, by bludgeons, hot irons, and hedgehogs.

These techniques were carried back to the Peninsula full measure, pressed down and running over, by Grisone's zealous disciples, there to brutalize and bastardize both schools of equitation. So seventeenth-century dukes and Infantas are shown riding steeds with mouths wide open, overbent, and often over the bit to a degree that even Newcastle might have deprecated; and to this day the noses of Spanish horses continue to be lacerated by the infamous *cerreta*.

(One must, however, question whether the use of the *cerreta* is any more cruel than the use, *ab initio*, of severe curb- or ring-bits by contemporary Moors, Arabs, Somalis, Gallas, and Texans. It does no permanent injury, though leaving its scars in the nose, and while sparing the mouth, it produces an undeniably handy horse.)

So one can, with a little historical imagination, discern two schools of horsemanship in sixteenth-century Spain and Portugal. It would be unnatural for these to co-exist without some intermingling and interchange of methods, just as today the teaching of Saumur, Vienna, and Pinerolo is blended (mistakenly, in some people's opinion) in Combined Training.

It is amusing to contrast this sophisticated Iberian horsemanship with riding in Japan, where the Samurai sometimes hunted and fought on horseback, but were not, in general, great horsemen, preferring perhaps to entrust their honour to their own valour rather than to that of a horse. They rode very short, and are reported by a European traveller to hold the reins 'merely for form, the horse being nevertheless led by one and sometimes two footmen, who walk on each side of the head holding it by the bit'. The merchant or common traveller was transported by a horse, but can hardly be said to have ridden. From a pack-saddle, secured by breastplate and crupper but no girth, was slung the traveller's two portmanteaus, one on each side. Between them was a small, coffin-shaped trunk, resting on the horse's back, filled with cushions, in which the traveller sat precariously balanced, either cross-legged or with his legs hanging down on either side of the horse's neck. 'Particular care must be taken to sit right in the middle, and not to lean much on either side, which would make the trunks fall or else the horse and rider. In going up and down hills the footmen and stable-grooms held the side-trunks fast, for fear of such an accident. The traveller mounts . . . by the horse's breast, which is very troublesome for stiff legs.'

Another peculiarity of Japanese horsemanship was that horseshoes were made of grass-rope, which were soon worn out, so many spares had to be taken on a journey or bought from poor children selling them in villages *en route*.

A 16th-century gentleman on his horse

From about the Restoration onwards the character of English hunting changed. The red- and fallow-deer almost disappeared from the greater part of England, exterminated by wholesale poaching during the Civil War and the interregnum and by the destruction of the forests for the requirements of shipbuilding.* The fox, previously regarded as vermin to be destroyed by any means, was now almost deified and, with no protection from the law, was preserved far more effectively by public opinion. Hounds were bred lighter and faster to kill him. At the same time enclosures were changing the face of the English countryside. The commons and strips of unfenced cultivation over which packs of harriers had circled at a modest pace, enabling the squire and his tenants to watch, without undue exertion, hounds work out a line, were gradually parcelled into individually owned fields, the boundaries of which were at first marked by lines of young blackthorn, ash, beech, or elm. To make a stock-proof hedge, farmers cut and laid these, and dug ditches along them to drain the field and water their roots. Soon the field boundary ceased to be a mere landmark through which anyone could push a way, and became an obstacle which had to be jumped.

There are practically no references to jumping as we know it before the Restoration. Occasionally, one reads of a fugitive from a battle escaping his pursuers by a leap which they could not emulate, but no one dreamed of teaching his horses to jump: a 'leap' meant one of the manège airs above the ground, a *croupade*, *ballotade*, or

* It took 4,000 mature oak trees to build one of Nelson's ships-of-the-line.

capriole. But from about the Restoration onwards jumping became first a rare, then a common, and finally by the late eighteenth century almost an essential feature of hunting. During the same period the improvement in English horses, largely due to the import of Arabs and Barbs by Cromwell and the Stuart kings, produced a horse which could gallop and jump at speed.

It is impossible to give a date for the start of jumping. But we read that James II, when Duke of York, one of the earliest fox-hunters and one of the first gentlemen to keep a pack of foxhounds, lamentably addicted to boring his friends with accounts of his exploits, 'kept pretty close to the hounds, though the hedges were high and the ditches deep and wide'. When, as king, he threatened to repeal the Test Act and Habeas Corpus Act, it was remarked that not even the loyalest Tories, 'men who wear red coats and have jumped hedge and ditch in all else', would stand for this. So although in the mid seventeenth century jumping was unheard of and, writing in 1666, the Duke of Newcastle does not mention it, by 1688 it had become so common-place as to be employed as a metaphor in a Parliamentary debate.

During the eighteenth century fox-hunting became enormously popular, partly because it was not, like shooting, restricted by law to a few privileged people. The Prince of Wales, later George IV, had a favourite story of his own pack, which displays as nothing else the democratic nature of hunting. 'There was a butcher out, God damn me, ma'am, a great big fellow, fifteen stone, six feet two inches without his shoes, and the bully of all Brighton. He over-rode my hounds several times, and I had spoken to him to hold hard in vain. At last, God damn me, ma'am, he rode slap over my favourite bitch, Ruby. I could stand it no longer but, jumping off my horse, said "Get down, you damned rascal and pull off your coat, none shall interfere with us, but you or I shall go back to Brighton more dead than alive." God damn me, ma'am, I threw off my coat and the big ruffian, nothing loth, did the same by his. By God, ma'am, we fought for an hour and twenty minutes, my hunting field forming a ring round us, no one interfering; and at the end of it the big bully of Brighton was carried away senseless, while I had hardly a scratch.'

No doubt His Royal Highness was drawing on his imagination rather than his memory, but his story neatly illustrates the fact that, while most fox-hunters were squires and farmers, anyone – butcher, baker, candlestick-maker – who could ride, could hunt. It was regarded in the eighteenth century as a very rough-and-ready, bucolic diversion, associated with drunkenness and, indeed, immorality; but in the nineteenth century it acquired a certain snob-value which is now, happily, almost extinct in the hunting-field, though it still survives and flourishes exotically in the minds of the anti-field-sports lobby.

On the Continent the pattern of agriculture was different; the countryside was not transformed into a chequer-board of fields separated by jumpable hedges; the red- and fallow-deer survived in far greater numbers, and hunting was largely con-fined to open rides cut through forest. De la Guerinière dismissed jumping in half a page, giving only the most perfunctory advice on how to train a horse to it.

English hunters 'out all day, always on the tail of hounds in their fox-hunting, jumping hedges and ditches' were, de la Guerinière noted, totally different even in conformation from manège horses. Their 'hunting-gallop', 'more extended than raised', developed good shoulders and a natural head-carriage unknown in the manège. A hunter should be allowed to gallop 'as he would without a rider'.

The irresistible thrill of hunting and the fascination of hound-work quite extinguished the English rider's interest, never very strong, in scientific equitation. Why waste time prancing round a riding-school like a damned circus-rider when one could be watching hounds work out a difficult line, or galloping at breakneck speed across field and furrow, jumping hedge, ditch, timber, and stone wall? So the English did not waste much thought on how to ride; they simply rode, in a slapdash, happy-go-lucky manner, their seat and hands the laughing-stock of continental experts who would concede to them only one equestrian virtue, that of courage – or, rather, since it was so conspicuously applied to lack of skill – rashness. But this was a false judgement, for English eighteenth- and early nineteenth-century horsemanship, transplanted with brilliant success in the American colonies, preserved some features of equitation which too much emphasis on the manège was in danger of destroying – impulsion, free forward movement, speed, dash, and control by a simple snaffle or the mild double-bridle which during the eighteenth century gradually replaced the long-armed, complicated curbs devised by Grisone, Pluvinel, and their contemporaries.

It is convenient at this point to summarize the history of horsemanship over some 2,500 years, up to the end of the eighteenth century.

From the earliest days there have been two styles of riding, each governed by the horses, the weapons, and the terrain of the people who developed them. In the open plains of Assyria, Scythia, and Tartary horsemen were primarily horse-archers. A man could not simultaneously handle a bow and ride collected. His pony was small, the country over which he rode was often desert or grassland. Whether fighting or hunting, he had no need to come to close quarters, no need to get the horse's centre of gravity back, his heels under him, for handiness in a mêlée. The system of riding which he developed unconsciously, with no consideration of theory, was based not on collection but on extension. His pony moved freely forward, on the forehand, head and neck extended.

In enclosed country such as Greece, cavalry riding bare-backed and therefore not coming to close quarters but relying on javelins hurled from fifteen or twenty yards away, developed a style of horsemanship based on collection. Without a curb-bit, Xenophon could not really make a horse bend at the poll, which is one-half of modern 'collection', but he could achieve the other half, getting the horse's heels well under him.

The invention of the saddle-tree and the stirrup greatly increased the efficiency of both forms of cavalry. The bowman rode 'short', standing in his stirrups to shoot: he had to let his pony have its head: with both hands occupied by bow and arrow, he could do nothing else, and in open country he did not need to. So there developed a style of equitation based on free forward movement, extension, and riding short, standing in the stirrups to shoot or to gallop. Assyrian bas-reliefs, Scythian carvings, Persian and Chinese pictures show the development, before and after the invention of stirrups, of this form of horsemanship. Adventurous English and French horsemen, travelling or serving as mercenaries against the Turks, might see

A 17th-century
cuirassier

it in action in eastern Europe, where it was practised by Poles, Magyars, and
Cossacks, all light cavalry. The horsemen of western Europe knew of this way of
riding: Blundeville more than once refers to 'riding short after the Turkey fashion';
but they saw no reason to adopt it.

For the horsemen of western Europe the saddle-tree and stirrups had an even
more important result: they made possible shock-action and hand-to-hand combat,
thereby promoting cavalry from an elegant irrelevance to the arbiter of battles.
Knights could charge with couched lances (far more effectively than using lances
overhand or, like ancient Persians, with both hands), then thrust and hack in the
ensuing mêlée. They rode 'long', indeed with almost straight legs, wedged into high-
pommelled, high-cantled saddles, because they found they could in this position

151

withstand the shock of impact of an enemy's lance – and, indeed, of their own. It seems very unlikely that they set much store by collection. In a charge, timing and impulsion are far more important, and in a mêlée no one has time or thought for equitation. In any case, a heavy lance held in the right hand and an even heavier shield in the left hand would have made any delicate handling of the reins absolutely impossible. The Bayeux Tapestry shows knights holding both reins with the shield in the left hand, shoulder high: the reins hang loose down the horse's neck. The long cheekpieced curbs are probably operated mainly by the weight of the reins to stop the horse, which was steered more by leg-action than by the bit.

A far greater degree of collection would be needed in hunting than in battle, for red- and fallow-deer were hunted mainly in forests, where a rider without control might smash his knee against a tree or meet the fate of Absalom. In hunting no shield was carried, so reins and bit could be more effectively used. It is possible – indeed I think probable – that the idea of collection was preserved through the early Middle Ages in the hunter rather than the war-horse.

The situation was transformed by another invention, the long-bow, which forced the knight to fight either on foot or on a horse so heavily armoured, and therefore itself so ponderous, that it could barely trot. The war-horse became, in effect, the jousting-horse. Plate-armour became heavier and heavier, its surfaces more cunningly angled so that an enemy's weapon just glanced off. The shield grew smaller and smaller, and was finally discarded as unnecessary or built into the saddle as an extension to the pommel. The rules of jousting became more and more artificial, and the arena smaller. So collection became both more important and more practicable. From the intellectual ferment of the Renaissance there grew a scientific interest in many things, including equitation. Grisone and other *maestros* were fascinated to discover that their ideas on collection had been formulated by Xenophon, 1,800 years earlier. Cavalry developed a new form of tactics, remarkably like Xenophon's but with horse-pistols instead of javelins, for which collection was necessary. So in the sixteenth, seventeenth, and eighteenth centuries all educated horsemanship was based on the principles of collection, which was carried to grotesque extremes so that the pleasure horse was in danger of losing all capacity for forward movement.

From this he was saved by the English fox-hunting man. In England forests and the wild deer were both so reduced that deer-hunting in forests almost ceased, and was replaced by hunting first the hare, then the fox at a much greater speed over fields, hedges, and ditches. For this the collected gaits of the manège-schooled pleasure horse were not merely unnecessary, but a positive hindrance, indeed a danger. So in England then developed quite spontaneously, without any thought or theoretical background, a slapdash, unscientific, but highly effective form of cross-country riding, based on free forward movement, extension instead of control, the snaffle instead of the curb. It was not the same as the 'Turkey fashion', the nomad's style of riding, since fox-hunters continued to ride 'long'; but in essentials the two styles were not far apart.

Thus by the end of the eighteenth century there were still the two ancient styles of horsemanship. The natural style developed by the horsemen of Eurasia who rode short, on a snaffle-bridle, with no thought of collection but allowing their horse free

Head of Charles I's horse
painted by Van Dyck

forward movement: and the style of western Europe, where educated, scientific horsemen rode long and concentrated above all on collection induced by spurs and a curb-bit. But there was also a third school of horsemanship, if anything so thoughtless and unscientific can be so pretentiously termed; that of the English (and American) hunting-man, who rode fairly long like his ancestors, but whose riding was based, like the Cossack's, on extension rather than collection. The history of horsemanship in the next 170 years is of the interaction and, in certain cases, coalescence of these three rival schools.

153

5

Mainly about the War-Horse

Frederick the Great is generally considered to have been the first modern cavalry commander to question the value of a high degree of collection, though Prince Rupert's tactics do not suggest that he thought collection was the be-all and end-all of cavalry-training. On ascending the throne of Prussia in 1740, Frederick found that his cavalry, huge men on massive horses, 'dared not walk on a bad pavement, nor move beyond that pace on even ground': it 'was not even worth the devil coming to fetch it away'. Promptly he ordered that manège-training be replaced by field-training, at speed, individually and in formation.

His cavalry general, Seidlitz, followed these instructions so conscientiously that the King reproached him for the number of fatal accidents during training. 'Sir,' replied Seidlitz drily, 'if you complain of a few broken necks, Your Majesty will never have the bold horsemen you require for the field.' To stimulate his cornets' ardour, Seidlitz himself used to gallop between the turning arms of a windmill. By sheer dash and speed the Prussian cavalry carried all before them.

We may, I think, assume that the victories of the 'Protestant Hero' interested British cavalrymen in his methods, especially as they seemed to vindicate the fox-hunter rather than the manège-rider. The best-known English horseman of the day was the Earl of Pembroke, Colonel of the Royals. He held strong views on the standard of riding in the British cavalry, produced by 'the common method of putting a man on a rough trotting horse to which he is obliged to stick with all his might of arms and legs'. Nor did the officers merit His Lordship's approval: they were, on horseback, 'a disgrace to themselves and the animals they ride'. In these circumstances, he wrote in 1762, it was quite impossible, and indeed a sheer waste of time, to teach manège-riding to soldiers, except perhaps selected remount riders.

Pembroke insisted on his troopers learning to jump, writing in his *Military Equitation* (1778), 'Riders must keep their bodies back, raise their hand a little in order to help the foreparts of the horse up, and be very attentive to their equilibre, without raising themselves up in the saddle or moving their arms. The surest way to prevent people, in leaping over anything, from raising up their arms and elbows (which is an unfirm and ungraceful motion) is to make them put a hand whip, or switch, under each arm, and not let them drop. 'Tis best to begin at a low bar covered with furze, which pricking the horse's legs, if he doesn't raise himself sufficiently, prevents his contracting a sluggish and dangerous habit of touching, as he goes over, which anything yielding and not pricking would give him a custom of doing.' It seems to be the first published description, in any detail, of how to jump, though this is not, of course, how it is done today.

Although Lord Pembroke was himself an expert manège-rider, it may well be that his faith in this form of riding had been undermined by an unseemly and ludicrous incident at the recent Coronation of George III. It was the duty of Lord Talbot, the Lord High Steward, to ride into Westminster Hall and up to the throne, swear allegiance to the King and ride out again. Talbot, who rather fancied his horsemanship, carefully schooled his great horse to back out of the royal presence, lest he turn a disrespectful rump on His Majesty. Unfortunately, the perverse creature learned the lesson wrong and, to the impotent rage of his rider (never a man of equable temperament) and the hilarious applause of the bystanders, insisted on approaching the throne backwards.

Pembroke also, incidentally, had hard words to say of docking horses' tails and cropping their ears. The latter barbarity was probably perpetrated as a prevention against a horse's ears being sheared off in battle, either by his own rider (a not uncommon mishap) or by an enemy trying to sever the headstall so that the bit should fall from the horse's mouth.

Sixteen years later Captain Robert Hinde, in *The Discipline of the Light Horse*, wrote, 'nothing can be more awkward than a country fellow, or perhaps an artisan, mounted, still stiff with their former occupations. The riding-master must therefore speak mildly to the recruits. . . . Though we may meet with great awkwardness, yet we find a desire to learn in almost every recruit.'

Robert Hinde's observations on recruit-training are quoted because they are hardly in accord with the usual military practice of his day, when discipline was based on unthinking obedience, pipeclay, and the lash: a desire to learn was more commonly attributed to the horse than to the recruit, and the discovery that private soldiers were actually capable of thought was a startling novelty.

But clearly Hinde agreed with Lord Pembroke that one should not burden a trooper's understanding with too much theory. He would teach horse and man in the school only to walk, halt, rein back, and passage* – all necessary for any sort of drill. Out of doors the recruit was taught to trot 'and even gallop'; he must practise galloping 'gently in file', the 'serpentine gallop', and how to escape enemy fire by leaning over and taking cover behind the body of his galloping horse. 'It would be scarce possible (nor is it at all necessary) to teach the many more difficult and refined parts of horsemanship, to the many different kinds and disposition, both of men and horses, which one meets in a regiment.'

Even in Pluvinel's and de la Guerinière's native country, some soldiers got the message. In 1776 Count Drummond de Melfort, a cavalry officer of Scottish Jacobite descent, wrote that it was enough for a troop-horse to be taught to go forward, stop, back, turn, trot, and gallop; while Mercier Dupaty de Clam said that a cavalry-horse was required only for fast work: slow, collected paces which did not carry the horse forward were quite unnecessary.

A change from the old, straight-legged manège seat was facilitated by a change in the typical saddle. Up to the early eighteenth century men rode in a saddle basically similar to that of the medieval knight. It had a high, stuffed pommel and cantle, both

---

* Using the word in its modern sense of moving sideways, not in the seventeenth-century sense of 'marking time'.

A 17th-century Japanese horseman. Note the
platform stirrup

carried well down so as to enclose the rider's legs in a sort of groove, almost a vice.
This was no use at all for jumping: indeed it was positively dangerous, for if the horse
fell, the rider could not be thrown clear. So during the eighteenth century men took
to riding in what, to all intents and purposes, is the ordinary civilian saddle of today,
with a flattish seat set on short, padded side-bars. For military use this was modified.
The seat was made deeper; the side-bars were made larger and wider to spread the
weight and carry the trooper's cloak, nosebag, spare shoes, carbine, and other
paraphernalia. There was really very little difference between the Universal Pattern
(UP) saddle used at Waterloo and the Crimea, and that used by British cavalry in
the First World War, except that the front- and back-arch (pommel and cantle),
made rather high so as to keep the seat well off even an emaciated horse's back,

were at first of beech wood, later of steel. It is a good saddle, comfortable for the rider, easy on the horse since it allows a current of air under the seat and distributes the rider's weight. Most of the things on it which are likely to break can be repaired with the aid of a clasp-knife, a strip of rawhide, and a screwdriver. The pads or 'numnah panels', which are detachable from the side-bars, can be altered in shape merely by lashing on, or fixing with sticking-plaster, extra strips of felt or folded blanket. It is adaptable, with a little ingenuity, to almost any sized horse or pony. It weighed, stripped, from thirteen and a half to twenty pounds. The officers' pattern or 'Colonial' saddle was a less robust article, flatter in the seat, really a hunting-saddle with long side-bars. Some found it more comfortable than the UP saddle, but it was less convenient for carrying arms and kit, and could not so easily be repaired or altered to fit a particular animal. Not having a high cantle, it allowed a tired rider to rest himself by sitting too far back, which is very hard on the horse.

John Adams, in his *Analysis of Horsemanship* (1805), described how men *ought* to ride at a gallop – standing in the stirrups which should be shorter than in the military seat, and inclining the body forward to an angle of twenty to forty degrees from the perpendicular, the instep, knees, and hip-joints serving as springs or shock-absorbers. His reason for this posture, to 'relieve the bottom from the friction and heat it would sustain from a strong and continued gallop', would not now be considered very

A 16th-century German knight

pressing, but the seat itself was not unlike that of modern horsemen as first developed by Caprilli.

But Adams was a voice crying in the wilderness: the 'forward seat' was still strange and alien to the horsemen of western Europe who sat either upright or leaning slightly back, as is illustrated by hundreds of contemporary pictures. There was some variation in stirrup lengths. Light dragoons, designed to be more mobile than heavy cavalry, were supposed to adjust their leather so that, standing in the stirrups, they would have four inches clear between crotch and saddle. But in 1773 a heavy dragoon regiment was reproved for riding too short. Some cavalry riding-masters were criticized for teaching a style which 'poked the man's chin up in the air, squeezes his arms and elbows close to his sides like a fowl trussed for the spit; pulls his legs down straight from the hips so that they hang on the saddle like a pair of tongs, throwing the man on his fork'. At the Battle of Laswaree, in central India in 1803, the British cavalry commander before a charge ordered his brigade to take up their

Austrian hussar of about 1814. From a water-colour by R. Ottenfeld

The Earl of Pembroke who pioneered proper
cavalry training in England

leathers three holes so that they rode short like Mahratta horsemen. But John
Gaspard le Marchant, a heavy dragoon and one of the few dedicated professionals in
the British cavalry, in 1796 wrote that the knee-joint should be nearly straight.

Throughout the wars with Revolutionary and Napoleonic France, British Army
equitation adhered to no common doctrine, indeed to no doctrine at all, but was
influenced mainly by the fox-hunting propensities of almost every cavalry officer,
rarely sullied by prudence, discipline, or the most elementary acquaintance with
tactics. 'Your horses', said a French cavalry commander, General Excelmann, to
a British officer, 'are the finest in the world and your men ride better than any

159

continental soldier. With such material the English cavalry ought to have done more. . . . The great deficiency is in your officers who seem to be impressed by the conviction that they can dash or ride over everything, as if the art of war were precisely the same as the art of fox-hunting.' Wellington admitted that the French cavalry won battles, but his generally got him into scrapes.

Their performance was indeed patchy, and was generally characterized by a headlong charge, inability to rally after the charge, and a total absence of formed squadrons in support.

In the Peninsula the most brilliant British cavalry actions, Villa Garcia and Salamanca, succeeded only because Le Marchant kept control of his squadrons. They charged at a swinging gallop, inflicting terrible losses on the enemy horse and foot, but rallied when ordered; and formed reserves, kept well in hand, provided the succession of shocks which kept up the impetus of the attack, the key to success in cavalry actions.

These charges would not have been so successful if the British cavalry had not recently been provided, by the versatile Le Marchant, with a proper sword and trained by him in its use. During the eighteenth century British swords were, by common consent, the worst in Europe. So blunt, ill-balanced, and heavy were the

160

To foreign horsemen, jumping was a daring and difficult exercise

cavalry swords in Marlborough's day that his troops often preferred, in a charge, to grasp their weapons by the blade and wield them like bludgeons. An Austrian officer in the Flanders campaign of 1793 told Le Marchant that British troopers' swordmanship put him in mind of chopping wood. Many of the wounds received by Le Marchant's men and their horses in that ill-starred campaign could have been inflicted by no swords other than their own: one dragoon captain in a mêlée almost severed his own foot.

Shocked by the contrast between the blundering amateurishness of his own men and the deadly efficiency of the Hungarian hussars, Le Marchant on his return home studied and worked out a system for training men in mounted combat, which he imparted to cadre courses and thence to the regiments. He also, with the aid of an intelligent Sheffield sword-cutter, devised a better sword for the British cavalry. Stripped of all superfluous weight, well balanced, razor sharp, and with a slight curve so that it was equally apt for the cut and the thrust, Le Marchant's cavalry sword (soon a regular issue) had such punishing powers that a French commander in the Peninsula protested at the terrible wounds it inflicted.

The whole mystique of the manège, based on collection, discipline, and an aristo-cratic concept of life, was totally alien to the egalitarian, romantic, permissive

161

atmosphere of Revolutionary France. Besides, in the frantic hurry of raising new armies to repulse the Kings of Europe, the French had no time for elaborate training. The trooper learned simply to stop or turn the horse by pulling on the reins, to drive it forward by kicking with his legs; and when it was going more or less to his satisfaction, to let the reins (and, indeed, the legs) 'float'.

These methods might not have answered with the better bred, better fed British cavalry horses. But the standard of horses in France was not nearly as high as in England, and the insatiable demands of nearly twenty-three years of war further reduced the quality of remounts. Moreover, the French practice during these wars was for an army to live off the country, which meant that the horses were largely fed on grass and crops cut green rather than on oats. Lastly, while the English cavalry habitually charged at full gallop, Murat was perfectly satisfied if his cavalry could 'walk on the march, and trot in presence of the enemy'.

So, as Wellington said, 'the French cavalry is often more manageable and useful than the English, because it is always kept in hand and may be stopped at a word of command'. To this it may be added, that French cavalry officers were better trained in their profession, sounder on tactics, than the British. They won battles not by speed and dash, but by weight of numbers applied at the right time and place, in co-operation with other arms.

At all events, it was these rather unfinished horsemen but fine soldiers who 'made the tour of Europe' until they were confronted by the natural horsemen of the steppes.

Though the Austrian Army was, as a whole, singularly unsuccessful in these wars, Le Marchant had the highest opinion of the horsemanship and swordsmanship of the Austrian cavalry which he saw in the unhappy Flanders campaign of 1793. It seems probable that these formidable horsemen were Magyar hussars, riding short, their horses extended rather than collected, in the nomadic fashion. Throughout the long war they maintained their reputation, though the Austrian infantry fought with singular ill-success.

The greatest surprise of the war was, however, the Cossacks. They rode short, in the fashion of central Asia, at the gallop and to use their weapons they stood in their stirrups leaning forward; using a plain snaffle, they never bothered about collection, but allowed their ponies to extend their heads in a natural manner. They rode rings round the French cavalry. 'These rude horsemen', wrote the French General Morand, 'keep their horses close between their legs; their feet rest in broad stirrups, which support them when they use their arms. They spring from a state of rest to the full gallop, and at that gallop they make a dead halt: their horses second their skill and seem only part of themselves; these men are always on the alert, they move with extraordinary rapidity, have few wants and are full of warlike ardour. . . . It was thus that the finest and bravest cavalry [i.e. the French] exhausted and wasted itself against men whom it deemed unworthy of its valour. . . . The Cossacks returned covered with spoils and glory to the fertile banks of the Donetz, while the soil of Russia was strewn with the carcases and arms of our warriors so bold, so unflinching, so devoted to the glory of our country.'

It is strange indeed, and indicative of that stubborn conservatism which seems to be characteristic of horsemen, that nobody west of Hungary thought of copying the

The English Galloper

Eastern short-stirruped seat, though Turkish, and in general Oriental, horsemen were the acknowledged experts in light-cavalry work. 'For ages', wrote Captain Lewis Edward Nolan, 'the light cavalry maniac' of the mid nineteenth century, 'the finest cavalry in Europe was undoubtedly that of the Turks. . . . The horses, though not large (seldom much exceeding 14 hands) were nimble, spirited, and yet docile, and so trained and bitted as to be perfectly under control. The hollow saddle was rather heavy, but all the rest of the appointments were light; the soldier rode in the broad, short stirrup to which he and his ancestors had always been accustomed, and on which they had a firm and (to them) natural seat, out of which it was most difficult to throw him; his scimitar was light and sharp. . . . Their tactics were few and simple.'

The natives of southern India are not generally considered the best horsemen, nor their mounts the best horses, of the sub-continent; but (wrote Nolan) the Mysorean cavalry of Hyder Ali and Tippoo* abounded in 'clever horsemen and

* It is likely, however, that many of these horsemen were Rohillas and other Pathan mercenaries from the north.

163

first-rate swords . . .'. Wellington, who fought against the Mysore horse in 1799, said, 'They were the finest of their type I have ever encountered, they hung about our flanks night and day, no movement of our column escaped them and they melted away before any attempt to engage them.' The Mahratta horsemen, who terrorized most of India for a century and gave endless trouble to the Honourable East India Company, were much the same.

When the long wars were over, cavalry reverted, almost unanimously, to the methods which had been discredited by active service. It is not difficult to see a reason for this: there was a reaction against the whole liberal, permissive, Revolutionary ethic; a feeling among those whose lives had been disturbed for twenty-five years of war that now they could return to the leisured elegance of the past; and officers could now get back to proper soldiering, without the tiresome irrelevance of fighting.

The Crimean War – the myth . . .

... and the reality

The Prussians forgot all that Frederick the Great and Seidlitz had taught them, and returned to the most rigid, scholastic manège-riding. The magnificent Russian cavalry, including the Cossacks, were adjured to follow the Prussian example. 'The officers found themselves in a great predicament, for they had merely heard of the manège and the special art of horse-trainers, but did not have any idea how to start the work. . . . Someone translated de la Guerinière's book into Russian. . . . Fast gaits were eliminated. . . . The incorrect conditioning and schooling of the horses became evident in the [Russo-Turkish] war of 1828–9, when the great majority were found to be completely incapable of field service.'*

However, the Turkish horses were not much better, as Nolan (who saw a lot of them) records, 'they too were by now disciplined *à la France*, in Western fashion,

* From *The Russian Cavalry Messenger*, 1906. Quoted by Vladimir S. Littauer, *The Development of Modern Riding*.

taught by foreign riding-masters to ride long and even dress in tight jackets and pantaloons. The men were always rolling off and frequently ruptured.'

As for the unhappy English cavalry, they suffered likewise, from the Prince Regent's unbounded admiration for everything to do with the Prussian Army. Subjected to Prussian riding-masters, they had to ride with legs absolutely straight, 'like tongs across a wall', which produced a positive epidemic of ruptures. To do the instructors justice, however, their post-war pantaloons were so tight as to make any more rational posture almost impossible.

In France, however, now that men could consider these matters without constant preoccupation with the immediate requirements of the battle-field, much more thought was given to equitation. From 1815 to the end of the century France, and particularly the great Cavalry School of Saumur, was the home of educated horsemanship.

There were two great masters of equitation, two rival schools whose differences, resulting even in duels, enlivened French equitation and military society.

François Baucher was born in 1796, studied equitation under his uncle, and, then started a school of his own. His interest was solely in manège-work, at which he showed an extraordinary talent in training horses, on one occasion, for a wager teaching an unbacked horse the High School airs in less than a month. His object was to perfect a horse's balance: and to do this, he expunged the horse's instinctive, 'natural forces' and replaced these by 'imparted forces'. The operation moved the centre of gravity back and got the horse on his haunches until the forehand was almost off the ground: then 'imparted force' drove the horse forward.

After a good deal of hesitation the French Army formally rejected 'Baucherism', though his influence remained strong. It was conceded – no one could deny – that in Baucher's hands it worked miracles, but for less skilful operators it was all too easy to destroy a horse's natural forces without imparting anything to replace them. Furthermore, the importance which Baucher attached to work 'in hand'* to supple and balance a horse was largely a waste of time: as soon as the horse had the weight of a man on his back, he must be rebalanced.

Baucher's great rival, the Comte d'Aure, three years younger, was primarily a cavalryman. He thought nothing of Baucher's extraordinary feats of schooling and believed that Baucherism was entirely fallacious – or, at least, useless outside a circus and positively harmful to the cavalry. 'It is perhaps a strange and rare thing to see a horse trot and gallop backwards but as use still requires a horse to move forwards, these are the principles which it may be well to know.'

As Chief Instructor of the Cavalry School of Saumur, he stressed cross-country riding, hunting, steeplechasing: he was himself a very bold rider, and his theme throughout was to simplify equitation, to improve the horse's natural forces and, 'while permitting him to retain all his natural energy', help him 'develop almost by himself those qualities which are proper to him'. It was a theme to which d'Aure returned again and again – the antithesis of Baucherism.

He tried to establish at Saumur a horsemanship which combined the good points

---

* i.e. with the trainer not riding, but standing beside the horse to work the reins and bit.

166

of German and English equitation, while avoiding the over-formalism and excessive collection of one, and the slapdash empiricism of the other. The English, he wrote, 'concentrate on hunting and racing, and consider speed the most important quality. In schooling young horses they use methods which push them forward; and English horses are generally more on the shoulder than on the haunches. . . . The Germans work particularly in the manège and concentrate on military riding. They want to have horses that are slow and handy, to obtain which they put their horses more on the hindquarters than on the forehand. . . . We should look for a middle way.'

But in the history of equitation one looks in vain for symmetry and regular patterns. Towards the end of his life Baucher used and recommended nothing but a snaffle, and d'Aure selected a manège-rider to succeed him at Saumur.

Nothing illustrates better the English lack of interest in educated equitation than the novels of Surtees. His fictional character, Facey Romford, is a fine horseman by English standards, constantly taking his own line across country, clearing the most formidable obstacles. How does he do it? Merely, it seems, by 'getting his horse hard by the head', 'letting in the Latchfords' [spurs] with his 'cart-whip brandishing on high', ready to give him 'a refresher on the shoulder'.

Nor is Lucy Glitters any more scientific.

'Dash it! But this is a rum customer', says Romford, examining the first obstacle to check him that day, a very rough, tangled boundary fence apparently made up of all the rubbish and refuse of the county.

'Oh, throw your heart over', says Lucy, 'and then follow it as quickly as you can.'

Simplicity itself! But, as the logicians would say, throwing your heart over may be necessary, but is not sufficient in negotiating a big place.

Nimrod, the sporting journalist, had a little more to say about equitation. His remarks on riding short come rather as a surprise: 'No gentlemen now, and very few servants, are to be seen with short stirrups and consequently a bent knee, which, independently of its unsightliness, causes uneasiness to the horse as well as to the rider; whose knees being lifted above the skirts of the saddle, deprive him of the assistance of the clip by the thighs and legs.' The short stirrup, he said, was supposed to help the horse, but in fact did the contrary, for it put the rider too far back. There was a great improvement in English riding since stirrups were lengthened, but perhaps this had been carried too far in military riding.

He could not have ridden with legs quite straight, for he advocated posting at the trot. 'The objection to it on the part of foreigners lies in the inelegance, if not indecency.' What minds they must have had!

One should generally, wrote Nimrod, ride slowly at fences, but 'put in some powder' at a brook. 'It is not the horse's rising that tries the rider's seat; the lash of the hinder legs is what ought chiefly to be guarded against, and is best done by the body being greatly inclined backwards.' In jumping brooks, the rider remains in his saddle with (one is relieved to hear) 'very little assistance from his bridle-reins'. It was considered elegant, when jumping, to raise the right arm as though calling a cab.

The one point in jumping on which the experts were unanimous was that one should lean back at the take-off, a practice now universally condemned. Even in the

Bodyguard of Ranjit Singh. 1814

1890s a very well-known, scientific horseman, Captain Horace Hayes, was writing, 'As the ability to clear height depends greatly on the power of raising the forehand, the rider should refrain from leaning forward when the horse is rising at an obstacle. He should, on the contrary, if anything lean back at that moment, so as not to put any weight on the forehand. . . . On landing he should try to avoid bringing his weight forward.'

Other experts, including Baucher, advocated not only leaning back over the cantle on approaching the jump, but pulling on the reins to help raise the horse's forehand, and loud repetition of the word 'Hop'.

In the Army there seems to have been a reaction against the dashing, rough-and-ready riding of Wellington's officers. Nolan found British cavalry slow moving and unhandy, largely because they never trained at a gallop: the trooper probably never broke into a gallop for the whole of his military career, until his first charge when his horse, not surprisingly, ran away with him. 'A troop should be able to go across country, for any distances required, at a rattling gallop, closing to their leader to charge when the signal is given. All fighting with cavalry is either done at speed, or you advance at speed to get at your enemy. . . . Speed is the only pace at which you can catch your enemy and destroy him.'

'All practical riders,' wrote Nolan, 'the Cossacks, the Circassians, all Eastern nations . . . all ride in a short seat.' He condemned utterly the sugar-tongs seat. 'Balanced on his fork, it is of no use pulling at the horse if he tries to bolt; for, with legs and stirrups behind him, the rider, at the slightest pull, falls forward, and has the greatest difficulty in keeping his balance.'

Hodson of Hodson's Horse, an outstanding leader of light cavalry, held, however, less flattering views of Oriental horsemanship. Enlisting into his newly raised regiment many veterans of Ranjit Singh's old army, he found them 'indifferent riders, as Sikhs usually are (till taught), and at least half of them used with one hand to clutch hold of the high knob in front of the Sikh saddle as they galloped along. All I attempted to teach them was "Threes right", or "Threes left" (never "Threes about"), and "Form Line, Charge." They had plenty of pluck.'

Lady Burton, wife of the traveller whose exposition of Oriental moral deviations so shocked his generation, described the Arab nineteenth-century version of the *jerid*, with which the Moors in Spain had once exercised themselves and kept their horsemanship up to the mark, but which the Sultan, in his singleminded search for military stagnation, had banned for the Turkish cavalry. 'When I say the men are riding *jerid*, I mean that they are galloping about violently, firing from horseback at full speed, yelling, hanging over in their stirrups with their bridles in their mouth, playing with and quivering their long feathered lances in the air, throwing and catching them again at full gallop, picking things from the ground, firing pistols, throwing themselves under their horses' bellies and firing under them at full gallop, yelling and shouting their war-cries. . . . The wildness of the scene is very refreshing, but you have to be a good rider yourself, as the horses simply go wild.'

How different, how very different, from our own dear Pony Club's gymkhana! But it certainly shows that, riding short, one could control a horse and perform remarkable feats of agility.

At the turn of the century, the man who most influenced European horsemanship was James Fillis, British by birth but French by naturalization, and emphatically a product of French equitation. He studied under one of Baucher's pupils, and for some years earned a great reputation and a handsome income as a circus-rider. This does not imply that he jumped through blazing hoops or rode on three horses at once. The circus was the recognized theatre for the display by professional riders of the High School airs and large audiences came to watch. To these classical airs he added other exhibitions of his own virtuosity, such as trotting and galloping backwards, or cantering on three legs, which High School purists dismiss as mere circus tricks. Having achieved fame by these performances and by the publication in 1890 of his *Principes de Dressage et d'Equitation*, he was in 1898 appointed Chief Instructor to the Russian Cavalry Officers' School at St Petersburg.

Just as d'Aure had aimed at combining the good points of German dressage and English cross-country riding, and at Saumur in the 1890s the teaching was a synthesis of d'Aure and Baucher, so Fillis tried to adapt to cross-country riding the principles of the High School. It seems to be a recurrent theme in French equitation. But of the classical equitation of the Spanish Riding School in Vienna he was extremely critical: 'the horse of Lippiza can do nothing outside the manège . . . can neither walk, trot, nor gallop'. In return, the Spanish Riding School still write Fillis off as a mere circus-performer.

For both High School and cross-country riding he constantly stressed the paramount importance of collection. 'My method of equitation consists of the *distribution of weight* by the height of the neck bent at the poll and not at the withers; *propulsion* by means of the hocks being brought under the body; and *lightness* by the loosening of the lower jaw.' (Author's italics.) This is very similar to the definition of collection in the 1937 edition of the British Army's *Manual of Horsemanship, Equitation and Animal Transport*. 'A horse is said to be collected when his head is raised and bent at the poll, his lower jaw relaxed and his hocks well under him, so that he has the maximum control over his limbs and is in a position to respond instantly to the least indication of his rider.'

Fillis's definition of collection holds good today. But modern doctrine disagrees with his ideas on balance. Fillis suggests that a horse's propulsion is produced simply by his hind-legs which must, therefore, be brought well under him so as to do the job. But this is only half the answer: he is also propelled forward by, so to speak, losing his balance at every stride, and having to stretch out a foreleg to save himself from falling. The faster this goes, the more forward his centre of gravity must be, to produce this effect, and the more extended must be his head and neck, so as to bring his centre of gravity forward. This, of course, implies that the position of head and neck must be constantly changing. But by Fillis's method they were static. Photographs show his horses carrying head and neck high and bent at the poll even when galloping.

According therefore, to modern ideas, Fillis erred in imposing on the horse a fixed head- and neck-carriage for all paces, instead of leaving him to adjust his balance according to his pace. This form of collection he achieved by a lot of work in hand. But Russian officers found (as the Earl of Pembroke had found a century earlier) that work in hand requires a judgement and delicacy of touch far beyond that of the average soldier. In the hands of rough peasants it produced a horse which, with a strong rider, performed adequately on parade, but moving across country, tucked his chin into his chest and set his jaw like iron. Moreover, the balance, laboriously produced, even by a good teacher, by weeks or months of work in hand, had to be altered as soon as there was a rider on the horse's back.

Nevertheless, Fillis was a great and very versatile horseman, across country as well as in the school. Nor were his horses, like Baucher's, purely school horses, restricted and overbent. Indeed, between his strong legs, they went, an eyewitness remarked, 'as though the devil were in them'. Russian Army remounts which passed through his hands – he personally schooled as many as sixteen a day – finished their school-training in June. In July they raced; in August they did a march of 150 miles in two days, carrying 175 pounds; and in September they hunted. According to

Horace Hayes, however, the hunting was not very strenuous, since all officers were obliged to keep behind their elderly and cautious colonel.

Fillis's advice on jumping was certainly an advance on that of instructors who taught their pupils to lean back at the take-off and pull on the reins in order to help raise his forehand. The rider, said Fillis, should lean forward at the take-off, but back on landing so as to keep his seat, to spare the horse's forelegs which might suffer if all his weight and that of his rider came suddenly on them, and to hold up the horse if his knees gave way. Many a riding-instructor in modern times has sharpened his wit on Fillis's jumping methods which, wrote Littauer, do not 'comply with the laws of nature which govern the movements of living beings on this planet'. Whatever the rider's position, nothing can prevent all his weight and the horse's from coming on the forelegs when landing. If these forelegs give at the knees and the horse pecks, sitting back and pulling on the reins will no more help him keep his feet than a monkey, sitting on one's shoulders, could prevent a man from stumbling by pulling on his ears. Nevertheless, it is human instinct to lean back on landing lest one 'go out through the front window'; many a rider has, in fact, saved his neck by doing so; and though there are, as we all now know, better methods of keeping one's seat, Fillis's jumping style was accepted and taught for many years and is still frequently seen in the hunting-field.

The fact is that Fillis was a genius who made the very best of the methods generally accepted in his day. But these methods were, in the half-dozen years before 1914, first questioned, then completely discredited by a radical reformer who discarded all the assumptions which had guided the west European horsemen since Grisone.

It was unfortunate for the British cavalry that its officers, hitherto supremely uninterested in anything to do with scientific equitation, should in the 1890s have suddenly developed a belated enthusiasm for High School riding. Their interest was, apparently, stimulated by visits and attachments to foreign armies, and at Saumur they saw 'a handful of horses and men, the pick of many thousands, go through a Riding School performance such as would be a credit to the finest circus in the world. The riding of these men is superb, the handling and management of their well-broken horses is something to remember, the whole carried out before a crowded house with the solemnity and silence that an occasion of such dignity demands.' What they forgot was that the Cadre Noire was a *corps d'élite* of professionals, utterly dedicated to their service and their art. But the average British cavalry officer was an amateur, filling in, without undue exertion, a few years before the call of sport became too imperative and he sent in his papers and retired, at an early age, to the family estates. (Horsemastership in the Royal Artillery and Indian Cavalry, whose officers were professionals, was notably better.)

The result of attempts to school British cavalry-horses on the methods of Baucher and Fillis was uniformly unhappy. 'At one time', wrote Major-General Smith, later Director of Army Veterinary Services, 'the cavalry-horse remained so long under training that his joints were partly worn out before he completed his elaborate education. The bulk of his work took place in the school, the result being that . . . not 10 per cent of the cavalry horses would go alone. If a man was wanted from the ranks to take a message, a volunteer had to be called for.'

The unencumbered Boer

The shortcomings of British military equitation were soon to be seen in South Africa.

In the mid seventeenth century the Dutch had introduced horses into their Cape settlement. There was a terrific demand for them: 'Send me more horses!' was Van Riebecks' recurrent cry: the tiny colony could grow and thrive only with the aid of horses. So they were imported from the East Indies, bred locally, increased and multiplied – until in 1719, like a bolt from the blue, the terrible African horse-sickness struck, killing nearly 1,700 in a year.

This is one of the scourges of the Dark Continent south of the Sahara. Only recently has the cause of the disease been discovered: it is carried by a small night-flying gnat. Only in the past few years has a prophylactic inoculation been invented. There is no known cure, and the recovery rate is not one in a hundred. It is interesting to reflect on the effect of African horse-sickness on human history. In Europe, Asia, and Africa the boundary of civilization, however that be defined, coincided to a remarkable degree with the boundaries of ancient horse-cultures. South of the Sahara, where horse-sickness is endemic, man for 3,000 years in his struggles to overcome a hostile environment was deprived of the assistance of this powerful and versatile ally. This may explain a lot.

Anyway, the Dutch persevered. It was 250 years before they conquered this terrible foe, but over the generations they learned, empirically, to mitigate its effects by reducing the exposure of horses to it.

The original stock of ponies imported from the East Indies were improved by stallions imported from Holland, Persia, and South America, bringing an infusion of Arab and Barb stock. The first English thoroughbred arrived in 1792.

The Cape horse was never a handsome animal, and although the Boers and British residents of South Africa thought the world of it, visitors found it dull and lifeless. 'In temper', wrote Horace Hayes, 'the South African horses are, as a rule, very quiet, spiritless, though good slaves, and are inclined to be obstinate. Their lack of life is no doubt due to their being kept during their youth in a state of semi-starvation. The cause of their tendency to be sulky I attribute to their being broken in at a comparatively late period in life. . . . The longer the inoculation of discipline is delayed, the more stubborn will be the horse. It is just the same with a child.'

Young horses were broken in by being ridden with the head tied to that of an old horse moving alongside: they were thus prevented from bucking, rearing, or otherwise making nuisances of themselves. 'This is a capital plan if one has a good break horse, and if one knows no better way. Its great fault is a tendency to make a horse unwilling to go alone. Of course it has no pretension to giving a horse a good mouth.' Again and again Hayes reverts to the extreme quietness of most South African horses, 'due to the fact of their being starved on arid pastures for a considerable portion of each year, and to the non-stimulating quality' of their food – generally maize or oat-hay. Nevertheless, they were good workers for their weight, and very game.

There may have been another reason for the South African horse being so quiet: the Boers like him that way. Boers were a nation of horsemen, living in the saddle; generally speaking they kept their horses not for racing* or hunting in the English sense, but for work – riding about the farm and into the nearest *dorp*, visiting, and, above all, for shooting. They did not need good roping- and cutting-horses, for African cattle are far quieter and tamer than Texas longhorns or Herefords, and can

---

* There was, of course, racing in the Cape, as everywhere the English went. But while breeding for racing may have marginally improved the Cape horse, it was not of much importance.

more easily be handled, sorted, thrown, and branded by African herd-boys on foot. There was no need for a Boer's horse to jump, for the country across which he rode had no fences. But he must ford or swim rivers in spate, and carry a dead buck tied across the saddle. He must stand stock-still while his rider aimed for a long shot, from the saddle, at an eland or springbok; he must face without flinching a charging lion or buffalo. For elephant-shooting the muzzle-loading *roer*, firing a huge lead ball, was so heavy that it could only be used with any accuracy with the aid of a ramrod as a rest. So the hunter must dismount, take a carefully aimed shot at close range and then mount quickly – and his horse must stand stock-still until given the office to gallop away as the wounded elephant, with ears spread like great sails, shrilly trumpeting with rage and pain, pounded after them. No horse bred for speed and spirit would do for this sort of work.

So the 'cold blood' of the Cape horse which Hayes and other English sportsmen rather despised, when translated into French, *sang-froid*, indicates precisely the quality which the Boer most valued – a stoic courage and steadiness. Besides, Cape horses, as an East India Company officer remarked, 'surpass any horse I have seen out of Europe in their untiring and unflinching endurance during the longest and hottest months of the year'.

The Boers needed a horse who was quiet, hardy, and could cover long distances, on little food and water, at a fairly slow pace. 'The Boer's pony', wrote an English journalist, 'hardly knows how to trot or gallop, but goes loping along in a leisurely, monotonous way.'

Frankly, I am not quite clear as to the Boer names for the paces of a horse. I believe the *lope* and the *gang* is the same pace, a loose, uncollected canter. The *tripple* is an amble, which some Cape horses did naturally. The amble is the subject of one of those interminable arguments in equitation. Most horsemen, in most parts of the world, condemn it, though it is undeniably comfortable for the rider. Hayes suggests that Boers liked it because a heavy rifle (which they always seem to have carried in the hand or slung across the back) is an awkward load at any pace, but less awkward at the smooth amble than at a trot.

The Boers' equitation earned only the grudging approval of Captain Hayes, though he admits that it served the Boers' purposes. 'As Afrikanders are broad in the beam and often have to remain several hours on horseback, they like their saddles to be particularly wide towards the cantle and have a good dip in them. South Africa being a very open country, little attention is paid to jumping. As the young men connect riding chiefly with shooting, they almost all ride with only the left hand on the reins, while the right is supposed to be occupied with a rifle. The use of a sharp curb or Pelham is a natural consequence of this one handed form of equitation.'

The new settlements in Australia and New Zealand, as they developed during the early nineteenth century, desperately needed horses, which were at first supplied from the Cape. In their new homes, horses flourished exceedingly, particularly in Australia. There were neither beasts of prey nor horse-sickness:* the hard ground and

---

* It is fortunate indeed that this scourge was not introduced from the Cape.

The Charge of the 11th Lancers at Cerizy,
28 August 1914

dry, sparse range-grasses produced animals sound in wind and limb. The original Cape stock was improved by imported thoroughbreds, and by mid-century there had developed in New South Wales the famous Waler, toughest and best of all working-horses. The Waler was the mainstay of the Army in India, replacing by the 1860s the Cape horse, and proved equally staunch in war, hunting, pig-sticking, and racing. But essentially the Waler was, and is, a working range-horse of the highest quality.

We have seen that the horsemanship of America, North and South, was strongly influenced by the Iberian horse-culture introduced by the *conquistadores*. The horsemanship of South Africa was influenced by the Boer's need for a quiet, steady shooting-pony, and by the fact that horse-sickness inhibited the import of expensive thoroughbred stock. Australasian horsemanship was quite different from both these, being the product of Victorian England. The stockman rode exactly like nineteenth-century fox-hunters, rather straight in the leg, holding his well-bred, spirited horse hard by the head and driving him into the snaffle-bit. His saddle was an ordinary English hunting-saddle, with an enlarged weight-bearing surface and sometimes fitted with knee-rollers to help with a buck-jumper. His sports were flat racing, steeplechasing, and riding to hounds after kangaroo. Since in the early settlements timber was plentiful, he was accustomed to jump his horse over deadfalls, stout

post-and-rail fences, and even wire. Like the 'crackers' of Georgia and Kentucky (whom he probably resembled in his ranching methods) he used a stock-whip, rather than a lariat. The Australian aboriginal took remarkably well to riding: by the 1860s, the 'abo' horsebreaker was commonplace, and now on many cattle stations the majority of riders are of that race.

In Australia and New Zealand cattle- and sheep-ranching are increasingly mechanized, but there are still vast areas where horses are necessary. Some of the roughest riding in the world is in Queensland and the Northern Territory: so hard is the going that horses have to be shod daily; so rough and rocky that most people would think it impossible to move out of a slow, stumbling walk. But these fine horse-men, driving, herding, or rounding up cattle as wild as deer, cover it at a gallop, still doing a job as tough as any horseman's in the world.

English and Irish foxhunters such as Whyte Melville, Adam Lindsay Gordon, and Captain Horace Hayes found themselves perfectly at home among Australian horsemen and horses, whom they admired quite as much as they despised those of South Africa. What escaped their notice was that in war now dominated by smoke-less powder and the magazine-rifle, the small, docile Boer pony and its slouching, slovenly rider were just the job. British cavalry-training, for horse and man, was concentrated mainly on the charge. So a troop-horse had to be able to cover the final, desperate furlong at a fast gallop, to be handy in a mêlèe, and heavy enough to keep his feet in shock-action. None of this was remotely relevant to war in the veldt, where the ideal horse was one which would go twenty-five miles a day, however slowly, on half-rations and one drink of dirty water.

The burger on commando carried only his rifle and ammunition, some mealies for his horse, a canvas bag contained a little biltong, coffee, sugar, flour, and a billy-can. He needed no more, for he was accustomed to short commons, knew how to hunt, what berries were edible, what leaves would cure a girth-gall or colic, and where water could be found in hollow trees or by digging in sandy river-beds. A friend of mine who, as a boy of eight, saw the Lichtenburg Commando riding into Vryburg, thus describes them: 'They looked just like what they were – farmers, slouch hats, any old clothes, the older ones bearded, riding loosely with long stirrups at a quiet pace. Keen eyes under shaggy eyebrows, dour, silent, seeing everything and noting all. They settled on Vryburg like a swarm of locusts.'

Their ponies carried about sixteen stone, and when a burger rode off on commando he was generally accompanied by a pack-pony and a spare. He could obtain, at least in the early years of the war, fresh but fit remounts at any veldt farm. In contrast, the British troop-horse carried about twenty stone, his rider had no spare animals and could not replace him unless he collapsed or dropped dead.

This alone would suffice to account for the extraordinary difference in quality between the Commandos and the Imperial forces who, although outnumbering them by nearly six to one, took three years to persuade them to lay down their arms and accept full compensation for all they had lost in the war. But there were many other reasons, mostly connected with horsemanship.

The Boers were bred to the saddle and to the veldt. So were some of the Colonial troops, and a few of the Imperial Yeomanry; but even they were not used to cherishing and keeping fit a *single* horse in campaign conditions, a very different technique to the *remuda* system to which they were accustomed, in which a tired, lame, or sore-backed horse can simply be, temporarily, discarded. For instance, as Lord Methuen reported, 'One never saw an irregular man go except at a gallop, he thought it was

French spahis riding short. First World War

Opposite
French dragoons riding long. First World War

A 20th-century Mongolian horseman

the normal pace for a horse.' A gallop may serve well enough when you have half a dozen spare horses awaiting their turn, but not when you have only one, and he is overloaded.

The regular cavalry had at least been taught, and were disciplined enough to obey the order on horsemastership given by their officers. But in general the Imperial Yeomanry, though in a sense able to ride, were in no sense horsemen, and were quite ignorant of looking after a horse in war conditions.

Unpractised horsemen, when tired, rest themselves and ease their sore behinds by sitting too far back, weighting first one buttock, then the other. They do not dismount nearly often enough: it is too much effort to clamber up again. When they do dismount, they seldom think of loosening the girth, and never of unsaddling the

178

horse. In any case, it took two men to saddle a horse with all the paraphernalia of war, a serious matter in case of a sudden alarm: so horses often remained under the saddle all night. All this resulted in sore backs; and the only way really to cure a sore back is to rest it; even an hour's riding, whatever dressings and pads were improvised, makes it worse; but on active service horses cannot always be rested just because they need it. The British Army's horsemastership – described in Chapter 11 – was even worse than its riding.

So, purely by their superior horsemanship, a few thousand Boer farmers made the greatest Empire on earth, at the height of its power, look supremely ridiculous.

Appalled by the wastage of horses in South Africa, the cavalry and veterinary authorities paid far more attention to horse-management. A great effort was made to cut from about twenty to about eighteen stone the weight carried by the troop-horse, though under active service conditions it tended always to creep up. Squadron and troop officers were strongly impressed with their responsibilities in horse-mastership. When I was a cavalry subaltern in the 1930s, we learned a golden rule: 'Look after the horses first, the men next, the officers last'. Whether or not this rule had been formulated in the nineteenth century, it was certainly not observed much before 1914: but it was observed in the First World War. The greatest importance was attached to dismounting, leading the horses, resting, off-saddling and grazing when-ever possible. British cavalry and artillery were never better ridden or better looked after than in their last large-scale appearance on the battle-field.

The results were striking, and of historic importance. In the advance to the Aisne the German cavalry was almost brought to a standstill not by battle casualties, but by horse-wastage. The presence of a French Metropolitan cavalry division, who sel-dom dismounted and hardly ever off-saddled, could be detected a mile away by the overpowering stench of suppurating saddle-sores and girth-galls. But in their long retreat from Mons and advance from the Aisne the British cavalry, by superior equitation and horsemastership, remained operational throughout and had a decisive effect in the First Battle of Ypres.

The last great campaign of British mounted forces was in Palestine where in the advance to Gaza, to Jerusalem, and to Damascus they performed brilliantly, largely owing to supremely good horsemastership. (A small French cavalry force, operating with them, suffered severely from sore backs and proved unable to keep up.) On many occasions, and nearly always with success, they charged large, unbroken formations of infantry, armed with all the weapons of the day.

Mileage statistics in a pursuit mean little, for they can take little account of reconnaissance, manœuvre, and fighting; cavalry formations, complete with machine-guns, horse artillery, and even the lightest transport, necessarily move much slower than individuals and small parties on long endurance-tests. Nevertheless, to cover nearly 170 miles in four days, as the Desert Mounted Force did over rough, waterless country in 1917, was by any standards a remarkable feat. In the Indian Cavalry Division's final pursuit to Damascus my own regiment, Hodson's Horse, having led the breakthrough on the coast and outpaced messengers sent to slow down its advance, rode fifty-six miles on the first twenty-six hours, in great heat, fighting several stiff actions. Thirteen exhausting days later the regiment reached Damascus

Mounted tribal police-
man during Kenya
Emergency, possibly one
of the last men to have
ridden to war

after a final day's march of sixty-three miles with negligible horse-wastage. Indian *sowars* rode lighter than British or Australian troopers whose horses had to carry, in this fodderless, waterless country, more like twenty-one stone than the eighteen stone carried in France.

One of the main difficulties of the Palestine campaign was shortage of water, and the slowness of watering from desert wells 150 feet deep of which the retreating enemy had destroyed the pumps. To meet this difficulty, the Australians deliberately cut down their watering to once a day, then to once every other day, in order to harden their horses and accustom them to go long distances without drinking. As a result, their Walers looked thin, but were certainly hard. It is interesting to compare these methods with those employed by some accomplished horsemen, the Turcomans of trans-Oxus, in preparing their horses for a raid. Alexander Burnes, an East India Company officer who travelled among them in 1832, wrote:

'Before a Toorkman undertakes a foray he . . . "cools his horse" with as much patience and care as the most experienced jockey of the turf, and the animal is sweated down with a nicety which is, perhaps, unknown to these characters. After long abstinence from food, the horse is smartly exercised and then led to water. If he drinks freely, it is taken as a sign that the fat has not been sufficiently brought down, and he is starved and galloped about till he gives this required and indispensable proof. A Toorkman waters his horse when heated, and then scampers about with speed,* to mix the water and raise it to the temperature of the animal's body. Under this treatment, the flesh of their horses becomes firm.'

---

* A sure recipe for disaster, according to Western horsemasters. The British Army manual lays down, 'horses should never be made to work faster than a walk for a quarter of an hour after a full drink'.

He goes on to quote examples of Turcoman horses covering 600 miles in as little as six days, in extreme heat and much of the way over heavy sand. Australian methods also paid off: there are many examples of units on long advances and flank marches going for as long as seventy-two hours between waterings.

Allenby's advance to Damascus was the last great cavalry campaign except in Russia, where there was ample forage and water but very poor road communications. The Russians used cavalry divisions and even corps with remarkable success in 1924–5 riding, of course, in the manner of the steppes. Elsewhere the day of the war-horse is over.

Perhaps the last men ever to ride to war were the members of the Kenya Police and Tribal Police mounted sections – increased eventually to several troops – who operated against the Mau Mau from 1952 to 1956. The plains country around the forests of Mount Kenya and the Aberdares are good cavalry country and prophylactic inoculation had considerably reduced the risk of horse-sickness. Besides the hard-core gangs in the mountain forests, many smaller gangs operated in the savannah country of the Rift Valley, Nanyuki, Masai, and the Northern Frontier. To harry such gangs, to stop them stealing cattle and ripe crops, to protect farms and loyal tribesmen, to dominate this open countryside, horsemen were ideal; and as the gangs had few if any automatic weapons, the horses were not particularly vulnerable. The need was first seen by a few farmer-horsemen, who formed mounted sections more or less on their own though incorporated into the Kenya Police Reserve. The Director of Operations, General Hinde, a 15/19th Hussar and international polo-player, soon appreciated their value and saw that they were properly organized, armed, equipped, and expanded.

Operating generally in section – sometimes in troop – strength, these mixed patrols of European and African horsemen did an extraordinarily good, if unspectacular job. Like the Boers, they could ride light, based on and obtaining remounts from farms and ranches.

The last charge ever carried out by British mounted troops was by a section of Northern Frontier Tribal Police, Somalis and Boran, employed on anti-Mau Mau operations near Isiolo in 1953. They came upon a large, well-armed gang in open country. Armed only with rifles, they should have dismounted and opened fire: but Serjeant Yusuf Abdulla, with a well-founded distrust of his men's marksmanship, ordered a charge. They galloped down the gang and killed the lot, shooting from the saddle at point-blank range or bashing them with rifle-butts. Their only loss was one broken rifle.

6

The Sporting Horse

For nearly 4,000 years the horse had been man's partner and comrade in work, war, and sport. During the eighteenth and nineteenth centuries, as though in anticipation of the horse's disappearance from the farm, the street, and the battle-field, there was an extraordinary development, improvement, and elaboration of the partnership in the one field in which, by the mid twentieth century, the horse was to retain his proud place. All horse-sports, in all countries, are characterized by a premium on nerve, skill, and complete co-operation between horse and man, who seem to share the excitement, danger, and fierce competition. There is an immense variety of horse-sports, all of which require a high standard of horsemanship, courage and initiative – qualities which make up what used to be called 'the cavalry spirit'. Some account is given in a later chapter of very tough sports associated with 'western' riding in America.

FLAT RACING

In its early days racing was neither organized nor conspicuous for probity, taking its tone from the general style of the Restoration Court where kings, statesmen, women, and horses were all to be had at a price. Races were generally 'matches' between individual owners, often run in several heats totalling several miles.

A notorious race took place, or is reputed to have taken place at Newmarket early in the eighteenth century between horses belonging to Sir William Strickland, a Yorkshire magnate, and a Mr Tregonwell Frampton, a Westcountryman and 'Keeper of the Running-Horses' to William of Orange. The rival owners, in order to ensure adequate return on their respective wagers, privily arranged a secret trial carrying equal weights. Unfortunately, each double-crossed the other by carrying seven pounds extra. Neither party kept its secret well: each tipped off his friends, and innumerable gentlemen plunged heavily on what, they were assured, was a safe thing. The consequent losses, charges, and counter-charges resulted in an Act of Parliament which made it impossible to recover in law more than £10 of a gambling debt.

In early days horses running at Newmarket were a very mixed lot, but gradually it became obvious that although imported Eastern horses – Arabians and 'Turks'* were not always themselves particularly fast, the Arab-English cross was far faster than anything hitherto known. These simple facts resulted in the English thorough-bred horse.

None too soon, the Jockey Club was established as the authority which controlled

---

* Probably also Arabs, captured or bought from Turks.

182

racing. It took some controlling in days when a Newmarket tout was hanged for poisoning a favourite, and the 'First Gentleman of Europe' had to be warned that if he 'suffered Chiffney to ride his horses, no gentleman would start against him'. More than once it was suggested that a horse of His Royal Highness was 'supposed not to have been made to exert his utmost efforts'.

Samuel Chiffney, the Prince's jockey, set out his racing theories in a book. He pioneered the use of a snaffle, when everyone else rode races in a double-bridle. On the analogy that a man carrying a heavy stone prefers to shift it from hand to hand, he believed that a horse went better if the rider kept shifting his centre of gravity, now backward, now forward. It is not a view which commends itself to modern jockeys, nor does his practice of riding on a loose rein: a jockey should ride, he wrote, 'as if you had a silken rein as fine as a hair, and was afraid of breaking it'. A horse ridden so 'can run considerably faster when called upon, to what he can when he has been running in fretting, sprawling attitudes with part of his rider's weight in his mouth'. In a finish, the horse's mouth should be 'eased of the weight of the rein'. Despite these heresies, Chiffney was by far the most successful jockey of his day, but unpopular with his colleagues because, he confessed, 'I don't talk to grooms about horses. What I have to say about horses, I say to noblemen and gentlemen.'

In France there had, of course, been informal races for centuries, and it is difficult to fix a definite date for the start of organized racing. Some put it at 1651, when the Prince d'Harcourt and the Duc de Joyeuse raced through the streets of Paris for a stake of 2,000 écus. Another possible start for racing in France was in 1766, a race between an English horse which 'ran with a speed hitherto not seen in France, and a French horse which failed to complete the course and died a few days later, poisoned, so it was proved, by the emissaries of "perfide Albion". Cela fit beaucoup de bruit.' Thereafter racing increased in popularity, receiving the patronage of Louis XVI. A French Jockey Club was formed, and judged it prudent to reserve certain races solely for French horses.

In the first flush of Revolutionary ardour, patriots condemned racing as a waste of time. But singularly enough, as the Revolution prospered, so did the Sport of Kings. Among the jockeys' names appears the improbable one of Jacqueson. Was he a Republican refugee from England? Riders wore tricolour sashes, to show that their hearts were in the right place, and were distinguished one from the other by long plumes, in their caps, of different colours. Races were run under the authority, not of any effete aristocrats, but of the Director-General of Public Instruction, and were open to all, disputes and objections being decided by the judges of the Revolutionary Tribunals, who perhaps regarded them as a welcome relief from condemning people to the guillotine. Prizes for winners were deprecated as being contrary to the spirit of the Revolution: citizens should be stimulated only by their 'passion for glory'. Perhaps this was why Jacqueson was not conspicuously successful, his mercenary race requiring a more material incentive.

To continue the story of French racing, the course at Longchamp was opened in 1857 and the first Grand Prix run in 1863, won by an English horse, The Ranger. But two years later a French horse, Gladiateur, more than squared the account by winning the Triple Crown – the Two Thousand Guineas, the Derby, and the St Leger.

For most of the nineteenth century book-makers could gain access to French courses only by qualifying as owners, but punters were still quick to suspect 'les intentions machiavéliques des jockeys'.

Among the more notorious English owners during the Regency was the Duke of Queensberry, 'Old Q', an infamous old lecher whose practice it was to sit, rouged, bewigged, and laced-up in stays at his club window, ogling the females who passed by and sending his footman with improper proposals to any who seemed likely to accommodate him. In his younger days he was hero of a racing story which displays him in a more endearing light. His jockey confessed that he had been offered money to pull a horse. 'Take it', advised Q, which the lad did. Then at the very last minute, just as the jockey was about to mount and ride down to the start, Q stripped off his greatcoat and, clad in his racing colours, said, 'I think I'll ride this race myself'. He won. He usually won – unless he intended to lose.

He was a great man for fantastic wagers, but the most unusual riding wager I have seen recorded is reported by Mr Wilkes, the famous rake and demagogue. 'Hartley, the nabob, for a wager rode thirty miles, drank three bottles of champagne and did what I dare not mention with three different women, all in three hours.' It must have been difficult to decide on the order in which the various elements of the contest, the heats as it were, should be attempted.

Presumably, Hartley, the nabob, rode long, like most other riders, with a great deal of arm- and leg-action. *The Sporting Magazine* commented on 'gentlemen riders', 'You see nothing but waving arms and yellow leather breeches in convulsions.' Professional jockeys like Chiffney may have been more restrained in their movements, but the style of race-riding did not alter much between the mid eighteenth and the late nineteenth centuries. Fred Archer, probably the most successful jockey of all time, developed no new style: his skill lay in his judgment of a horse's capability, in superb timing of a race, and in ruthless, indeed often brutal determination and will to win. This sometimes recoiled against him, as on the occasion when he was riding against a very young and nervous apprentice who had been instructed not to expose his horse which had no chance of winning. 'Come on', said Archer at the start, 'we'll put this young b . . . . r over the rails.' The terrified lad shot off like a bullet from a gun, and won by lengths, much to his owner's indignation.

But Archer rode in the Derby exactly as he had ridden to hounds as a boy. He, and all other jockeys of his day, sat down in the saddle, body upright or even leaning slightly back, reins in the left hand, whip hand raised on high. The stirrups, wrote Nimrod, should be of moderate length 'so as to enable him to clear the pommel and have a good resisting power over the horse'. One should not, he explained, ride too long because at top speed a racehorse's forehand sinks down by several inches, so without the 'power of resistance from the stirrups', the jockey would be pulled over the horse's head. A jockey must never ride with a loose rein. 'Exclusive of the necessity of restraining a free horse, who would run himself to a standstill if he were suffered to do so, or of "making a waiting race", all horses feel relieved by a strong pull at their heads, and many will "shut up" at once if their heads were loosed.' They seem to have used a double-bridle as often as a snaffle. The seat is familiar to us from a thousand sporting prints.

In 17th-century Japan in one kind of race the rider had to
dismount and run the final stage with his horse as is done
in Pony Clubs today

The jockey's art lay in judging speed and following the trainer's instructions to
'wait' or to 'make running'. He should win if possible, and not do more than win.
'A very clever one, if he is opposed to another of less science, will "gammon" he is
beat; and then if his opponent eases his horse or becomes at all careless, he catches
him on a tremendous "Chiffney" rush on the post.' Despite those flailing right arms,
the jockey should seldom actually use his whip, which might make a horse 'shut up'.
Riding long, he could make much more effective use of his spurs. A jockey rode most
of a race standing in his stirrups, but sat down in the saddle to ride a finish, 'moving
his hands as if describing a circle by way of rousing the horse'.

'The seat of the jockey', wrote Nimrod, 'is one of peculiar elegance, heightened
by the almost universal quality of his form or figure, for very few ill-proportioned men

185

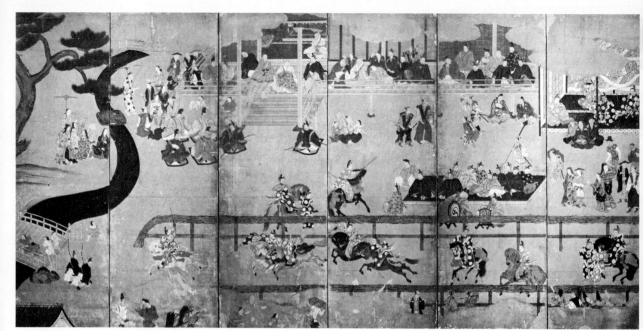

Classical horse-race. Japan

are found in the racing-saddle. The good appearance of the jockey is also increased by the neatness of his clothes; his costume appropriate to his calling; the extreme cleanliness of his person produced by his necessary attention to it during the preparatory course of exercise; and his utmost affinity with the noble animal we see him mounted upon.'

The man who changed all this was an American, a queer, 'mixed-up kid' named Tod Sloan who was terrified of horses, frequently run away with but still went on riding – generally those animals which trainers thought had no chance of winning whoever rode them.

According to his own story, Sloan was clinging to the neck of a horse which was running away with him, and had the presence of mind to notice that the animal ran much better with the rider in that position. Forthwith he determined to use the 'crouch seat' in races.

Without animadverting on the probability of this story, one may note factually that others had used the crouch seat in the past. There is a fifteenth-century picture of the annual race through the streets of Florence with some of the boy-jockeys crouched on the horse's neck; and a picture in the fifteenth-century manuscript, *Les très riches heures du Duc de Berri* shows the same thing – a horse-dealer's boy-rider crouched on the neck of a horse whose paces he is showing off to a client. Tartars and other central Asian tribesmen raced in this position, as did Red Indian boys. Tod Sloan would be unlikely to see Tartars, Red Indian boys, or medieval pictures, but there is evidence that some Negro riding-boys in the States used the crouch seat for practice gallops long before Sloan 'invented it'. A coloured jockey named Simms had used it, not very successfully. However, it was unquestionably Sloan who, by his remarkable successes, popularized it in America in the mid 1890s, and in Europe from 1897, when he first raced at Saint-Cloud.

His racing career in England lasted only from 1898 to 1900, and was marked by scandal after scandal, for he was a bad, if infrequent, loser, financially unreliable, and 'could not hold his oats'. He was not exactly warned off the English turf, but decided it would be imprudent to apply for a 1901 licence. However, before he died in a charity ward, every flat-race jockey in the world was riding 'like a monkey-on-a stick'.

The essence of Tod Sloan's crouch was to bring together the horse's and the rider's centres of gravity. Since at full gallop the horse's centre of gravity is well forward, the jockey's must be also, a position achieved by riding very short, seat right off the saddle, body lying almost parallel with the horse's neck, arms stretched forward. Besides advancing the rider's centre of gravity to conform with the horse's, this seat reduced wind resistance and, by freeing the horse's loins, allowed him to reach well forward with his hind-legs, thereby lengthening his stride. The drawbacks at first urged against it were that it almost deprived the jockey of the use of leg-aids, and reduced control by the hands, the ability to hold back in a waiting race. The contemporaries of Fred Archer and George Fordham generally rode the first half of a race quite slowly, manoeuvring for position and sometimes conversing, more or less amicably, *en route*. Such a leisurely progress was impossible for Sloan, but this hardly mattered; for horses ridden in his style went twelve or fourteen pounds better than those ridden by older methods, and could therefore race from start to finish – another novelty introduced by this American.

STEEPLECHASING

It is odd that people took such a very long time to think of racing over jumps. They raced on the flat: they jumped when hunting: but they did not combine the two. Jump-racing seems to have developed from the wild-goose chase. As jumping became more common, so in this game the leader would naturally take his horse over hedge, ditch, and timber. By the early nineteenth century this had developed into half a dozen riders trying 'which could set the others the most desperate or cramped or

The English racing seat before Tod Sloan

difficult leaps, and the rider who could within a certain time keep forty yards ahead was the winner.'

Apart from wild-goose chases, the first steeplechase on record was in 1752, in Ireland, when Mr O'Callaghan and Mr Edmund Blake raced over four and a half miles of hunting country from Buttevant Church to St Leger Church.

All early steeplechases were run from steeple to steeple, or point to point, the riders being free within certain defined limits to choose their own line. They might, for instance, in one race be prohibited from diverging more than fifteen yards from the direct line, in another be bound only to follow as direct a line 'as possible'. The first race over made-up fences seems to have been at Bedford in 1811.

One of the reasons for the gradual increase of racing over jumps was that owners wished to race their hunters against one another, and no matter what rules were made about qualifying horses by hunting, it proved impossible to prevent thorough-bred non-hunters from infiltrating and winning such races so long as they were on the flat. This was the origin of the Bedford race, someone having suggested that the only way to restrict the race to genuine hunters would be to run it over eight fences, four foot six inches high with a strong bar along the top. Both the winner and the runner-up had 'certificates gained by being in at the death of three foxes in Leicestershire'.

By 1839, when the first Grand National was ridden, a steeplechase was no longer a privately arranged race across natural country, but had assumed more or less its present form.

Steeplechasing came rather slower to the Continent, where the winter climate in central Europe and the pattern of farming elsewhere produced conditions inimicable to fox-hunting: there was no tradition of cross-country riding over obstacles. But Comte d'Aure deliberately encouraged it at Saumur. French horsemen, ever jealous of their country's traditions and pre-eminence in equitation, could not long neglect this new, exciting, and dangerous sport. From about 1836 races *au clocher* became popular around Paris. Flat-racing purists still regarded steeplechases as *illegitimes*, but Auteuil became the centre of the sport in France.

For a long time steeplechasing was in considerable disrepute, infamous for crooked riding, pulled horses, 'jockey boys on cast-off racehorses, riding round and round a course, jumping hurdles, sham brooks and other artificial fences . . . a burlesque'. It was condemned in *The Sporting Magazine* as cruel to the horses, a criticism which Nimrod was to repeat twenty-four years later and, indeed, in these early races an undue proportion of horses – indifferent jumpers, who should never have been entered – were killed. The vexed question of gentlemen riders and professionals stirred up much ill-feeling, and the Duke of Beaufort declared that the former could be identified only because they wore gold rings and kept their hands out of their breeches pockets. The first Grand National, intended only for gentlemen riders, was won by a blatant professional, Jem Mason; and the most talented amateur, Captain Beecher, achieved immortality by his misfortune in falling arse-over-tip into water. It was, incidentally, Jem Mason who defined the height of human misery as riding 'a ewe-necked horse galloping over a mole-hilly field, downhill, with bad shoulders, a snaffle-bridle, one foot out of the stirrup and a fly in the eye'.

The sport was becoming the refuge for human and equine outcasts because there was no over-all, national control; stewards were appointed *ad hoc*, so their heaviest sanction was the insignificant one of suspending an offender for the remainder of a single meeting. As a result stewards – like, as Surtees observed, churchwardens and sheriffs – seldom volunteered for a second tour of office. 'There is always something wanting or forgotten. Either they forget the ropes, or they forget the scales, or they forget the bell, or – more commonly still – some of the parties forget themselves. And the very horses were lean, lathy, sunken-eyed, woebegone, iron-marked, desperately abused brutes, lacking all the lively energy that characterized the up-to-the-mark hunter, and having a peculiar air about them – neither hunters nor hacks, nor yet exactly racehorses.'

An American journalist, writing from his pinnacle of transatlantic rectitude, observed austerely that in England steeplechasing 'fell into disfavour because the integrity of the rider could hardly ever be depended upon. . . . They would practice a long pull and a strong pull when money could be made by such an operation; and so in two senses the sport was properly termed "cross-country work".'

In Surtees's Grand Aristocratic Steeplechase the hero, Soapy Sponge, certainly practised 'a long pull and a strong pull', he and Mr Buckram having 'got uncommonly well onto the losing tune'. The delicate question of 'gentlemen riders' reared its ugly head in the case of Buckram's rough-rider, 'Captain' Boville. Eventually it was settled that he was 'an undoubted gentleman. Everything about him shows that. Does nothing – breeches by Anderson – boots by Bentley – besides which he drinks wine every day and has a whole box of cigars in his bedroom.'

Jack Spraggon, having after weighing out handed his extra weight to his patron, Lord Scamperdale, had a fatal fall at a five foot wall built of heavy blocks. 'As he nears it, Jack sits well back, getting Daddy Longlegs well by the head and giving him a refresher with the whip. It's Jack's last move. . . . "Oh, poor Jack! Such a fine, natural blackguard!"'

Of fifteen starters, only three finished: one rider was killed, one horse broke his back, one was drowned, and one 'cut all to pieces'.

Tom Colman, a Newmarket hotel-keeper closely connected with the promotion of the sport, admitted that he only ran one horse, 'a very vicious beast who had killed a boy. I should have shot him had I not been stopped; and ran him to punish him, not with an idea of winning. I was disgusted to see horses ridden to death in them, as they were by people knowing nothing about it.'

More temperately, Nimrod thought steeplechasing 'an unreasonable demand' on a horse.

One is left with a feeling of amazement that, on such animals, they could have cleared the five- and even six-foot timber and walls which, apparently, figured in Victorian steeplechases. Riders who, by leaning well back to take their weight off the forehand and by a 'soft opposition of the hands' hoisted their screws over these enormous, solid obstacles deserve our respectful homage, diluted perhaps by a dash of scepticism. Nimrod recommended the ordinary hunting seat and observed, not without reason, that 'the steeplechase jockey has one evil to guard against, which the racing jockey is comparatively but little subject to, and this is a fall'. 'That horse has the best chance to win which is the stoutest runner and the surest fencer, and whose

20th-century Boran
horseman mounting on
the off side

rider is good enough, and strong enough, to give him all the assistance he requires.'
Yes, indeed.

The situation was reformed by the constitution, probably in 1866, of the Grand National Hunt Steeplechase Committee. It is not crystal clear exactly when this body, later known as the National Hunt Committee, assumed control of the sport on a national basis; but by the 1870s it had taken, to the general relief, powers analogous to those of the Jockey Club in flat racing.

By putting the minimum weight up to twelve stone seven pounds, they got rid of the weedy thoroughbreds and encouraged gentlemen riders, somewhat rigidly defined by profession and club membership. In 1889 steeplechasing received the seal of respectability by the establishment of a House of Commons race.

Nevertheless, it was very far removed from its original purpose of a race for hunters. This was entirely forgotten, though a few chasers could be found who had hunted and a few hunters who had raced under National Hunt rules. The race for hunters developed into the modern point-to-point, a meeting locally arranged generally by a hunt. Even these, in the interests of a large gate and of specialization, are frequently more of a steeplechase than a test of genuine hunters, though horses must qualify by appearing at a meet and following hounds for a minimum of three hours on not less than seven days – rules which are interpreted by various Masters with varying degrees of elasticity. They are, however, genuine amateur events, and it would be rare indeed to find a point-to-point rider who did not regularly ride to hounds.

A few hunts still run their point-to-points over banks: but the overwhelming number, and all National Hunt races, are run over standard brushwood fences, with or without a ditch on either side. These fences of packed birch are stiff, but not nearly as solid as timber, which figures prominently in continental and American courses; on the other hand they are stiffer than American spruce fences, which horses can easily brush through.

In the United States steeplechasing made a comparatively late start. What is generally recognized as the pioneer meeting – though hurdle races had been run for some twenty years – took place in 1865, two months after the end of the Civil War. The course was a circular one, over a variety of obstacles including timber, a wall, a bank, an in-and-out, and several hurdles.

There was always in American steeplechasing a formidable variety of jumps. At a Virginia meeting in 1875, for instance, these included a blind ditch; two high, stiff Irish banks, and a fence over four foot high with the 'points of the limbs trimmed and set *outwards*', like a *chevaux de frise* – a formidable obstacle this, for, as with a hayrack, it is very hard to pick a take-off point. The Maryland Hunt Cup was run over a course with eighteen unbreakable post-and-rails fences up to four foot nine inches. It is unique in that it was until recently open only to amateur riders.

The Grand National is run over a terrific course, in all respects but one more formidable than the Maryland Hunt Cup course: the one exception being, of course, that its jumps are not of solid timber but of packed birch, high, wide, and stiff but still possible to brush through in the top six inches, especially the second time round. There are sixteen separate jumps, all except two taken twice, making thirty jumps in all, over four and a half miles. The jumps average four foot ten, and the highest is five foot two inches. These are not the biggest steeplechase jumps in the world: on the Hanover course between the wars there were jumps of six foot. But Aintree is more like a gigantic hunting country, full of hazards which a horse can neither see nor anticipate, such as the eighteen inch drop at Beecher's Brook, and the Canal Turn so sharp that a horse jumping the fence immediately before it must change direction almost in mid-air. To these hazards must be added an enormous field, drawn by the fame of this race, which greatly increases the risk of being bumped, ridden off, or brought down, perhaps by riderless horses. It is these which make the National probably a greater test of horse and rider than any other steeplechase: to win, one must not only be very, very good, but very, very lucky. To ride – let alone finish – in the National is the highest ambition of many a horseman, amateur and professional.

Throughout the nineteenth century and well into the twentieth old-fashioned jumping methods were preserved, like flies in amber, in National Hunt racing. The bigger the fence, the more important it seemed to lighten and even to lift the horse's forehand at the take-off. Nowadays, steeplechase jockeys lean back and slip the reins at the take-off only if they see they are coming at it wrong and likely to hit the fence; but late Victorian and Edwardian pictures show all the jockeys in a race doing so, often without slipping the reins, long after the practice had been abandoned in the hunting-field. We, better informed than our grandfathers on a horse's requirements in clearing a big jump, can regard these methods with superior knowledge and tolerant disdain; they rode *all wrong*; yet it is worth recalling that horses ridden in this way *did* get round at Aintree, Hanover, and in Maryland. Perhaps our forward seat will look equally irrational to our grandchildren who have learned that a horse goes better if the rider sits back-to-front, or performs a hand-stand on the withers.

FOX-HUNTING

There is a sound, long-established belief that riding in general and hunting in particular are good for body and soul. The Duke of York in the early fifteenth century argued eloquently that hunting diverted a man's mind from unwholesome thoughts, and when he came home dog-tired in the evening, had wined and dined, washed his arms and legs 'and peradventure his whole body', he was in no mood for carnal pleasures. 'Live in the saddle' advised an eighteenth-century physician. 'That riding is the most wholesome of all exercises I do not doubt. Despite all the vile stuff that finds its way down his throat, whoever heard of a bilious postboy?' 'The best thing for the inside of a man is the outside of a horse.'

This English attitude, shared in France and Germany only by the aristocracy, finds an echo in the Sahara, where the noble of the tent, who prides himself on his descent from men who fought the Crusaders, quotes (or used to quote):

> 'The mounting of horses,
> The letting slip greyhounds from the leash,
> And the clinking of ear-rings,
> Draw the maggots out of your head.'

More specifically, though perhaps not all foxhunters will find themselves in total agreement:

> 'The paradise of earth is to be found on horseback.
> In the study of books,
> Or on the bosom of a woman.'

George III, his mind wandering hopelessly in the labyrinths of the royal malady, was heard to admit, rather endearingly, 'I love hunting, but I fear leaping. A King and the father of a family should not ride bold.'

But Dr Johnson, alas, did not approve. After trying it on the Downs, 'I have now learned,' he said, 'by hunting to perceive that it is no diversion at all, it not even takes a man out of himself for a moment. It is very strange and melancholy that the paucity of human pleasures should persuade us even to call hunting one of them.' He was, however, wrote Mrs Piozzi, 'proud to be among the sportsmen, and I think no praise ever went so close to his heart as when Mr Hamilton called out one day, upon the Brighthelmstone Downs, "Why, Dr Johnson rides as well, for aught I see, as the most illiterate fellow in England."'

Up to about 1940, English riding was based really on hunting: our ideal horseman was the man who could ride to hounds across country, taking any obstacles in his way. *How* he took them was not very material. Since the late eighteenth century, the fox has been regarded as the most satisfactory animal to hunt, for (to quote again the Duke of York) 'he stinketh ever more'. To the fox-hunting purist riding is really irrelevant: a horse is simply the most efficient vehicle for keeping him in touch with hounds, and he would as soon follow on foot or on a bicycle if it served that purpose better. But, to be honest, there are few foxhunters who really ride in order to hunt, though many say they do: most, if they were honest with themselves would admit that they hunt in order to ride. Indeed one, in a moment of confidence, admitted to me, 'All I ask of hounds is that they keep out of my way.'

Foxes have to be kept down in numbers, but no doubt gassing them during the breeding season would be a more efficacious, if less humane, method of control than chasing them across country with twenty couple of hounds and a hundred horses. Why, then, should not cross-country riders follow a drag or a paper-chase, which does much less damage to farmland and does not offend the anti-blood sports lobby? This is a difficult question to answer. Some, of course, do; and no doubt by the end of the century drag-hunts or paper-chases across carefully planned courses will, per-force, replace fox-hunting in many places. Most hunting people, however, feel that it is the uncertainty of hunting a fox rather than an aniseed bag which gives their sport its unique excitement and flavour.

Fox-hunting during the eighteenth and nineteenth centuries was the democratic sport: shooting the snob sport, as many stories testify. Lord Rosslyn, his pheasant battue interrupted by the activities of a pack of hounds whose Master (shades of Jorrocks!) was a mere grocer, exclaimed angrily, 'Don't talk to me, Sir! How dare you bring your hounds here? Go home at once, Sir, and sand your sugar!' Queen Victoria begged her erring Bertie to 'do away a little with the *exclusive* character of shooting. . . . With hunting, (much as I dislike it on account of the danger) this is the case, and that is what makes it so popular.'

So, in the hunting-field, *anyone* is welcome, provided only that he can pay his cap or subscription (which farmers and children are rightly excused), and provided he behaves himself.

Seventeenth- and early eighteenth-century fox-hunting was a slow, methodical, patient business. Peter Beckford thought it a poor hunt if the fox had not 'stood up to hounds for four hours'. Then, with enclosures, fences multiplied and thickened into impenetrable obstacles which had to be jumped, Regency bucks took to hunting on thoroughbreds and hounds were bred for speed.

The farmer's need, before the invention of barbed-wire, to make a really stock-proof fence produced in the nineteenth century, the Golden Age of fox-hunting, a wonderful variety of obstacles. There were plain fences, such as we now have but more strongly cut and laid, generally with a ditch on one or both sides. But where the modern farmer can easily and cheaply put up a strand of wire to prevent cattle tread-ing down the ditch and running into the hedge to escape gad-flies, his great grand-father had to build a post-and-rails fence along the edge of the ditch. The result was the single- or double-oxer, a terrific obstacle rarely seen outside the specially con-structed jumping-course and the show-ring. These were solid park palings, five or six feet high and running along a turnpike road, and four-barred stiles on footpaths, both of which are now mercifully rare. Farmland is now too valuable to be wasted, so the wide bank, with a post-and-rails fence along the top or a ditch running down the middle, is now very seldom seen and even less frequently negotiated. Brooks seem to

Peter Breughel's painting of troops sacking a village

have been wider, their banks more rotten, than in modern, well-drained farms. Without wire, banks had to be higher and more sheer sided. So did stone walls, now greatly respected, which Nimrod considered 'the least dangerous fences. . . . Their height varies from three to five feet, but those even of the last-mentioned height may be taken with safety by a good horseman.'

H'm. I hunt in a stone-wall country, and while I am the first to acknowledge my own timidity, I do not recall many of my friends, good horsemen though they be, habitually leaping five-foot walls. The highest fence on the Grand National course is five foot two inches, the average four foot ten inches, and the top six inches can be brushed through, while a wall cannot.

Here is a description of a Victorian foxhunter, jumping the highest timber Whyte Melville ever saw attempted. 'The leap consisted of four strong rails, higher than a horse's withers,* an approach downhill, a take-off poached by cattle and a landing into a deep muddy lane. I can recall at this moment the beautiful style in which my leader brought his horse to the effort. Very strong in the saddle, with the finest hands in the world, leaning far back and sitting well down, he seemed to rouse, as it were, and concentrate the energies of the animal for the last half-stride when, rearing itself almost perpendicularly, it contrived to get safely over.'

Leaning far back – sitting well down – rearing itself perpendicularly – it sounds, to modern ears, exactly how not to do it, but the horse got safely over. Which only goes to show!

Elsewhere, however, Whyte Melville advises, 'When business really begins, men are apt to express in various ways their intention of taking part. Some use their eyes, some their heels and some their flasks. Do you trust your brains, they will stand you in better stead than brandy diluted with curaçoa.' Brandy and curaçoa indeed! Excellent nerves, had our fathers of old – and heads, too, evidently.

Such are the imperfections of our nature that most people, I think, exaggerate the size of fences they have negotiated hunting. Last season a bit of unbreakable timber, leading out of a lane, stopped or sent on a detour three-quarters of a good, hard-riding field. The trouble was a bad, sloping take-off, and the fact that it had to be jumped almost at a walk. But next day one of those who had got safely over took the trouble to measure its height. Under four foot! One is forced to the conclusion that our ancestors rode harder and jumped bigger fences than we do, despite those bodies leaning back over the cantle, those legs stuck out in front, those right hands upheld on high.

After nerve and a good jumping-horse, the first requisite was an eye for country. One could ride and jump almost anywhere – anywhere, that is, within the capacity of the horse. So a man with a good eye for country would plan ahead how to keep with hounds – here cutting a corner, there avoiding a field of heavy plough, choosing one place because his horse was good at timber, another because no one else is making for it. He rode with a 'knee not very far from straight, his foot well out in front of it', advised Nimrod. 'However good his mouth, never ride him in chase with quite a slack rein. . . . He requires your support, and should have it.' Good hands, Nimrod con-

* i.e. at least five foot two inches.

Pig-sticking in India

sidered, were almost a prerogative of the upper classes, a status-symbol. 'The generality of servants are deficient in that first essential to good horsemanship, a fine and sensitive hand. Nor is this a matter of surprise. The nervous influence proceeding from the organs of touch may be said chiefly to constitute what is termed the 'hand' of the horseman; and that influence may easily be supposed to be greater in a person whose situation in life has not subjected him to rough and laborious employments which must necessarily tend to deaden it.' One hears nowadays much the same explanation for the widespread belief that women riders have better hands than men.

In the century since 'Facey Romford' and 'Lucy Glitters' rode over English fields, fox-hunting has greatly changed. Everyone under forty and most people over it make some attempt at the 'forward seat'. No one, unless they have been 'left behind', leans back on approaching a fence, or 'calls a cab' on clearing it. Except in very expensive countries, with big Wire Funds, hunting is dominated by the presence, or absence, of barbed-wire. To cut-and-lay or stake-and-bind a hedge and protect it with single- or double-oxers against cattle is extremely expensive and labour-consuming: a strand of wire serves equally well. Similar considerations apply, though not nearly so strongly, to stone-wall country, and to banks. More and more – always excepting the best and most expensive countries – those who ride to hounds are compelled to do so over a line of 'hunt-jumps', built by the hunt in a fence otherwise impassable because of wire. Horses can be taught to jump wire: in Australia and New Zealand they frequently do so; but they can only jump wire which is clearly visible, or so close to a wall that in clearing one they clear the other. No horse can be expected to clear a strand of wire half-hidden in a hedge. So in most countries riding to hounds does not now generally mean taking one's own line level with, and two fields

Detail from Peter
Breughel's painting of
the sack of a village

Opposite
The Trooper by Benjamin
Cuyp

down-wind, of the tail hounds; rather, it requires a good deal of local knowledge of what farms are likely to be wired up, where are the jumpable places, or how to get round. Motorways and tarmac roads in general are a further hazard. Nevertheless, an increasing number of people find riding to hounds the best of all sports and would still agree with Jorrocks that ''unting is all that's worth living for – all time is lost wot is not spent in 'unting – it's like the hair we breathe – if we have it not, we die – it's the sport of kings, the image of war without its guilt, and only five and twenty per cent of its danger.'

PIG-STICKING

In all ages and in most countries the wild boar has been a most prized hunter's trophy. In Europe he lives generally in thick forest and has been hunted mainly on foot; but in much of Asia and Africa he can be found in country where a horse can gallop. The boar himself moves surprisingly fast: even on a level plain it takes a very good horse to catch him within half a mile, and the rougher the terrain, the greater his advantage over the horse, for the boar's centre of gravity is nearer the ground. He is brave and bad-tempered; when hunted he will turn at bay and fight sooner than most animals. When he fights, he does so to his last gasp, charging in with little red eyes glowing with rage. There are plenty of known instances of a big boar, standing thirty-six inches

high and weighing 300 pounds, killing leopard or tiger. He has a nasty bite, and his curved, razor-sharp tusks can easily disembowel a horse or a man.

It is significant that in the legend of Venus and Adonis, the young man was slain by a boar – the most dangerous animal known to the ancient world. Iberian horsemen, Moors and Christians, sometimes rode down the wild boar. But apart from these and from an occasional Crusader, the first Europeans to ride down and kill the boar with a spear were probably the servants of the Honourable East India Company in the eighteenth century. It was they who (perhaps in imitation of Rajput chiefs) developed the modern sport of pig-sticking or hog-hunting, which consists of riding across country after the wild boar and killing him with a spear, unaided by hounds or fire-arms.

First find your boar. This is done either by a beat, or by positioning yourself along one of his regular routes, say between the stream where he drinks and the cover where he lies up in the heat of the day. Then hunt him – a breakneck chase often over country which in cold blood you would consider absolutely impossible for a horse to cross at any pace faster than a walk. The hunt may last half an hour, and take you over two or three miles. It is a test not only of bold and skilful horsemanship – the best hog-hunters ride on a loose rein, leaving it to the horse to balance himself over rocks and ravines, through eight foot grass and soft sand – but of field-craft. He disappears. What should the 'spears', probably two or three of them, do? Keep together or separate? Gallop on in case he has gone forward; right or left, in case he has turned? Or stay still, in case he has squatted in thick cover until he thinks the coast is clear? He is making for thick cover: should one hustle him, in the hope of a quick kill before he gets to it? Or slow down and nurse him through to the open ground on the far side?

Finally—but in not more than about one hunt in three or four – comes the moment of truth. The boar is tired, the horses have caught him up and several things may happen. He may go on running to the last, so that the hunter can gallop alongside and drive his spear home in the loins or behind the shoulder. If he is old, heavy, short of temper, and short of breath, he will turn to fight, his stern protected by thorn or cactus, defying the world. Then there is going to be trouble, for a charging boar is not easy to stop: his head is impenetrable to a spear-point, and the vital target, the spinal cord between the shoulder-blades, is a small one. If you miss, graze his head or spear too far back, someone is going to get hurt. That is pig-sticking. The combination of riding at full speed over rough, blind country, and personal close-quarters combat with a formidable, wild animal, make pig-sticking, in the opinion of most of those who have done it, the finest, toughest, and most dangerous of all horse-sports.

MOUNTED BULL-FIGHTING

During the Dark Ages there had been wild cattle both in North Africa and in the forests of Germany, France, and Spain. Charlemagne, among others, hunted them on horseback, as did the Moors; but it is recorded that Haroun el Rashid's Ambassadors to Charlemagne found the sport too robust, and declined an invitation to take part. It is difficult to know when wild cattle became so scarce that they were no longer hunted across country, but it seems that by the eleventh century bull-fighting was an arena game. In Spain it was a gentleman's sport, practised by both Moors and Christians: knights such as El Cid Campeador fought on horseback, killing their bulls with lance and sword. In the fifteenth century Pope Alexander I, of Spanish blood, introduced this aristocratic diversion to Rome, and his son Cesare Borgia (more celebrated in other fields) was a noted bull-fighter. The sport was banned by a pope, but the ban was later removed.

Mounted bull-fighting was at its height in the sixteenth and seventeenth centuries, when at great Spanish and Portuguese fiestas scores of bulls were slain in the city squares and other public places, a spectacle which rivalled even the burning of a batch of heretics. Two weapons were used. The *garrocha* or bull-spike had a point which could be driven only half an inch or so into the bull's hide; the *rejon* or bull-spear, was a broad-bladed, lethal weapon. The bull could either be killed on horse-back with the *rejon*, or bowled over by a powerful thrust of the *garrocha* into his hind-quarters: the cavalier then dismounted and fought him on foot, with the *rejon*. In the seventeenth century the *quebrar rejon* was first used, a spear designed to break, leaving the head in the bull's withers while the shaft, embellished with a fluttering flag, was left in the rider's hand so that he could divert or play the bull.

In 1700 Philip of Anjou came to the throne of Spain. He was French, detested bull-fighting, and wished to wean aristocrats from this rough, bloody business to the more refined and elegant vices of gambling and adultery as practised at Versailles. So in Spain the sport ceased to be a gentleman's pursuit and became, instead, a spectator sport practised by professionals, which developed into the modern Spanish bull-ring.* But in Portugal the tradition of the mounted bull-fight was preserved, by both professionals and amateurs. It is of the latter and their horses that I shall write.

In Portuguese bull-fighting the bull may not be killed in the ring. The bull's horns are sheathed with leather, which reduces the risk to the horse. The cavalier's weapon now is a dart, to be planted in the bull's withers, the shaft remaining in the rider's hand. The object is not death, but a dazzling display of skill, courage, and horsemanship.

For the bull means to kill: there is no doubt of that. He is bred to it, and specially selected from his breed for his savagery and agility. The horse, generally a Barb-nosed Peninsula stallion but sometimes a thoroughbred cross, is also bred to it and schooled for five or six years until it is superbly collected, handy, and obedient. He fears and hates the bull: as between horse and bull there is no make-believe: only the skill of the rider makes it a contest in which neither animal is seriously hurt, for a dart in the bull's thick hide is a mere pinprick.

The horse generally, and regrettably, receives his initial training on the spiked noseband so as not to harden his mouth. His manège-training – very long, very thorough – is on a double-bridle. In the ring itself he is ridden on a plain curb, and generally on a loose rein, so well schooled is he by now.

---

* Sometimes in Spain the bull is killed by the *rejoneador*, a cavalier on a fine, well-schooled horse. This is the real survival of the ancient tradition, but I know too little to write of it.

When he is handy in stopping, turning on his haunches, passaging, and all the relevant High School movements, he practises on a sort of artificial bull, a pair of horns mounted on a bicycle wheel and propelled by a boy who imitates all the bull's charges. Then he works with a tame bull, who has learned to obey all the cavalier's commands, 'Charge! . . . Chase me! . . . Stop! . . . Turn quickly! . . . Back!' The bull is a genuine, fighting bull who has been trained to this work after appearing in the ring. Finally, he is entered to the real thing, his life and his rider's at stake.

In the ring itself two assistants on foot play the bull for a minute or two so that the cavalier can study his habits, temperament, and action. Then they leave. The contest is on.

To display his and his horse's skill the cavalier must challenge the bull, provoke him to charge like a thunderbolt from various angles – head-on, from (so to speak) the starboard bow, beam, or quarter. At each charge the horse must, at the last possible moment, be swung away from the horns while the cavalier leans over and plants a dart-head which breaks off in the bull's withers. The most difficult is the frontal approach: horse and bull charge head-on: only as they are about to meet does

Persian cavalry crossing
a river

An early game of polo

a squeeze of the leg, a touch of the neck-rein, swing the horse out of danger – but not so far that the rider cannot plant his dart. The more technique the cavalier can show, the more dazzling his display, the higher his reputation. A superb display of virtuosity is to leave the reins knotted on the horse's neck, controlling him only by the leg-aids and weight distribution, and plant two darts simultaneously in his withers; but some purists deprecate this as a trick to gain cheap applause by sacrificing complete control of the horse.

When he has placed enough darts, the cavalier withdraws from the ring and the bull is caught – also a great display of skill and agility, not unlike ancient Cretan bull-dancing – by a team of men on foot.

One cannot compare bull-fighting with pig-sticking. They are entirely different. The latter is a field-sport practised, as a rule, far from spectators, for the sportsman's own diversion. The former is a spectator-sport, practised in public with great ceremony and in gorgeous eighteenth-century uniforms. It is difficult to say which is the most dangerous or skilful. The bull is a larger, more formidable enemy than the boar: the bull-fighting horse must be far more educated and schooled than the pig-sticker, for this art (like the Californian rodeo) is the climax of *gineta* horsemanship. But there is no risk in the bull-ring of a bone-smashing fall as the horse puts a foot in a hole or

Bull-fighting – the acme of skill in horse and man

drops into a blind watercourse; no need for field-craft, cunning, or endurance hour after hour under a blazing sun; man and beast do not fight one another to the death, tusk against steel. Both derive from a very ancient idea; the idea of man and horse, in partnership, pitting themselves against the fastest and fiercest of wild creatures.

AFRICAN HORSEMEN

There is no indigenous horse-culture in Equatorial Africa. The tsetse fly, added to horse-sickness, weighs the odds too heavily against the horse: during the campaign in German East Africa, four regiments of South African cavalry, largely composed of Boers who fifteen years earlier had fought so successfully against the British, lost 98 per cent of their horses in the first ten months. But from the Horn of Africa, through Ethiopia and the Sudan there is a wide belt of mountain and desert country where horses have flourished for many centuries.

Their horse-culture may, perhaps, be traced to the people known to archaeologists as the X Group.* It seems likely that it is from them that the horse-culture of the Sahara and the Horn of Africa is derived.

* See Chapter 2, p. 60.

Presumably the Somali and Galla pony is of Arab origin, though it cannot be said that he looks much like an Arab. He is small, generally under 14 hands, rather common-looking, rather slow and lazy. But his virtue is in his toughness, his ability to keep going with little water and scant grazing. The horseman from the Horn of Africa belongs to the flapping legs and waving arms school of equitation, but he can gallop: he can even make his pony gallop, no mean feat. His tack is Arab in origin – a ring-bit and a home-made, wooden-framed saddle with high pommel and cantle, similar to those found in X Group tombs in Nubia. He mounts, curiously enough, on the off-side. This is because in the days of swords – seldom now carried – he wore it slung on his right hip, drawing it back-handed. The best pony I had in that part of the world, a 14·2 grey, was quite impossible to mount from the near-side, but quiet as a lamb when mounted on the side to which he was accustomed. It is said, though I have not personally seen it, that Galla and Boran giraffe-hunters have trained their ponies to eat giraffe-meat when grazing is scarce. They ride down and spear giraffe exactly as do pig-stickers, but with less danger for the giraffe has no real defence but speed.

Further west is the desert and savannah country of the Dongola horse, a much bigger animal running up to about 16 hands, raw-boned with a sheep's nose. It is supposed to be descended from Barbs brought from Egypt by the Mamelukes. Some of the Sudanese tribes hunt – or used to hunt – elephants on horseback. The best-mounted man of the party would provoke the animal to charge and then gallop away, closely pursued. Others then raced up behind to hamstring the elephant with sharp swords. When the elephant was immobilized and helpless, he could easily be killed with spears.

Even more remarkable was lion-hunting on horseback. The hunters would track

An eastern
hawking
expedition

Opposite
Anatolian
nomads going
out hawking

and follow the lion until he was brought to bay, the horsemen making a wide circle round him. One brave man then dismounted, holding in one hand, like a shield, a small string-bed, the legs pointing towards him, and in the other hand a sword. He received the charge on the string-bed and, falling back under it, the bed-legs taking the lion's weight, thrust his sword through the string into the animal's vitals.

The Moslems of northern Nigeria are perhaps the best African horsemen, riding short, with ring-bits in the Arab style. They are the only Africans who have taken to polo; and one of them, doing an army officers' equitation course at Melton Mowbray, used to appear in the Leicestershire hunting-field dressed in the robes of his people.

POLO

In the early seventeenth century Sir William Sherley, an adventurous English traveller, watched a game of polo played on the Great Maidan at Ispahan. His

Cowdray Park,
1966

impressions were recorded in *The Journey into Persia* by George Mainwaring, one of his companions, published in 1613.

'The King of Persia and his nobles take exercise by playing pall-mall on horse-back, which is a game of great difficulty; their horses are so well trained to this that they run after the ball like cats. . . .

'Before the house there was a very fair place to the quantity of some ten acres of ground, made very plain; so the King went down, and when he had taken his horse, the drums and trumpets sounded; there was twelve horsemen in all with the King; so they divided themselves six on the one side, and six on the other, having in their hands long rods of wood, about the bigness of a man's finger, and on the end of the rods a piece of wood nailed on like unto a hammer. After they were divided and turned face to face, there came one into the middle, and did throw a wooden ball between both the companies, and having goals made at either end of the plain, they began their sport, striking the ball with their rods from one to the other, in the fashion of our

The Earl of Pembroke at Wilton House by
David Morier

George IV as Prince of Wales by George Stubbs

football play here in England; and ever when the King had gotten the ball before him, the drums and trumpets would play one alarum, and many times the King would come to Sir Anthony to the window, and ask him how he did like the sport.' The King was so keen that he tired out half a dozen horses in one afternoon's play.

This seems to be the first description by a European of polo, though Christian captives or enterprising travellers in times of truce between Franks and Moslems may have seen it played at the Court of Saladin in Cairo or Damascus. For it is a very old game, probably the oldest in the world. After all the idea of hitting a ball on horseback is a simple one: Red Indian boys seem to have invented spontaneously their own version of the game when their tribes took to horses. There is some evidence that it was played at the Court of Darius, the Great King. Its home seems to have been Persia, whence it spread eastwards to China and westwards to Constantinople. Innumerable Oriental pictures and carvings, principally from Persia, show it being played by men and women. The combination of riding, hitting a ball at full gallop, teamwork, aggression, and pageantry seems to be irresistible.

Besides, there is an undeniable snob-value in polo. As Kai Kaus of Ispahan advised his son 900 years ago, 'If once or twice a year you find pleasure in polo, I regard it as permissible. But you should not indulge in a great deal of riding, because in that there is danger. The men riding should number not more than eight in all; you should be stationed at one end of the field and another man at the opposite end, with six men in the field actually playing the ball. When the ball comes in your direction, return it, and bring your horse up; but take no part in the scrimmage, thereby avoiding collision. You can achieve your purpose merely by looking on. That is how men of distinction play polo.'

Well, some men of distinction, perhaps.

The game reached India from two directions. A Chinese version was played at Manipur in the far north-east; and over the north-western passes the Mongols brought their Persian-Turkish form of the game. During the full glory of the Mogul Empire it seems to have been played by many emperors, nawabs, and maharajahs, but with the break up of the Empire it disappeared: perhaps life was too insecure. It survived only in Manipur and in the remote Himalayan kingdoms of Ladakh, Baltistan, Gilgit, Astor, and Hunza.

There it is still played, in what one must suppose is the ancient, traditional way. Any village with pretensions to importance boasts its polo-ground, perhaps 100 or 200 yards long and 40 or 50 yards wide, and that in a land where every steep hillside is laboriously terraced and every other square yard of level ground is zealously cultivated.

It was from Manipur that British officers got the idea, forming in that neighbourhood the first Polo Club in 1859. The game quickly gained popularity, spreading with the British Army. The first game in Europe, between the 9th Lancers and the 10th Hussars, was played at Hurlingham in 1871.

At first it was played with eight a side, one being a goal-keeper, probably much as in the days of Kai Kaus. This was reduced in 1873 to five, and in 1882 to four a side, each reduction speeding up the game. At first it was played on tiny ponies, apparently under 13 hands. Pictures of the historic Hurlingham game show these big, moustachioed cavalry officers with their legs hanging almost to the ground. Gradually the height limit was raised, until before 1914 it was set at 14·2 hands and in 1919 it was abolished altogether: there is nothing in the rules to prevent one playing a horse of 17 hands. In fact, however, the general experience is that ponies above 15·2 are not handy enough, while those below 14·2 are too slow: so most polo-ponies are between these heights, except in China where the local Mongolian pony is ridden, which is much smaller. Many people regret the abolition of a height limit, which has certainly made the game more expensive; but it has also made it much faster and, therefore, more exciting both to play and to watch.

By far the best description of an early polo-match is given in Kipling's story, *The Maltese Cat*. From this it is evident that the tactics of the game was based on Association Football: one man guarded the goal, while the others played as forwards, passing the ball to one another across the ground. Of course the smaller and slower the pony, the easier are cross-shots. Beauvoir de Lisle, writing when there was a 14·1 height limit though most polo-ponies were smaller, describes two cross-shots which would surely be impossible on a modern polo-pony. One was to hit the ball at a right angle to the pony's course by leaning forward and swinging the stick *in front of* the pony's nose; the other, with the ball on the *near* side, to lean well forward and hit it to the left rear by an under-the-neck shot.

The man who transformed modern polo was John Watson, in the 1880s. He invented the backhand shot which was, of course, much quicker than turning the pony round to take a forehander. More important, he conceived the idea of a team lined up not across the ground, passing across to one another like football forwards, but up and down the ground – back hitting it up to 3, 3 to 2, and so on. This, too, greatly quickened the game.

Another change was the abolition, at first by the Americans, of the off-side rule. This so speeded up the game that, to the pained surprise of the Island Race, the Americans first beat the British in the international match for the Westchester Cup in 1909. So they too abolished the off-side rule and copied from the Americans their handicapping system.

Polo is a game played at very high pressure, galloping, stopping, swinging, and turning: it is extremely exhausting for both horse and man, which is why a match is divided into four or six 'chukkers', each of seven and a half minutes, with intervals for changing ponies. No pony can regularly play more than three fast chukkers in one day, and two is the usual ration.

Opinion differs on the subject of horsemanship in polo. One would have thought that it required a pretty high standard of horsemanship to place a pony for shots at all angles, ride off, stop and turn in an instant – all at a gallop. Oddly enough, however, this does not seem to be so. A good polo-player must, of course, be a reasonably good rider, but there are some first-class polo-players who are not first-class horsemen, and some first-class horsemen who are indifferent polo-players. It is more important to have the eye and aggressive instinct of a games-player, to be able to hit the ball hard and accurately and, above all, to have the gift of anticipation, to estimate in an instant where the ball and other players are going next, and to place oneself accordingly. The man without this essential games sense, however good a horseman, will too often find himself galloping madly in the wrong direction. Many equitation purists view polo with faint disapproval: it is, they say, impossible to ride properly in the stress of a fast game, which is, therefore, hard on the ponies. There is some truth in this: ponies do undeniably get pulled and knocked about in fast polo. Perhaps this is why on the whole women do not take to polo as they do to other equestrian sports. Nevertheless, most polo-ponies seem to like it: without a pony's active and intelligent co-operation (in, for instance, riding off or placing himself exactly the right distance from a ball on either side) it would be quite impossible to play; so one can be quite certain that no pony who hates and fears the game will play it for long.

What does require horsemanship of a high standard is to *make* a pony, that is to say to bring on a pony who has been trained merely as a hack or charger to the standard at which he can take part in a game. Once made, he can be played by any strong and reasonably competent rider. A good polo-pony must be supremely handy, obedient, well balanced with the ability to stop and turn 'on a sixpence', and

Horses at Wilton House by David Morier

great powers of acceleration from a halt. He must have a good nerve, for he is useless if he shies away from a swiftly moving ball or an opponent; and he must be robust, welcoming, not flinching from, a shoving match at full gallop with another pony. He must, of course, be controllable only with the indirect rein, leg-, and weight-aids, for the rider's right hand is fully occupied with the stick.

Whatever your hands or the elegance of your position in the saddle, for polo you must have a strong and independent seat. You cannot rely on balance. It must be strong so as to ride off and resist an opponent who is riding you off, particularly the man who comes charging up behind and tries to get his knee under yours to weaken your grip and force you to draw away from the line or be unseated. It must be independent so that you can twist your body right round to the left and bend it over, right shoulder pointing at the ball, to take those tricky near-side shots.

The central Asian horse-archer discovered that he shot best not sitting down in

A Bay Horse by Sawrey Gilpin

the saddle, but riding short and standing in the stirrups. So does the polo-player, perhaps because with this 'polo brace' he can twist, turn, and bend the upper part of his body without weakening his seat. 'Shorten your leathers' is advice often given to a player who is inexplicably mishitting.

7

In the New World

There was a prehistoric horse in America, but we have no evidence of prehistoric man domesticating it. Between 9000 and 5000 B.C. some epidemic or natural disaster exterminated it and, the land-bridge between Siberia and Alaska being destroyed about the same time, no replacements migrated across from Asia. The horse did not return until the *conquistadores* came 6,000 or 7,000 years later. The first to arrive, when Columbus landed on Haiti, were some 'sorry hacks' which his mounted escort had prudently exchanged, on advantageous terms, for their expensive chargers before embarking on this perilous voyage. Later arrivals, cast overboard to swim half a mile to shore through shark-infested waters, were of better quality, probably with Arab or Barb blood. In 1509 Cortez brought the first horses to the mainland, bringing ashore in Mexico eleven stallions, five mares, and a foal.

Thirty years later a robust adventurer, Hernando de Soto, set off from Florida to explore westward in search of mountains, cities and rivers of gold. He searched in vain for two years, and of his 200 horses some foundered, some starved, some became so footsore that they had to be slaughtered for food. By the time he died, on reaching the Mississippi, there were only forty left, the expedition's last food reserve. They set off down-river in canoes, but the poor emaciated horses, hobbling along the bank, delayed their progress and impeded them in their fights with hostile Indians. At last it was decided to kill the survivors and dry the meat, but five horses escaped the butchery, on the west bank of the great river. From these and some stragglers from the contemporary expedition of Francisco Coronado, are supposed to be descended the vast herds of feral mustangs who grazed the western prairies two or three centuries later.

These mustangs did not cross the Mississippi and spread eastwards. The horses and horsemanship in the Thirteen Colonies came not from Arabia and Spain, but from north-west Europe. In 1541 Jacques Cartier landed twenty French horses on the site of Quebec; in 1585 Raleigh established some in North Carolina. Throughout the seventeenth century increasing numbers of French, English, Irish, Dutch, and German horses were landed on the eastern seaboard. We do not know much about these: probably farmers tended to bring useful work-horses, while the Puritan and Cavalier gentry brought their favourite hobby-horses, hacks, hunters, and racehorses. But clearly the horse-stock of the Thirteen Colonies and Canada was an amalgam of European stocks. The first English thoroughbred to be imported is believed to be Bulle Rock, reputedly sired by the Darley Arabian and brought to Virginia in 1730.

While the Lord Protector was ruling England, a Puritan gentleman named John Pynchon, a Yorkshireman, pioneered American ranching by driving a herd of fat cattle from his farm at Springfield into Boston, for shipment to the West Indies. His 'cowboys' as they were already called, were local lads and 'boucaniers', skilled cattle-handlers, from Jamaica. Around Springfield grew up a ranching industry in minia-ture, where Pynchon raised both half-wild cattle herds and fatstock stall-fed in winter. His practices spread. Long before the 'Wild West' of the nineteenth century, ranching techniques were being developed in the 'cow-pens' of Pennsylvania, Virginia, Carolina, Georgia, Tennessee, and Kentucky. Their favourite tool, and weapon, was the fifteen foot stock-whip, with which one could kill a man, bring down a steer, or snap the head off a rattle-snake. Hence the expression 'Georgia cracker'.

The demand for saddle-horses for long journeys popularized the Irish hobby-horse, which readily learned to amble, and a distinct breed, now vanished, called the 'Narragansett Pacer'. 'These are very spirited and carry both head and tail high. But what is most remarkable is that they amble with more speed than most horses trot, so that it is difficult to put some of them upon a gallop.' Their smooth paces and sure-footedness made them 'greatly sought after by females who were obliged to travel over the roots and holes in the New Countries'.

Careful horsemastership was not a characteristic of these early Americans. It was fair enough, in the absence of metalled roads, to leave their horses unshod, but in 1688 a clergyman of Jamestown felt so pained by his parishioners' neglect of their horses that he actually reported it to the Royal Society. 'They neither shoe nor stable them: some few gentlemen may be something more curious, but it is very rare. Yet they ride pretty sharply, a Planter's Pace is a proverb, which is a good, sharp, hard gallop.' A French visitor at the same time wrote indignantly, 'All the care they take of them at the end of a journey is to unsaddle, feed a little Indian corn and so, all covered with sweat, drive them out into the woods where they eat what they can find, even though it is freezing.' This suggests that in Virginia at least horses were plentiful and expendable.

There was, curiously enough, no synthesis between the Spanish horse-culture in Florida and western European horse-culture further north. That synthesis did not take place until Americans began to crowd into Texas and California.

The eastern Indian tribes took rather slowly to riding. But the Chickasaw tribe in Georgia and South Carolina took and developed from Spanish stock a special breed of small horses, seldom over 13·2 hands, but 'high, active, and beautiful'. These were much in demand among the settlers, but 'a person runs too great a risk to buy any to take them out of the country, because every spring season most of them make for their native range'.

Meanwhile, 2,000 miles to the south and west, the Apaches, fiercest and most warlike of all Indian tribes, were already taking an unhealthy interest in the horses belonging to Spanish colonists in New Mexico. In 1680 there was a massacre of the Spaniards, hundreds being slain, their livestock looted. The Apaches took to horse-manship like ducks to water, and even devised armour of stiff bull-hide in imitation of the Spaniards' breastplates, cuirass, and morions. From the Apaches and Navahos, horsemanship and horses spread northwards to the Utes, Pawnees, and Comanches. These tribes no doubt rode at first Spanish horses, in the Spanish style, using Spanish saddles and bridles. They naturally replenished their stock from the feral mustangs,

Horse-race through the streets of Florence. Early 15th century.
Note the modern seat of the jockeys

and eventually relied mainly on the wild herds. The Apaches, great riders and raiders, never went in much for breeding horses: it was less trouble to ride other people's.

The northern Indians were slower to take to the horse. They all have legends of the first appearance on their prairies of the wild mustang herds, which at first they regarded solely as an animal to be hunted, like bison. Then they must have seen, or heard of, Apache war-bands riding ponies up from the far south. French *coureurs du bois* arrived with horses, trading and exploring. No doubt some of their horses, of French or English stock, escaped, some were stolen. Perhaps foals were caught and kept as pets, mares might have been milked. The women would see that a tame mare was a far more powerful animal than a dog for pulling the poles of the *travois*. One pioneer has pertinently remarked that he never saw an Indian herd-boy on foot. The value of these swift animals for buffalo-hunting and raids would be obvious to a people who, before they began to enjoy the blessings of civilization, were virile and enterprising.

Only about the Blackfoot tribe, one of the last to be horsed, have we a recent and circumstantial account of the beginnings of this horsemanship. Until the early nineteenth century they were a forest tribe, ignorant of the horse. Then some Kootenays traded them their first ponies, and within twenty-five years, presumably mounting themselves mainly on wild mustangs, they were said – but it sounds unlikely – to have been able to put 40,000 light cavalry into the field.

As they took in succession to the horse, the tribes' entire culture and way of life changed. The Blackfeet gave up agriculture and supported themselves by buffalo-hunting. They emerged from the forests and lived on the plains. Wigwams replaced timber huts. The horse, not the dog and the canoe, became their transport. A man's wealth and honour were measured by the horses he owned or stole. Medicine-men's fees and brides' prices were all paid in horses. Horses pervaded the tribes' religious ceremonies. Like the Scythians, dead chiefs took their favourite horses to the Happy Hunting Ground. It was an extraordinary, and amazingly rapid trans-formation.

In considering their remarkable skill, we must remember the characteristics of horses and riders. The feral mustang flourished exceedingly on the short, tawny, crisp buffalo-grass of the prairies, which is sweet as a nut to taste and has a good food value. The survival of the fittest, through summer drought and bitter winters, hunted by wolf, bear, and mountain-lion, produced a remarkably tough, hardy, intelligent, self-reliant animal. Their Arabian and Barb ancestry, and the hard, dry plains over which they roamed, gave them good bone, small hooves as hard as iron, and a singular absence of leg- and foot-unsoundness. But running wild for 300 years, with neither grain-feeding nor selective breeding, the big Spanish war-horse had degenerated in size: the average Indian pony was only about 13 hands. He was also pretty quiet: ponies were plentiful, so any who proved intractable could simply be turned loose or killed for food. The average Blackfoot brave, however, was a strapping five foot ten inches, lean and active. Large strong men on small, docile ponies could perform feats of equitation which looked, perhaps, more remarkable than they really were. An ancestor of mine, J. H. Lefroy, travelling in the West in 1840, rode an Indian pony for a hundred miles with nothing but a thong tied round its lower jaw. 'Though scarcely at all broken in,' he wrote, 'these horses are good-tempered, completely free from vice and much more easily managed than our own.'

We know a lot about Indian horsemanship from George Catlin, an artist who travelled in the West in the 1840s when many tribes were still almost unaffected by the white man, and still had recent legends of the arrival of the first horses.

The Indian's saddle, unless he had acquired something better from the white man, was a blanket or buffalo-robe laid over the pony's back and secured by a surcingle. His bit was a rawhide thong tied tightly round the pony's lower jaw. He steered his horse by leg-pressure, not with the reins, since his hands were occupied with his weapons; but Catlin observed that this somewhat primitive bridle was very effective in stopping a horse. If he could get hold of them, he liked wearing spurs, the sharper and crueller the better, with which he 'nettled his prancing steed until its sides were a gore of blood'.

At a walk or trot he sat bolt upright, riding down to the crotch, not quite straight-legged but with a forward slant to his thighs which rested on the pony's barrel, his lower leg vertical. At a gallop, he leaned forward, his long thighs gripping like a vice, his lower legs slightly behind the vertical. In races the jockeys, stark naked, rode very short, leaning well forward, thighs almost horizontal, lower legs bent sharply back: sometimes the knees were secured by a strap binding them to the horse's barrel. Can there be any connection between this racing seat, evolved naturally on the great plains, and that of the modern jockey, developed by the American Tod Sloan?

Some Indians carried a lance, which they used not couched, but two-handed, like ancient Persians; but their principal weapon was the bow, short and very stiff, made of wood, horn, and sinew. They used this not, like Asian horse-archers, as a long-distance weapon, but at point-blank range, galloping up alongside a quarry and shooting it, from three or four feet away, with such force that it was not uncommon for an arrow to pass completely through a buffalo.

The tiny hunting-pony was trained to gallop at breakneck speed on a parallel course to the great, lumbering beast so that the rider could shoot to his left, then, at the twang of the bow, to swing away out of reach of the wounded buffalo's horns. Spills were frequent, and to help him catch his pony after a fall, the Indian rode with a rawhide lassoo tied round its neck and trailing along the ground.

Indians would pay very big sums for good 'made' ponies: a chief of the Fox tribe bought one from a trader for $300. But to keep up numbers they had to catch and tame the wild mustang. Catlin often watched this done. Riding his best pony, raw-hide lassoo coiled over his arm, the brave would gallop 'under the full whip' into a wild herd and cast the noose over a pony's neck; then instantly dismount, leave his own horse and, running after his quarry, let the fifteen yard lassoo out as slowly as possible until the pony, half-throttled, fell and lay helpless on the ground. Advancing slowly, keeping the lassoo tight, the Indian fastened a pair of hobbles on the mustang's legs and a thong round its lower jaw. Then he loosened the noose, giving the terrified animal a chance to breathe. As soon as it got its breath, it started rearing and plunging; but the thong tight round the lower jaw soon got it under control. Hand over hand the Indian advanced, holding the thong so that the pony could not rear up and fall over backwards, until he could put a hand on the nose and over the animal's eyes. Then, according to this reliable witness, 'it soon became docile and conquered; so that he had little else to do but to remove the hobbles and lead or ride it into camp'.

'The "breaking down" or taming', he wrote, 'is not without the most desperate trial on the part of the horse, which rears and plunges in every possible way to effect its escape, until its power is exhausted and it becomes covered with foam; and at last it yields to the power of man and becomes his willing slave for the rest of his life. By this very rigid treatment the poor animal seems to be so completely conquered, that it makes no further struggle for its freedom and is led or rode away with very little difficulty.'

Catlin observes, however, that only the slower mustangs were caught in this way: the faster ones galloped away from their pursuers. Perhaps they caught more mares in foal than anything else, which was probably what they most wanted.

Robert Denhardt describes another method of breaking a wild horse, using a sort of thin rawhide halter which when the rein was pulled, tightened on the horse's nose, like a hackamore. The chosen horse was roped, and held by several men. As in the examples Catlin saw, one man then gradually worked up the rope 'talking' to the horse with low grunts which sounded like hoh! hoh!, deep in the chest and seemed to intrigue and soothe the terrified animal. When the horse became accustomed to the man, he was shown a blanket, and handled all over, the Indian talking to him continuously. The hackamore was then looped over the horse's nose and behind his ears in such a way that a pull on the rein tightened the nose-loop. Being very strong, but no thicker than a bootlace, it exerted a cruel pressure on the nostrils and nerves, and the horse soon learned not to defy it. The helpers could then leave go.

There followed handling, particularly of the back and flanks, and a sharp jerk at the rein whenever the horse objected, the Indian talking to him all the time. The man would press his hands on the horse's back, harder and harder; then rest his elbows on the horse and raise his feet off the ground. Finally, not more than an hour or so after catching the horse, the rider would swing his leg gently over and the horse would be backed. It usually stood still for a moment, petted and soothed, then trotted awkwardly away.

Frederick Remington, drawing Indians in the 1880s, shows an Indian boy riding a newly caught colt while a man hangs on to it with a lariat fixed round the pony's muzzle, so having the same effect as a hackamore. Sometimes a horse was backed girth-deep in a stream, a practice the prudence of which I can appreciate, for I used to back remounts in a stockyard two feet deep in soft cattle dung which exhausted a plunging horse, cushioned his bucks and provided, if necessary, a soft landing-pad for bronco-busters of riper years.

Clearly there were many methods of catching and breaking wild mustangs.

Of all the tribes, the most spectacular horsemen were the Comanches. Rather shorter and more squat than most Indians, the Comanche on foot was heavy,

221

The start of the chukka

ungraceful, slovenly-looking, and 'almost as awkward as a monkey on the ground without a limb or branch to cling to: but the moment he lays his hand on a horse, his face even becomes handsome, and he gracefully flies away like a different being'.

They were passionately addicted to horse-racing, gambling heavily on it. They had one astonishing feat which, Catlin states, almost every young man in the tribe could perform. The rider slid down the off-side, keeping only his left leg hooked over the horse's back, and then, protected by the horse's barrel, his right arm taking his weight by a neckstrap braided to the mane, shot a stream of arrows either over the back or under the neck – all at full gallop. It sounds more like a circus trick than a useful operation of war, until one recalls that the shooting was at point-blank range. Its greatest value was probably in concealing the riders as they approached an enemy, so that a war-band looked like a troop of wild ponies.

Although wonderful riders, most Indian tribes were singularly bad horsemasters, callous, neglectful, and cruel. They knew nothing of selective breeding and instead of castrating or putting down worthless stallions, turned them loose to perpetuate their runtish stock. The best animals were reserved for riding, not breeding. Only the Flatheads castrated their colts, in the belief that geldings did not tire so quickly as

222

Reward for
a good chukka

Below
The start (detail)

entires. The Sioux and Comanches slit their ponies' nostrils up to the gristle, to facilitate their breathing at a gallop. They neither grain-fed nor shod their ponies – and if one went lame, got a sore back, or broke down, he was simply ridden till he dropped, turned loose, or killed for food.

Yet there is no doubt of the Plains Indians' mobility. On short distances, in a few days' chase, the big horses of the U.S. Cavalry might outrun them; but for sustained mobility there are few cavalry marches in history to compare with that of the Nez Percé tribe, who in eleven weeks rode 1,600 miles to evade converging U.S. mounted forces. If the main body of the tribe, encumbered by baggage, women, and children, averaged nearly twenty-one miles a day, the fighting men must have covered twice that distance, besides finding time for thirteen battles and skirmishes.

The Nez Percés were the only Indian tribe to breed horses genetically. They developed the grey horse with black and brown spots and vertically striped hooves, known now as the 'Apaloosa'. His peculiar colouring gave him a natural camouflage on the summer prairie; his turned-in forefeet made him very sure-footed along narrow mountain-paths across the face of a precipice; his wide heels with well-developed frog gave him a good grip on slippery or rocky ground, while his thin tail would not get caught as he galloped through thorn bushes.

But other tribes were almost as mobile as the Nez Percés: raiding Indians were notoriously difficult to outrun or intercept. They achieved their mobility by the *remuda*, a remount system. While the U.S. Cavalry trooper had to rely on a single horse for a campaign, the Indian had a string of ponies, herded by boys, so that none need be ridden for more than three or four hours a day. Any who broke down could be abandoned and easily replaced.

Fifty years after George Catlin, Frederick Remington drew Indians riding in much the same way, except that most of them had acquired the white man's saddle and curb-bit, and others used a sort of home-made version of the stock-saddle. Armed with rifles instead of lances and bows, they now fought at longer range circling round their enemies and shooting at the gallop – obviously without much accuracy – in tactics reminiscent of Turks and Mongols; but they were still great horsemen. It is curious that so few of them made a name as rodeo-riders. Perhaps defeat and subjugation just broke their spirit.

Shortly before the Civil War it was discovered that the Texas longhorn cattle not merely survived, but flourished on the great plains through the winter, and in the spring, when the fresh grass gave rich feeding, would actually put on condition while being driven hundreds of miles to slaughterhouses. This made possible the Western ranching industry, the short-lived 'cattle kingdom'.

Before the Civil War the ranch-riders were mainly Mexican *vaqueros*; after it, Americans, mainly from Texas and the defeated South, moved by thousands into the new industry, many no doubt bringing ranching skills they had learned in the 'cow-pens' of Tennessee and Kentucky. They brought their horses too, but not in sufficient numbers to provide the seven horses which every cowpuncher needed for his *remuda*: most rode mustangs.

The horsemanship of the cattle kingdom was to some extent a synthesis of East and West, but the Mexican style, tack, and language prevailed; saddle and bit were almost identical with those used by medieval knights, brought across the Atlantic by the *conquistadores*.* The general appearance of the saddle is well known. It is secured by two girths or *cinchas*, for and aft. It has a high pommel and cantle, the former rising to a horn to take the strain of the lariat. The seat slopes sharply from front to back, like Henry V's and Pluvinel's saddles, throwing the rider's weight back against the cantle. The stirrups are slung well in front of the rider's centre of gravity. so that he sits with a straight leg, his feet well forward – just like the knight at Hastings and Agincourt. The saddle sits high off the horse's back, on several thicknesses of blanket, so that one saddle can fit many horses even those with prominent spines or withers. The seat at the canter is comfortable and relaxed, the rider leaning slightly back against the cantle. Rising to the trot, the buttocks are thrust back against the cantle, the body raked stiffly forward. The range-rider on a long journey generally trotted over hard ground and cantered on grass. Nowadays some people hold that a Western horse should never trot.

The most important thing about the stock-saddle is that its long, wide skirts – extending well behind and below the actual seat – spreads the rider's weight over about eight square feet of the horse's back, while with the ordinary English hunting-saddle the weight is concentrated on two or three square feet. Thus, although the stock-saddle alone weighs forty pounds or more, because of this weight distribution the horse feels the rider's weight much less than with a small saddle.

Modern European horsemen, brought up to the 'balanced seat', have plenty to say against the old-fashioned Western stock-saddle. The rider's weight is placed too far back; the saddle is useless for what foxhunters call 'riding across country', since one cannot jump with it and merely climbing a steep bank one is butted in the midriff by the horn as one leans forward. I have myself ridden on long safaris in a very ancient 'Cheyenne' saddle, a real museum piece with very high pommel and cantle, a monstrous vertical horn. After two days the inside of my knees were raw and I felt in grave danger of a ruptured diaphragm or emasculation. But these criticisms of the old stock-saddle are the objections of ignorance, and are usually voiced by people who have tried to ride with bent leg on a saddle not designed for it. A hundred and thirty years ago nearly everyone in Europe and North America – cow-punchers, foxhunters, soldiers – rode with a more or less straight leg, the feet rather far forward, leaning rather far back: any hunting or military print proves the point. The weight-distributing stock-saddle was admirably designed for its purpose and for the contemporary seat.

Its great weight and strength was necessary to take the terrific strain of roping, and for hard wear far from a saddler. Cowpunchers were not always good horsemen, though with constant practice many became good: when they started they were beginners, with no riding-school to teach them. The stock-saddle is very comforting for beginners: the deep-seat and the bulge just in front of his thigh gives the beginner confidence, and keeps his weight stable, for he cannot shift about on a long ride, now backwards, now forwards, giving his horse a sore back. In moments of crisis he can

* Some of the conquistadors had ridden short, *à la gineta*. But this, I am told, now survives only in a few remote areas of Brazil and, perhaps, Argentina.

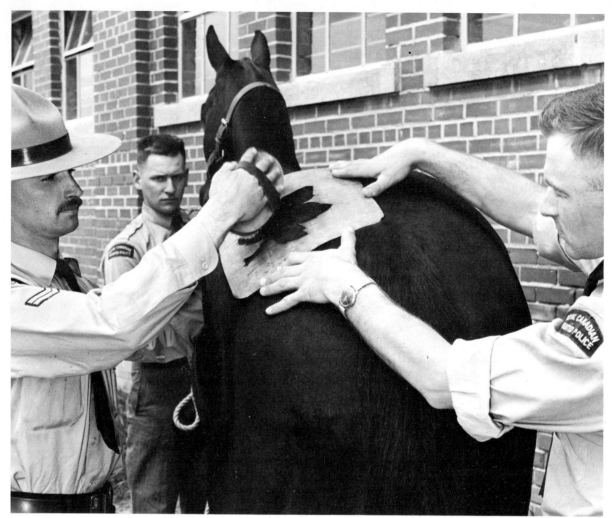

Brushing up the maple leaf

grab the horn; even the best riders do not disdain this help when, for instance, a cutting-horse whips round at full gallop; it is a great deal better than hanging on by the reins. Above all, by distributing the rider's weight, the stock-saddle is perfect for long-distance riding.

A few statistics bear this out. An Australian stockman, on an American stock-saddle, without changing horses rode from the Murray River to Melbourne, 143 miles by the route taken, in twenty-six hours. A constable of the Royal North-West Mounted Police, on a forty-two pound stock-saddle, rode from Regina to Wood Mountain Post, 132 miles, by sunlight, without changing horses, and his horse bucked him off at the finish. Most of the Mounted Police constables and ranch-hands moving between Fort Macleod and Calgary in the 1890s covered the distance, 108 miles, in a day. Kit Carson with a party of five Mexican gentlemen rode from Los Angeles to San Francisco, 600 miles, in six days, and only two of the party changed horses.

Outlaw gangs such as the Robber's Roost after a bank or train hold-up thought nothing of covering a hundred miles a day for several days. But they generally had relays of fresh horses waiting along their escape-route, and so could easily outdistance the sheriff's posses pursuing them.

Some of the West's best horses as well as mustangs were organized in the early 1860s into the Pony Express. The riders were 'young, skinny, wiry fellows, not over eighteen, willing to risk death daily'. On joining the company they had to swear not to use profane language, not to get drunk, not to treat animals cruelly, and not to do anything incompatible with the conduct of a gentleman. By pony-stages of twenty-five miles, the Express covered 200 miles a day. At the staging-points were stables, the best of oats, hay, and bedding, ostler-crews to groom the horses and keep them fit for their next run through drought, blizzard, and Indian ambush.

These rides with English hunting-saddles would be considered phenomenal feats for man and horse, to be undertaken only after weeks of training. They were – except for those of the outlaws and the Pony Express – carried out by ordinary cowpunchers and police constables, on ordinary range-horses – but using the weight-distributing stock-saddle.

In the 1920s the emphasis in Western riding naturally shifted from work to sport. Trail-riding and the rodeo did not require such a rugged horn, and the theory of the balanced seat affected the design of Western saddles. The pommel and cantle have been lowered, the horn reduced to a bare minimum and raked forward so as not to endanger the rider's midriff. The seat no longer slopes sharply backwards, and the stirrups are hung nearer the centre of the saddle. As a result, the modern seat on the modern Western saddle is not so very different from the balanced seat developed by Eastern and European horsemen. The saddle retains its priceless quality of weight-distribution, and if I were ever to take to long-distance riding again, in a country where jumping is not necessary and the sole aim is to cover the miles at a steady pace without distress to myself or my horse, it would be on a modern Western stock-saddle. I wonder how it would show up in the Golden Horseshoe ride.

To adapt the medieval war-saddle to work on the cattle range, Americans strengthened the front arch with a tempered steel fork and roping-horn shaped rather like an inverted Y. They widened the arch to keep it clear of the horse's withers, giving the saddle heavy shoulders or 'swells' which also served to hold the rider's thigh in place. Instead of a single girth, they fitted it with two *cinchas*, fore and aft, made of horsehair, lamp-wick, or leather with a ring at each end through which the *latigo* or cinch-strap is run and tightened with a two to one mechanical advantage. There is no saddle-flap, nothing for the knee to grip; and the stirrups are hung not from narrow stirrup-leathers, but from wide sweat-flaps called *sudaderos*, designed to protect the rider's legs from the horse's sweaty flanks. Metal stirrups become uncomfortably cold in winter, uncomfortably hot in the Mexican summer, and were replaced by a stirrup made of hardwood. To protect the rider's foot against acacia thorns, the wooden stirrup is sometimes enclosed in a hard leather box called the *tapadero*.

At first Western range-horses were generally ridden on a Spanish spade-bit, a very severe curb with long checkpieces and a port so high that it acted on the roof of the horse's mouth, causing acute pain if applied roughly. Except when used by a horseman with very light hands, it could be an instrument of torture; but in good hands it is a delicate and sensitive aid. The mouthpiece, acting on the bars of the mouth, makes the horse bend; and if he overbends, the port, acting on the palate, corrects the fault. With such a bit the range-rider rode with a very loose rein, held high between the fingers of one hand, guiding his horse by the indirect rein.

Although horsemen bred to the European style of equitation disparage loose-rein riding, quite a good case can be made for it, on the grounds that a horse can pick his way over rough country much better if left to himself. A case in point is, surprisingly enough, that of the evangelist, John Wesley, who in the course of his fifty-three-year ministry rode some 228,000 miles, and may therefore be considered an experienced long-distance rider. Unable to afford good horses, he used to buy, dirt-cheap, screws with a reputation for stumbling. He always rode with a loose indirect rein, reading the Bible as he went, and found that quite soon his screws were cured of stumbling, and he could sell them for a good price – profit and piety combined.

Another, even more striking example of loose-rein riding comes from the Russian front in the last war. A Red Army cavalry division was ordered to advance over a snow-covered minefield. The divisional commander ordered his men to ride with loose reins, leaving the horses to pick their own way. Most of those who did so got through; most of those who rode collected were blown up. I do not vouch for the truth of this story, but I do know that in India some of the pig-sticking experts maintained that, galloping over the roughest country, studded with hidden boulders and seamed with blind pot-holes and nullahs, one was far safer riding with a loose, indirect rein.

In discussing horsemanship on the open range one must remember always the quality of the horses. The average mustang or range-pony was very different from the prancing, spirited steed of glorious Technicolor. A few may have been like that; but most, as portrayed by realistic contemporary artists, were small and quiet, with largish, common heads, ewe-necks, and falling away behind. The U.S. Cavalry, the Royal North-West Mounted Police, the Mormon elders, and many 'cattle barons' gradually improved the breed by introducing thoroughbred, Standard Bred, and Morgan stallions. Homesteaders too brought large, common work-horses. So the modern Western horse is infinitely larger than the horse of the Wild West. These larger, better bred horses did not take kindly to the spade-bit in rough hands, so by the end of the nineteenth century many range-riders were using an ordinary snaffle, a 'half-bred' bit or a 'Western curb'. The half-bred also has a high port, but its severity is mitigated by a copper roller in the port, like those used by Xenophon but without the spikes, which stimulates the flow of saliva and keeps a horse's mouth moist. The Western curb, with its moderate port* is similar in effect to the Wey-mouth from which it differs mainly in its ornate appearance and in having a leather strap instead of a curb-chain. Many Western riders firmly believe that horses like the taste of copper, and that by inlaying the mouthpiece with it the horse's mouth is kept moist and the severity of the bit thereby mitigated.

---

* It should be explained that the smaller the port the milder the bit, because a horse can lift it with his tongue off the bars of the mouth.

In Mexico the *Charros* on their vast patriarchal ranches preserved the ancient traditions of Iberian horsemanship. But the Mexican Revolution of 1911 swept away the *Charros*, so it is in California, long isolated from outside influences and shielded from the consequences of that Revolution, that an extremely sophisticated form of Spanish horse-culture, probably of Arab and Moorish origin, survived and developed.*

The young horse is trained on the hackamore (Spanish *jaquima*; Arabic *hakma*), a bitless bridle which acts on the nose, not the mouth. It consists essentially of a light cavesson, the noseband of which is shaped rather like the frame of those very old tennis-rackets, wide and rounded at one end, narrow and pointed at the other. The rounded end encircles the horse's nose, the pointed end is closed with a heavy raw-hide knot, several inches behind the horse's chin-groove. The function of the knot is to act as a counterweight, holding the noseband clear, when the rein is slackened, of both the tender skin above the nostrils and the sensitive portions of the lower jaw. The reins are attached, together, just in front of the knot. The horse is stopped by pressure on his nose and steered, necessarily by the indirect or neck-rein, without any help from the rider's legs.

Occasionally, the effect of the hackamore is increased by a couple of blunt nails, but this is generally deprecated.

After about ten months the breaking hackamore is replaced by a lighter model known as the two-rein bosal and a bit. At this stage all four reins are held in the bridle hand, but the bit-rein allowed to slip very easily between fingers and thumb. A year later the two-rein bosal is replaced with an even lighter bosal with no reins, similar in action to a dropped noseband but running obliquely from the chin-groove, *above* the bit and round the nose well clear of the tender gristle above the nostril. But neither bit nor reinless bosal is fitted until the horse performs perfectly with a vertical head-carriage, in the hackamore.

Why, then it may be asked, bit him at all, if he puts up such a finished perform-ance in the hackamore or bosal? The answer is, apparently, that if kept too long on the hackamore or bosal he hangs on it, becoming heavy on the hand. But premature bitting, before a horse learns to obey the lightest touch of the rein, produces a hard mouth. It is a question of exact timing.

Finally, after long and very patient training, even the bosal is removed, and the horse is ridden just on the bit. Thereafter, if properly handled, he will retain his training for life.

Traditionally the Californian horseman uses one of various forms of spade-bit. In the early days of the Conquest, when silver and gold were abundant, the *Charros* (themselves, of course, born with silver spoons in their mouths) had discovered that horses, like humans, preferred the taste of silver and gold to that of steel. They often used spade-bits made of solid silver, and even solid gold; but nowadays spade-bits with a copper inlay have been found to serve the same purpose.

---

* The alert and percipient reader will suspect that I have no personal knowledge of Californian horseman-ship. My information comes from Mr John Paget who, with a wide background of other horse-cultures, has studied the art under the Californian *maestroi* and traced its origin into prehistory. I hope that the result of his studies will appear in book form: meanwhile he has kindly allowed me to anticipate his publication.

The spade-bit acts, of course, like any curb, on the bars of the mouth; but having a very high port, it acts also on the palate. So, automatically, the horse is kept correctly bent by these two opposing but very light pressures. It usually contains a copper roller or 'cricket' with which the horse can play; and the noise of the cricket is a familiar feature of the spade-bit country. This keeps the bit at the proper angle and helps the horse to hold it as steady in his mouth as a dental plate. He flexes only at the poll.

In rough hands this instrument can mutilate a mouth, and the rider be rewarded for his horse's pain by a bloody nose or a mouthful of broken teeth. But if the horse has been well made on the hackamore before bitting, there is no need for more than the slightest touch of the neck rein to turn him, a fractional increase in the weight of the reins, caused by a very slight movement of the bridle hand, to stop him. In de la Guernière's words, he is ridden 'by the sole weight of the reins'. So free moving is the hackamore-trained horse that leg-aids, other than an occasional touch of the spur, are considered by the Californian horsemen to be totally unnecessary. Really the horse is controlled not physically by the ironmongery in his mouth, but psychologically by a respect for the reins implanted during his early training on the hackamore. This is proved by the ban, in Western bridle-horse horse competitions, of any form of noseband, even though no reins be attached to it.

Modern Californian horsemen are more catholic in their choice of bits, using the spade, the ring (*chileno*), the Pelham, or a cutting-horse bit* to suit individual horses and the work they are to do.

The thoroughbred responds to these methods far better than any other breed, because of his beautiful economic action. The finished product of three years' hackamore-, bosal-, and spade-bit-training is a superb saddle-horse, a supremely efficient cow-pony or rodeo-performer who at the touch of the rein turns on a dime or comes from full gallop to a sliding stop.

Some wonderful polo-ponies have been trained by these methods, but few have come to Europe or the East coast. The reason for this is probably that the horseman bred to the flat saddle, bent leg, leg-aids, and riding a horse into the bit cannot readily adapt himself to the hackamore-trained horse who, wrongly handled, may make a most uncomfortable ride and lose his servo-brakes.

Surely Californian methods, applied not, as they once were, to small, cold-blooded range-ponies, but to well-bred horses, are the quintessence of Spanish horsemanship, derived from Arabs and Moors, brought to perfection by American breeding and specialization.

In the early days, over most of the West, when a pony could be bought for $10, it was not worth spending time and trouble in 'making' him. So, for $5, a bronco-buster was hired to 'break' him. Often no effort was made to win, by patience and kindness, the pony's confidence. He was roped, thrown or hobbled, saddled by force, ridden by force, the bronco-buster sitting on him through his terrified bucks and plunges until he was exhausted, his spirit broken. The principle was to provoke a horse's resistance, then smash it. Sometimes the process was expedited by tying up

---

* A form of curb with fixed mouthpiece, similar to the 9th Lancer but with longer, swept-back cheekpieces.

the victim for a couple of days without food or water, a process known euphemistically as 'gentling'. The bronco-buster was a wonderful athlete, and a very brave man; he was generally killed or smashed up internally within three years; but he was hardly a horseman in our sense of the word, since he all too often broke horses instead of making them.

However, with the small, cold-blooded range-ponies, these methods worked: ponies which did not respond to them were termed 'rogues' and reserved for rodeo-work or for taking the Mickey out of a stranger who laid claims to horsemanship.

As range-horses became larger, better bred, and more valuable, these robust methods fell into disrepute. In modern times the range-horse is made very much like any other horse – handled, longe-ed, long-reined, backed when he is ready for it, and so schooled gradually until he has completed his education. Schooling must include some tricks unnecessary in Eastern horses. The range-horse has to stand still when his rider, to do some job or other, had dismounted and left the reins (not joined at the end) hanging. He is taught to do so by tying the reins to a sack, on which he treads if he moves. The range-horse must be expert in cutting out an individual animal from a herd, and for this he must be schooled as carefully as a polo-pony in sudden, sliding stops, turns, and circles, all on the correct leg. In roping, which involves a sliding halt and reining back to tighten the rope, a young horse is made to practise with a sand-bag or heavy log to represent the roped calf. Then he graduates to roping a goat at a walk, and finally to the calf or steer taken at a gallop. Good stock-horses seem to have inherited or developed a 'cow-sense' which enables them to anticipate the moves of a frightened or stubborn calf. The cruelty of the bronco-buster is a thing of the past; though eyebrows may be raised at the practice, during schooling, of leaving a horse unshod in front so that, in sliding stops, his forefeet hurt and he gets his weight well off his forehand, his quarters well under him.

I cannot discover whether, in the days of the open range, the cowpunchers and other range-riders shod their horses or not. Possibly the practice varied from area to area and from ranch to ranch, but I am inclined to think that most rode unshod. Roger Pocock lists the items he carried in his saddle-bags and on his pack-horse for a long journey: they do not include spare shoes, nails, rasp, buffer, hammer, or pincers. Shoeing probably came in with larger, more expensive range-horses. In the Thirteen Colonies horses were worked unshod until about 1750, when the increase of metalled roads necessitated shoeing. On the Argentine pampas they are still generally worked without shoes.

The cowpuncher, like the Indian, based his mobility not on one well-schooled horse, but on the *remuda* system. For a round-up he used not less than seven ponies – two morning, two afternoon, and two night horses, so that each rested every other day, and one was kept as a spare or for his visits to church, saloon, or dance-hall of a Sunday. The last had, perhaps, the most exacting task: he would be tied up, without food or water, outside the saloon if his rider was of a convivial nature, and must remain there until the barrel of whisky, purchased by his master and a few friends, had been consumed. He must then (on, one assumes, a loose rein) convey his precious burden back to the ranch-house without dropping it *en route*.

Although thousands of horses are still used on ranches, their use is declining.

231

Cutting out and roping has largely been replaced by driving animals into separate pens and crushes for sorting, inoculation, castration, and branding: the round-up, immensely simplified by paddocking, is often carried out more expeditiously by jeeps and motor-cycles. Increasingly the emphasis in Western horsemanship is on trail-riding (Anglice pony-trekking) and on the rodeo.

The latter is a wonderful display of horsemanship, in which all the old-time cowpunching skills have been perfected to a degree unknown to the Old West. The best performers are not, of course, cowpunchers doing it for fun, but full-time professionals making very large incomes. Some have never worked on a ranch at all, or have worked only on dude ranches in the Eastern States. Their mounts are nothing like the little mustang, but well-bred horses, as professional as their riders, trained to the highest degree.

Some events in a Western horse-show are intended not for the professionals, but to give a bit of fun to the ordinary owner of the ordinary horse. Racing in a zigzag figure-of-eight, or clover-leaf course round poles or barrels requires no specifically Western technique, and is very good training for polo-ponies. Trail-horse competitions are eminently practical. The competitor must be able to box and unbox his horse in the ring, and to ride it, in Western gear, through, past, or over any obstacle likely to be encountered in a trail-ride – opening gates, stepping over logs, fording streams, carrying awkward loads such as fishing-tackle or a dead deer – all without jumping. It is a good test of horsemanship, but well within the capacity of almost any horse or rider, given patient, proper training.

The rodeo events in a Western show are displays of superb, specialized horsemanship and professional skill. In small rodeos, of course, working cowboys and amateurs enter, but in the big shows they are the preserve of the professionals.

In the calf-roping contest the object is, on horseback, to catch, throw, and tie up a calf, in the shortest time, as though for branding or inoculation. It is the most popular of rodeo contests. A very active half-grown calf comes bouncing out of the chute and scampers across the ring. When the starting flag is lowered, the rider gallops after it and throws a noose over its head. The horse must stop dead, if necessary backing to keep the rope taut, while the rider leaps off, throws the calf, and ties three feet together. A first-class performer can do all this in under thirteen seconds. The record time is 11·5 seconds.

In the bull-dogging or steer-wrestling contest a longhorn steer is released from the chute and two riders, the bull-dogger and the hazer, gallop after it. While the hazer rides alongside the steer on its off-side to prevent it turning away, the bull-dogger comes up on the near side, leans over to grab the steer by the horns, swings out of the saddle, and twists the galloping steer's head round to throw him on his side. To throw in this way a steer weighing 800 or 900 pounds requires considerable strength and a very high standard of horsemanship. A lot depends on the horse and in bull-dogging, as in other rodeo contests, an outstanding performer is often leased by the owner to several competitors, in return for a share of the winnings.

The object of 'cutting' is to separate a very active calf from a herd and then frustrate its determined efforts to get back again. Originally the chosen calf had to be driven out of the middle of a tight-packed mob of long-horn cattle, described by

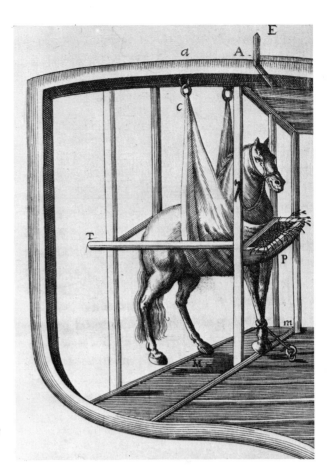

How the *conquistadores*
took their horses to
America

Theodore Roosevelt as the most dangerous animal in America. That, in a rodeo, is
no longer done. The horse is supposed to do the work with no assistance or guidance
from its rider, who must use neither rein nor leg to help. (The best cutting-riders
sometimes use both, but so cleverly that the judges cannot detect it.) A cutting-horse
in action reminds one of a sheepdog, stalking a calf in an almost menacing way,
anticipating the victim's every move, and dodging this way and that to block its
escape. The cutting-horse can spin till the rider is giddy, 'rolls over on his hocks',
turn on a sixpence with the rider's inside stirrup almost scraping the ground. The
qualities needed are speed and agility equal to the best polo-pony's; faultless stopping, turning on the haunches, leg-changing and, above all, highly developed
'cow-sense'.

Finally, there are the spectacular bronco-riding contests in which a cowboy
must remain on a horse, with or without the Western saddle, for eight or ten seconds
during which he gains points for spurring a horse *in the shoulder* to make him jump
and buck higher and higher. Here the horses are professionals as well as the riders,
animals who are almost unridable, either unbroken range-horses or saddle-horses
who like bucking better than they like being ridden. Their efforts are stimulated
legally by a strap drawn tight round the loins and stomach, illegally (or so it is
rumoured) by a thorn concealed in the saddle-blanket.

233

This section would certainly be incomplete without a mention of Western riding-clothes, which are *de rigueur* in Western horse shows and rodeos. Whatever their occasional present-day extravagances, they were developed for practical use.

The cowboy's hat shades his head from a blazing sun and prevents the rain dripping down the back of his neck. He can use it – I have often used it – for watering a horse from a well, or giving him a feed of grain. Squashed flat on the seat of the saddle, it makes a tolerably soft pillow if one has to sleep out on the cold, hard ground. I have found it most useful in pushing through acacia thorn. In Kenya, the branches are often of such a height that a horse can duck his head under them, and the skin of a horse's neck, chest, and shoulders is pretty tough: but the rider's face, shirt, and trousers unless protected, are ripped to pieces by these wicked, hooked 'wait-a-bit' thorns. Wearing a wide-brimmed, tough felt hat, the rider can bend low over his horse's withers and fairly butt his way through, shielded by the hat.

At the same time leather chaps keep the thorns out of his legs and stop his trousers being torn. They are also useful as a ground-sheet at night, for giving a grip on the saddle, and for protection against the front of the stirrup-leather, a kick, or snake-bite. What one wears under chaps is pretty well immaterial. Trousers are cooler and more comfortable than breeches, and under chaps do not ruck up. They need not be tight, though that is the modern fashion: nineteenth-century cowboys wore quite wide trousers.

A large silk or cotton square, knotted round the neck, serves as a sweat-rag, handkerchief, towel, dust-mask, bandage, or water-filter. At night it keeps midges and mosquitoes off the face. A lariat is useful not only for roping cattle, but as a halter rope, for making an enclosure into which to drive ponies for catching them or to keep them in at night, for hanging card-sharpers and horse-thieves, and for many other worthy purposes. Lariats are made of cotton-rope, rawhide, or plaited horse-hair. The latter are very expensive, but never kink and are said to have the useful property, when laid round a rider's blankets as he sleeps on the ground, of keeping off rattlesnakes.

Horsemen, since Xenophon, prefer high boots to shoes. Spurs can be fitted to boots, and one can leg a horse better with boots. They, like chaps, protect the leg against thorns, snakes, kicks, and the stirrup-leather. High heels are convenient for the cowboy who wants to dig his heels into the ground and haul back on a roped steer, and for the Lilliputian film star who wants to tower over the leading lady. They also serve to prevent the foot slipping through the big wooden stirrup.

Mexican spurs, huge and cruel-looking, are not in fact cruel. The larger in diameter the rowel, the less the spikes mark or hurt a horse, and the spikes of the Western spur are always blunt. A Roman prick-spur, or its modern Eastern equivalent, even blunted, is far more severe if clumsily used than a Western spur. The object of those three-inch, jingling rowels and silver spurs are partly swank and show, partly so that a range-horse, approached in the dark, would recognize the sound of his master's spurs and stand to be caught.

Long hair in a man is a matter of fashion, not necessarily connected with drugs, decadence, depravity or student protest. In the mid nineteenth century most men wore their hair long. American frontiersmen wore it longer than most for pride and

Red Indian lassoing a wild horse by G. Catlin

prestige: Indians despised a man who had no scalplock. Also, no doubt, cowboys were far from a barber and reluctant to submit to the ministrations of a friend with a pair of blunt scissors.

There were few vets on the cattle range, so it was perhaps providential that leg- and hoof-unsoundness was very rare in range-horses. Saddle-sores, due no doubt to poor horsemastership and the knowledge that horses were cheap and expendable, were more common. The range-rider rode with a light-coloured sweat-pad between the saddle and the horse's back. Inspecting this when he off-saddled, he would be warned by hairs rubbed off an incipient sore, and could then take the heroic remedy of riding a horse to sweating heat, dismounting, and dashing cold salt water over the part affected. Of course the *remuda* system enabled the cowpuncher to apply the best cure for any equine ailment – rest.

I recall an old Scottish vet who insisted on applying to my mare's shoulder a blister for which I, in my superior wisdom, could see no necessity.

'But what's the point of it?' I asked.

'To stop ye riding for a month,' he growled.

It is only when you live hundreds of miles from a vet that you realize how many things can be cured by rest, hot or cold water, and some simple disinfectant like salt or spirits. A vet was called out on a bitter cold night to look at a horse's eye which was scratched.

'Have you some brandy?' he asked the owner.

'I have.'

'Then bring me some – a large glass, mind, of your best liqueur brandy.'

The next stage

The owner, somewhat mystified, brought this nutritious beverage. The man of science drank the brandy, spat in the horse's eye, remarked 'He'll be better tomorrow' – and sent in a bill for five guineas.

In 1865 a vet in the West recommended for the treatment of glanders 'one powder and one blue pill. Take one tablespoonful of Dupont's best rifle powder and put in the muzzle of a good musket and ram down the paper on top of it; then take one blue pill of lead of an ounce or less in weight and ram down on top of that; and then go to the patient in the stable and go through the military manual of firing; but be sure to kill the horse and burn him, and the stable, bridles, and everything that has come in contact with him.'

Western horsemanship was a logical development for a specific purpose, cattle-ranching and trail-riding in the Western States. Under the influence of the cinema and television, it has spread far from its native ranges, to the Eastern States and even to Europe where dude ranches and Western riding-clubs are to be found. It is, to Europeans, the best-known branch of American equitation, but it is by no means the only one.

The early colonist imported horses for sport and work. They rode in the same style and in the same sort of saddle as their English contemporaries, but developed some local specialities.

One of the earliest was the 'Quarter horse'. Widely scattered planters and farmers could not construct full-sized racecourses but, like all horsemen, they were fond of racing. So from thoroughbred stock, they developed a sprinter to race only a quarter of a mile. All quarter horses are supposed to be descended from Janus, a smallish, stocky, thoroughbred stallion imported into Virginia in the late eighteenth century; but as the breed was standardized only with the formation of the American Quarter Horse Association in 1950, one must suppose that it has been considerably diluted by outside strains. The quarter horse is heavier built than a thoroughbred, and measures 14·3 to 15·1 hands, with a shortish neck and legs, rather heavy shoulders, and well-muscled quarters which give him a good start in a short race. He makes a good polo-pony, and a first-class ranch- or rodeo-horse for roping, barrel- or pole-racing, and particularly for cutting. To see a good quarter horse in a cutting contest is one of the great spectacles of equitation. Rich ranchers imported quarter-horse stallions, particularly to the South-western States, to add size, speed, and quality to the mustang's intelligence, hardihood, and endurance. Sam Houston was a quarter-horse lover, and in Texas they are sometimes known as 'Copperbottoms' after his favourite stallion.

In 1795 Justin Morgan, a Vermont farmer, schoolteacher, and composer of music, acquired in settlement of a bad debt an undersized bay colt named Figure. Figure turned out to be the sort that all of us are looking for but few of us find – the horse that does everything and costs nothing. He pulled wagons round the farm; he carried Justin Morgan at a brisk, smooth trot or fast walk to school or market; he raced under saddle and in harness; he won wagers for his master by hauling enormous logs which had defeated animals twice his size. He was phenomenally strong, willing, and intelligent, and his progeny, known as 'Morgan horses', have inherited to an extraordinary degree his colour and characteristics.

After Justin's death, Figure fell on evil days; and in his old age an unfeeling master turned him out all one winter in the snow – and found in the spring all that the wolves had left of poor Figure. His fame came posthumously. Years after his death the extraordinary versatile performance of many dark bay horses was noticed, and all were traced back to Figure.

The typical Morgan horse is never over 15·2, generally under 15 hands, but rather heavy for his height. He has a short neck, a high head-carriage, a deep, wide chest, short legs, good sloping shoulders, and strong quarters. His breeding is shown in his head, for he has inherited the dished face, small muzzle, and wide-set, gentle eyes of his remote Arab ancestors, though only his most fanatical admirers now claim that Figure was clean-bred. He is the supremely versatile horse. Former cavalrymen will recognize in this description the ideal troop-horse or officer's charger, and the Morgan horse has always been a favourite in the U.S. Cavalry for all ranks from General Sheridan downwards.

The famous American Standard Bred is bred for trotting-races in harness, and does not generally make a good saddle-horse, so is no concern of this book. But the Tennessee Walking horse has been scientifically bred from Morgan, Quarter horse, and Standard bred strains, and schooled by the most expert, meticulous horsemanship. Plantation-owners wanted a comfortable horse for riding between rows of crops. The typical walking-horse has inherited three gaits, of which the third is peculiar to the breed. He has an ordinary flat-footed walk, accompanied in show specimens by a cadenced nodding of the head; an easy, luxurious canter; and an extraordinary

Red Indian method of breaking a pony by F. Remington

running walk, smooth, high-stepping, and very fast, which carries his fortunate owner at a phenomenal nine miles an hour. For trail-riding and ranch-work he is very popular, for his running walk is comfortable for the rider, and not, apparently, particularly tiring for the horse.

Finally there is the American Saddle Bred, a horse of thoroughbred ancestry, in some ways similar to the walking-horse, as fast and comfortable a hack but without the famous 'running walk'. There are two kinds of saddle-horses. One has the three ordinary gaits, walk, trot, and canter, but developed to a high degree of comfort, accuracy, and elegance. The other, known as the 'Five-Gaited horse', has, in addition, two other gaits, not natural but taught. These are the 'slow gait' and the 'fast rack'. Walking- and gaited-horses are ridden in an exaggerated High School style, with a straight leg. The slow gait is something between a trot and a walk: a horse almost trots in front and walks behind. The rack, with an even rhythm and considerable speed, is a faster development of the slow gait. Both are syncopated, four-beat paces, very comfortable for the rider but (the rack particularly) very tiring for the horse.

The running walk and the rack are taught and, when inherited, improved by methods which do not command universal admiration. A horse's feet are allowed to grow unnaturally long and he is shod for training with very heavy shoes which make him pick up his feet. For showing, both walking-horses and saddle-bred horses are sometimes beautified by cutting the depressor muscles of the tail so that it is carried glamorously high; by dyeing mane and tail and even by fitting false tails. But these devices are, rightly, coming into increasing disrepute.

Racing in America, both on the flat and over jumps, developed on the same lines as in Europe. Bloodstock flourished, particularly on the limestone soils where the famous 'blue grass' took. This wonderful grass, *Poa pratensis*, came originally from the steppes north of the Black Sea: it must have been the staple food of the Scythians' horses.

The first recorded race-meeting, apart from impromptu quarter-races, was held in Kentucky in 1788: gentlemen were advised to come well armed, owing to the danger from Indians. In 1793 horse-racing down the streets of Lexington had become such a nuisance that it was prohibited by a by-law. 'Horses and lawsuits', observed the newly appointed Consul for the French Republic in that year, 'comprise the usual topic of conversations. If a traveller happens to pass by, his horse is appreciated. If he stops, he is presented with a glass of whisky and asked a thousand questions.' In Charleston race-meetings were fashionable and social occasions: 'youth anticipating its delights for weeks before hand, lovers becoming more ardent, and young damsels setting their caps with greater taste and dexterity – the *quality* of the company in attendance – the splendid equipages – the gentlemen attending in fashionable London-made clothes, buckskin breeches and top-boots'. It was all a long, long way from John Pynchon's and his buccaneer cowboys.

It was, of course, in America that the modern racing seat was devised by Tod Sloan or, perhaps, copied by him from diminutive Negro stable-boys.

We have seen American horsemanship applied to work and to sport. Now let us see it at war, for in America as elsewhere horsemanship was developed largely by the requirements of war and, in its turn, influenced military tactics and strategy.

Despite the heroic ambitions of a few ardent cavaliers, American cavalrymen never deluded themselves with an exaggerated regard for *l'arme blanche*. They owed nothing to medieval chivalry, and drew no inspiration from Blenheim, Ramillies, Salamanca, or Waterloo. They formed at a time when the revolver and the breach-loading rifle were obviously about to dominate the battle-field, and made these their favourite weapons. Sabres, if carried at all, came in useful for signalling and for cutting grass and firewood. The great cavalry operations of Stuart, Sheridan, and Nathan Bedford Forest were carried out by troopers who realized, some fifty years ahead of European cavalrymen, that it was easier and safer to dismount and shoot an enemy than to try to prod him with a lance or sword. They suffered, however, from another delusion, almost as expensive – that every red-blooded American can ride and shoot, especially if he has done neither before. For a long time they were given quite inadequate training, and regiments on the Indian frontier spent on fort- and barrack-building most of the time which should have been devoted to instruction in equitation and musketry.

The most troublesome of the Plains Indians were horsemen, who could only raid in force in the months of good grazing. In 1832 the first regiment of dragoons – called at first mounted rangers, and later cavalry – was formed, for frontier operations. Each trooper provided his own horse and was assumed to be able to ride it. They

Coming and going of the Pony Express by F. Remington

carried out their first expedition, against the Comanches, in 1834. In a temperature of 105 °F in the shade, they suffered tortures from thirst, lack of grazing, heat exhaustion, and dysentery: ninety died, not one by Indian bullet or arrow. But they proved that, despite all difficulties, cavalry were, for plains warfare, a great deal better than infantry. The hostile tribes were healthily impressed, and many submitted. The cavalrymen learned two lessons – not to miss the May grass, and to carry oats.

The U.S. Cavalry has been criticized for never using a *remuda* system. Perhaps the Government boggled at the expense. Certainly a regimental *remuda* of a thousand horses (two spares for each man) would have consumed too much oats and grass, and been too vulnerable to attack when spread out to graze. At all events they opted for the orthodox Eastern cavalry system of one large, well-bred, grain-fed horse to each man.

They rode, as did most cavalry at that time, with a straight leg and a stiff back. They were issued with a double-bridle, but seem at times to have dispensed with either snaffle, or curb. Their saddle was the McClellan, brought from Hungary by an officer of that name. It was no more than the skeleton of a saddle consisting of two narrow pads, joined fore and aft to a steel frame and covered with a rawhide seat. At first the saddle did not have panels, and troopers suffered agonies from sores on the inside of their thighs due to rubbing against the horse's sweaty flanks. Later, panels were sometimes added. The wooden Western stirrup was used, sometimes with the *tapadero*.

The McClellan saddle, though the U.S. Cavalry retained it until 1940, has been much criticized. I have never used it. My mother bought one in the United States in 1903 and used it all over the world, on horses and ponies of all shapes and sizes, for thirty years. She says it would fit anything, and never gave her horses a sore back or herself a sore bottom. What more can one ask of a military saddle?

The story of the U.S. Cavalry belongs to a history of war rather than to a history of equitation, but it is a good story. They never fought against a first-class enemy, except of course during the Civil War; but for sixty years, suffering extraordinary privations from heat and cold, besides what must have seemed interminable boredom, they held and advanced the frontiers of civilization. They won no great victories and suffered, at Little Big Horn, one dramatic defeat, but they hold, deservedly, an honoured place in American history. It was a hopelessly prosaic cavalry general who calculated that, for less than the $3 million a year that it cost to run a frontier military district, he could have provided every Indian with a broadcloth suit, fried oysters, and all the poker, whisky, and tobacco he required, thus ending the Sioux Wars.

To South America also the Spaniards took the Andalusian or Barb horse and the medieval war-saddle. They founded Buenos Aires in 1535, but almost immediately deserted it, leaving there five mares and seven stallions. Their descendants, improved by imported stallions, were, like the mustang, sound, handy, hard as nails, and intelligent. But they seem to have been of much better quality than the mustang, 14·3 to 15·1 hands in size, short-backed, well ribbed-up. They may not have shown in their heads much thoroughbred blood, but they were a first-class stamp of working-horse, with a better natural balance than most. With legs and hooves like steel, they worked unshod, and still do, at roping, cutting, round-up, and all the usual jobs of the range-horse, which in the South American pampas have been much less mechanized than in the United States.

The gaucho makes his own bridle, of beautifully softened and plaited leather, innocent of metal buckles but fastened instead with leather loops and studs. His saddle, too, he makes himself; for he did not, like the Mexican *vaquero*, adopt and adapt the Spanish war-saddle, but produced something very similar (except for the decorations) to those found in Scythian tombs. It consists basically of two oblong cushions which lie along either side of the horse's spine, the whole being covered with a sheepskin or leather seat.* The saddle is flat and rather broad: it has no roping-horn, no noticeable pommel or cantle; but, like the Western stock-saddle, it is designed to distribute the rider's weight over a wide area of the horse's back. There is a single *cincha*. The stirrups are smaller than Western stirrups, just large enough to take the rider's toes. The gaucho wears huge, cruel spurs, not blunted like the cowboy's, but designed to cut and score a horse's flanks if the rider really uses them.

* Living in a tree-less country, he does not use a wooden saddle-tree.

Argentine ponies, like Red Indians', are bridled first with a rawhide thong known as the *bosado,* tied in a clove-hitch round the lower jaw. With rough hands this is very severe, for it tightens when the rein is pulled, but does not loosen when the rein is relaxed; but with good hands it is very gentle, and many a gaucho's pony works in nothing else all its life. Others graduate to the hackamore, and to various types of curb-bit, particularly the Western curb. No attempt is made to ride the pony into the bit, which would hurt and make it rear; the mere weight of the loosely hanging reins, which are sometimes made heavier near the bit, acting on the severe *bocado* or curb, does the trick.

Riding on a flat saddle, his horse balanced between those savage spurs and a potentially severe bit, the gaucho must, if he is not to hurt his horse or make it rear up, be perfectly balanced himself. So he rides not straight-legged but with a slightly bent leg, sitting very much as is taught in European and Eastern States riding-schools today.

To catch or throw an animal the gaucho uses a *bola,* which consists of three ropes joined like a starfish, a small heavy ball at each end. Skilfully thrown, the *bola* wraps itself round the steer's legs and brings it down. Sometimes, instead of the *bola,*

. . . and today –
Gregory Lougher
on Jack Hammer

a lariat is used. In default of a roping-horn, the gaucho gets a purchase on the lariat by jamming it under his stirrup-leather.

When a gaucho wants to stock up his *remuda*, he selects an unbroken horse (preferably a mare) and ropes her. She is then tied very short to a strong post, and left to kick and plunge until she is exhausted. A *bocado* is then fitted, and she is again left to struggle for a while; then a saddle. A couple of hours later the gaucho rides up to the *estancia* a quietly moving, collected, and apparently half-schooled mare. It is a remarkable feat, especially with such a large, powerful animal.

Thereafter, the mare takes her place in the *remuda* and earns her living with two or three hours' work every other day, lives off grass, and develops into a real expert at cutting, roping, or both. From the gaucho's point of view the trouble is that, if she becomes too good at her job, she may catch the boss's eye as a potential polo-pony, worth £800 or £1,000 at New York, Cowdray, or Deauville, for Argentine ponies, costing perhaps £50 unbacked, have the perfect conformation, training, and temperament for polo. The gaucho gets a commission on the deal, but it is still discouraging for a man who has devoted endless skill and patience on a mare to have her taken away just as she attains perfection. Some people believe that the gaucho no longer takes such pains over schooling his best mares as in the past.

According to the classical school of equitation, a horse brought up short while galloping must bend, that is to say, tuck in his chin so as to get his weight back on his haunches, a movement assisted by the curb-bit acting on the bars of his mouth and so making him lower his head. In recent years, however, the Argentine polo-experts have concluded that a horse halts quicker if he raises his head, like Xeno-phon's horses, even though he be almost star-gazing. Their ponies are therefore, schooled in snaffles and gag-snaffles, which raise the head by acting on the corners of the horse's mouth; and this has had an influence also on the training of the gaucho's ponies which are often now ridden in snaffles instead of *bocado*, hackamore, or curb.

No matter what bit he uses, the gaucho can still, by any standard, be numbered among the world's great horsemen.

The horsemanship of North and South America is remarkable for its excellence and its astonishing versatility. In the United States alone one sees the most artificial and the most functional horsemanship rubbing shoulders in the same ring: nothing could be more artificial than the making of a five-gaited horse, nothing more functional than a cutting-horse. Every horse-sport (except, I believe, pig-sticking) is practised in the Americas, and many are practised nowhere else except by travelling American horsemen. Nearly all are practised to a high degree of excellence. American

A two-rein bosal and
(*right*) a hackamore

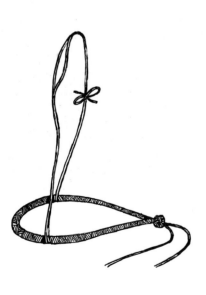
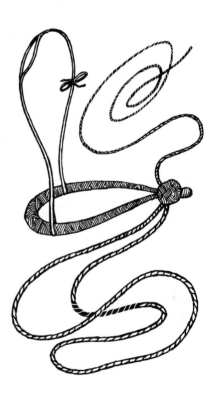

A Parade Horse at Santa Barbara National
Horse Show

and Argentinian polo-players are certainly the best in the world; American flat-racing and steeplechase jockeys are as good as those of any country; American show-jumpers and combined event riders are right in the top rank.

What produces this versatility and excellence? Partly, of course, money, the affluent society, partly sheer American efficiency, and partly the American characteristic of a consuming desire to *win*, not merely to play and enjoy. But there is more to it than that.

In the United States there met, and to some extent combined, three or four different horse-cultures: Spanish equitation both *à la gineta* and *à la brida*, in a slightly debased, rough-and-ready form coming up from Mexico and surviving in its purest form in California. From the east and south-east came English horse-culture based on fox-hunting and racing, but adapted to the needs of the early colonists and plantation-owners. American Indians, a brave and intelligent race, starting from scratch, produced a horse-culture very similar to that of the Scythians and nomads of the steppes.

Tennessee
Walking Horse

Similarly, there was a great variety of horses – thoroughbreds, quarter horses, Morgans, Arabs, Spanish horses, mustangs. A great part of the United States, Canada, Mexico, and the Argentine is perfectly suited to horse-breeding.

All these horse-cultures and horses met, by the accident of history, at a time when the horse was the most important single factor in the country's development, in war and peace. The pace of the Manifest Destiny was set by the horse.

All that was lacking to American horsemanship at the beginning of the twentieth century was the educated, scientific horsemanship of France and Italy. It is strange indeed that the country which produced the jockey's crouch in flat racing did not at the same time develop the forward seat for jumping.* But the deficiency was made good between 1920 and 1939 by some very gifted horsemasters and equitation instructors, notably Vladimir Littanev, formerly of the Imperial Russian Army who set up in New York a riding-school which profoundly influenced civilian riding, and Colonel Harry Chamberlin who brought the distilled wisdom of Saumur and Pinerolo to the U.S. Cavalry School at Fort Riley. They supplied the science and education which Eastern American horsemanship had hitherto lacked, so that Americans can now say of equitation, 'You name it – we've got it. And, what is more, we'll win it.'

* Tod Sloan and Caprilli are discussed in later chapters.

8

Caprilli's Revolution and the Counter-Revolution

The man who brought to equitation a far greater revolution than Grisone was an Italian cavalry officer, Federico Caprilli, who was born in 1868 and died at an early age in 1907, having taught his methods at the Italian Cavalry School at Pinerolo for the last four years of his life.

All previous educated horsemanship, that is to say horsemanship consciously thought out, has been based on the presumption that a horse, whatever his accomplishments in the state of nature, was incapable, without prolonged training in collection, of adjusting his balance to the weight of a man on his back, since this implied a change in his whole equilibrium. Caprilli's basic premise was that a horse was perfectly capable of adjusting his centre of gravity to changes of pace or to jumping, without any assistance from the rider, so long as the latter made his centre of gravity conform as near as possible with that of the horse and thereafter refrained from interfering. Horsemanship should, therefore, consist not of the rider instructing the horse, with aids, on weight distribution, but of the rider anticipating and conforming to the horse's movements in this respect. Rather than collecting a horse, bringing his forehand and quarters together 'like two ends of a curved whip', the rider should encourage and promote the horse's 'forward impulse'.

The teaching of all previous west European riding-masters, from Xenophon to Fillis, had been variations on the theme of collection. But Caprilli was really revolutionary: he discarded the whole concept of collection, which he thought not merely unnecessary, because a horse could, without interference from the rider, adjust his balance to all paces, but positively harmful, because it inhibited a horse's forward impulse. All that was necessary, in his view, was for the rider to interfere as little as possible with the horse's natural balance. This does not, of course, mean that a horse should be allowed to do as he pleases: he must always do what his rider wants. But whereas (to use untechnical terms) the classical rider told a horse what to do and how to do it, Caprilli believed that the rider should tell a horse what to do and then simply conform to the horse's way of doing it. After much thought and experiment, Caprilli evolved from these ideas the 'Italian seat'.

Consider first the simplest case, when the horse is standing still. His natural centre of gravity, that is to say his centre of gravity when he has no rider on his back, lies directly below his withers, so his perpendicular of body weight can be represented by a vertical line dropped from the withers. In the classical seat, the rider's centre of gravity lies well behind this and, depending on his exact position, his perpendicular of body weight can be represented by a vertical line dropped approximately through the centre of the saddle. As the horse's pace increases, his centre of gravity moves forward, so the gap between horse's and rider's perpendicular of body weight widens, making the horse seem clumsy and heavy handed and greatly increasing his difficulty in jumping.

Classical riders, from Xenophon to Fillis, all tried, in varying degrees and by varying methods, to narrow this gap, and make the two perpendiculars of body weight coincide, by bringing the horse's centre of gravity back.* Caprilli, on the other hand, made them coincide by bringing the rider's centre of gravity forward. This he did by shortening the stirrup-leathers, drawing back his lower leg to behind the vertical, and inclining his body forward – slightly at slow paces, but at fast paces or in jumping, as the horse's centre of gravity moved forward, raising the seat off the saddle, leaning well over the withers, and standing in the stirrups.

The classical rider held the reins with his forearm parallel to the ground, and made his horse bend at the poll by bending and twisting his wrist, raising his hand, and bending his elbow.

Caprilli taught that the forward impulse should always be encouraged, the rider's hands should conform to, not oppose, the movements of the horse's head which was naturally extended, the face keeping at medium paces an angle of about forty-five degrees to the ground. This was best done by so holding the reins that they, the wrist and the forearm, formed a straight line from bit to elbow. Only along this axis should the rider's hand move – conforming to the horse's head movements as pace is increased or restraining them to slow down the pace. The hand must follow the reins, the reins follow the horse's mouth.

To increase pace Caprilli simply advanced his hand along the elbow-bit line. Since this was done mainly by a movement of the shoulder and back muscles, it meant that the rider automatically leaned forward, imparting to the horse a forward impulse. Except with lazy, stubborn, or untrained horses, a squeeze of the legs was merely an auxiliary, often an unnecessary addition to this forward impulse. To restrain the horse, the rider leaned slightly back, withdrawing his hand along the elbow-bit line.

He did not ride on a loose rein, but always preserved contact with a horse's mouth. Since it was unnecessary, indeed harmful, to make a horse bend at the poll, no form of curb should be used, only a snaffle.

He allowed no sharp halts or turns, no sudden changes of pace, but easy circles and smooth transitions through walk, trot, and canter. Most of his remounts' work was individual, not merely following in single file; so there was no difficulty in getting his troop-horses to leave the ranks and go off on their own.

By observation, study, and logical thought Caprilli had evolved a seat and a style of riding not unlike those of the natural horsemen of the steppes and great plains. It also had obvious affinities to the jockey's crouch 'invented' a few years earlier by Tod Sloan, though it was not, of course, the same seat, for Caprilli's system was

---

* Either by raising his head and making him bend at the poll, or by getting his hocks well under him, or by both.

Show jumping, an extreme forward seat

designed essentially for riding across country at all speeds, Sloan's only for riding on the flat at a racing gallop. Whether Caprilli was consciously influenced by what he had read or heard of Tod Sloan, then engaged in making himself painfully conspicuous in the most expensive London restaurants, or whether he even knew how Cossacks and Comanches rode, is extremely doubtful. They had developed a style by instinct and experience: he thought it all out.

Caprilli's system, like many simple things, is far easier described than practised, particularly in jumping. Educated horsemen of his day believed that the rider must indicate to the horse when to increase his pace for the jump and when to take-off. He should steady the horse several lengths from the jump and, with an accurate judgement of pace and distance, squeeze with the legs (if not more) three strides from the jump; he must at the same time make a horse 'put in a short one', or lengthen his stride so that his last stride takes him to the correct take-off point, when another squeeze of the legs is given to make him jump. Without being 'given the office' a horse would inevitably mistime his jump, either taking off a stride too soon, or leaving it until he was too close to the fence. 'Quite unnecessary', said Caprilli's disciples. 'The horse who has been practised, with a rider on his back, jumping over obstacles at first very low but gradually increasing in size, is perfectly capable of

Steeple-chasing – the forward seat (same rider as on page 264 but a different style)

A trooper of Hodson's Horse. 1932

judging his distance, lengthening or shortening his stride accordingly, and of timing his take-off, provided you don't upset his balance or otherwise interfere with him. Just impart that forward impulse, make your centre of gravity conform to his, and leave the rest to him.'

All except the very old fashioned had, by Caprilli's time, given up leaning back as the horse approached a jump, took off, and rose over it. Like Fillis, they tried over a jump to keep their bodies vertical, leaning forward as the horse took off and rose, back as he descended and landed. To lean back as one lands is anyone's instinctive flinching from the unwelcome prospect of the horse pecking or oneself tumbling over his head. Practitioners of this style rationalized their instinctive reaction by saying that one must lean back so as to save the horse's forelegs from the sudden jar of landing and to hold him up and save him from a fall if he pecks. 'Not so', said the Caprilli-ists. 'However one sits, the inflexible laws of gravity ensure that the combined weight of horse and man must inevitably be borne by the horse's forelegs. This is particularly so if you land with your own legs stuck stiffly out forward to save yourself from falling. But the jar is reduced if your legs are correctly placed, with knee bent; for it is then absorbed progressively by your ankle, knee, and loins. By no power on earth can a rider save his horse from falling by a tug on the reins: if he could, flying would be a simple proposition. The attempt to do so will certainly make the horse raise his head and drop his quarters, with dire results if there is a ditch on the landing side. You are prevented from falling forward not by leaning back, but by knee-grip, which is assured by a correct position of the foot and ankle – toes up, ankle turned so that pressure comes on the inside of the stirrup-tread. By sitting forward, over the horse's centre of gravity, you allow him to stretch out his head over a jump and as he lands; then, with no pause for rebalancing himself and you, he resumes his forward gallop. In any case the horse will jump all the better if he is not interfered with and if he is not in constant fear of a jerk at his mouth.'

No one at first took much notice of Caprilli, though a few foreign visitors to Pinerolo, impressed by his methods, described them in journals such as *The Russian Cavalry Messenger*. But in 1907 exponents of his style startled the equestrian world by winning, with ludicrous ease, the show-jumping at the International Horse Show, and in subsequent years proved clearly that this was no fluke.

The conservatives soon thought of an answer. 'Ah yes, this monkey-seat may answer well enough for popping over artificial fences in a show-ring, but it must be quite impracticable hunting, with poached take-offs, blind and drop-landings. One must sit back on landing, to ensure against a big drop, an unexpected ditch, or a peck in heavy plough. As for this silly trick of leaning forward to slide down a steep slope, that is just showing off, to impress the spectators.' (In fact, Caprilli leaned

An almost perpendicular
slide being negotiated
by an Indian officer of
Hodson's Horse.
India 1937

forward for a slide in order to take his weight off the horse's quarters so that the hind-legs could function properly as a brake.)

What the conservatives would not see was that Caprilli's system had been developed specifically to enable cavalry-horses to move with ease and freedom across every sort of obstacle in every sort of country. This, not show-jumping, was the object of the exercise: in his own words, to produce cavalry-horses 'of good disposition, calm and confident of their riders and strong, accustomed to galloping for long periods over any kind of terrain, calm and alert in difficulty'. Caprilli himself and his most lucid disciple, Major Piero Santini, were pre-eminently cross-country riders, not much interested in show-jumping. The pre-1914 Caprilli-ists shone principally in the ring not because they were unable to ride across country, but because they had rejected classical dressage with which, in Combined Training, the cross-country events were linked.

However, although only the Italian cavalry adopted Caprilli's system in its entirety, his doctrines had a considerable influence elsewhere.

Caprilli's system covered the entire training and riding of cavalry-horses, not just jumping, though it was in jumping that its novelty was most conspicuous. His insistence on encouraging free forward movement and his rejection of restrictive manège-training, his belief in extension rather than collection, his insistence that a horse's obedience should never be enforced by fear or pain, seemed to produce a better cavalry-horse in less time than the methods of Fillis. Besides, Caprilli's habit of working remounts individually rather than in a squad, ensured that they would leave the ranks and go off on their own when required, a feat which was, we are assured by high authority, well beyond the capacity of most troop-horses at that time: 'When an officer wants to send a man with a message, he has to call for volunteers.' 'The men', said Sir Douglas Haig, 'must do less school riding. There are only six things you want to teach the individual man in riding – to start his horse, to stop his horse, to back, to turn, to circle, and to passage.' Why, then, waste time with work in hand, shoulder in, and all that rot? Besides, the poor performance of manège-schooled horses in the Boer War undermined faith in traditional methods. From about 1910 the British Army moved in the direction of Caprilli's system, though never adopting it completely. 'They shifted their centre of gravity forward and shortened the leathers, calling this the "balanced seat"; they stood in their stirrups in a position rather like the "polo brace", to gallop, charge sword-in-line, or thrust.' This may well have contributed to the greatly improved performance of British Cavalry in the First World War.

It was, ironically enough, when the horse had ceased to be of much significance in war, that the science, or art, of equitation made its greatest progress. In the 1920s the conservatives and the exponents of the forward seat waged a ding-dong battle in every country where equitation was seriously studied. The Italian school clearly had the best of it.

The Italian system made most progress in the United States, where a few ex-cavalry officers, mainly from the Tsar's armies, and the United States Cavalry School at Fort Riley under the influence of Colonel H. D. Chamberlin, had an enormous effect in educating young riders in forward-seat jumping and cross-country riding. When Americans take anything up, they do not believe in half-measures: indeed they were soon riding far too short for Piero Santini's taste. Above all, thousands of young riders, particularly in the United States and Britain, were taught by the Pony Club to ride in a sort of modified Italian style. Collection was not discarded, but Pony Club pupils shortened their leathers a couple of holes and sat forward over jumps.

By the mid twentieth century it was rare to find any educated rider under the age of thirty who rode in any other way. This did not, of course, make them all Caprilli-ists. Many, perhaps most, of those who believed themselves to be exponents of the Italian style should have been indignantly repudiated by purists like Piero Santini and Vladimir Littauer. But their jumping style, whatever their individual imperfections, was inspired by Caprilli.

In polo Caprilli's ideas did not, perhaps, make much impact. Standing in the stirrups to gallop was, to polo-players, no novelty: they had done that for years to hit the ball, just as horse archers had done it to shoot. It seems that the sudden stops, starts, and sprints of the game, the violent changes of direction and pace, are hardly compatible with Caprilli's ideas, but require curb-bits and a lot of leg-aid. Caprilli-ists advocate more emphasis in polo on extension than collection, on circling a pony rather than a sudden halt and turn, on snaffle or Kimblewick rather than a curb; and there has perhaps been some move in this direction, but not much, as you can see by watching any polo-match.

The principles governing the flat-racing seat are very similar to Caprilli's and in racing the Italian influence is seen mainly in the manner of 'scrubbing' a horse with hands and legs towards a finish. I am open to correction on this, but I do not think nineteenth-century jockeys bothered much about timing hand and leg movements to the horse's stride and head extension. 'Now', writes Nimrod of riding a finish, 'the set-to begins . . . he moves his hands, as if describing a circle, by way of rousing his horse.' The modern jockey's scrubbing seems much more in line with Caprilli's dictum that 'the hands must follow the reins, the reins the horse's mouth'.

Most remarkably, the Caprilli-ists made their mark in international dressage tests, for which before 1933 they could not enter. In that year their arguments persuaded the International Federation of Equitation to remove from the tests those collected gaits which required a high action and a change in the horse's natural balance, and to substitute for them tests in which speed was controlled or reduced, but natural balance left unchanged. Nor in tests was it required any longer to take-off from a halt into an immediate trot or gallop: increase of pace in future was to be by progressive transition through walk and trot.

English and Irish horsemen, who from 1921 must be considered separately, were sublimely satisfied with their own horsemanship, sure that they rode a great deal better than foreigners who never followed hounds, until with pained surprise they saw these foreigners winning from them every sort of jumping competition. They still, with a few exceptions, gave little attention between the wars to the theory of equitation, but they did take up the forward seat in practice, with results that began to show in international competitions. The Cavalry Schools of Weedon and Saugur taught it

255

An 18th-century
exponent of the
classic seat

for jumping, but retained the concept of collection while discarding artificial manège gaits and movements.

Many foxhunters of the old school still sit back on landing, though not to take-off – except inadvertently.

Steeplechase jockeys take Caprilli with a pinch of salt. They ride more or less in his style over hurdles and park fences, if only because of the speed with which a horse can get away after a jump. But they do not accept his methods for riding at racing pace over really big jumps. If a horse hits one of these (and the bigger they are, the more likely this is) his speed is instantaneously reduced from about twenty-five miles an hour to about fifteen. Caprilli, they say, would go out of the front window, so while leaning forward from the hips as he advocated, they stick their legs forward in a manner which he would have deprecated. Moreover, they sit back on certain occasions: if they see a horse is coming to it wrong and likely to hit it, if a horse is apt to over-jump and fall at speed, if there is a heavy or drop-landing which the horse

256

cannot see and anticipate. On all these occasions they sit, they even lean, right back, as any photograph of Beecher's Brook will show.

A sophisticated opposition to Caprilli-ism built up at Saumur, traditional home of scientific equitation and of the famous Cadre Noir. These accomplished, supremely polished horsemen very soon recognized the merits of the forward seat over fences; but still, faithful to the tradition of Pluvinel and de la Guerinière, insisted that collection was necessary for a cavalry-horse or, indeed, any horse required to go at various gaits across country. A horse, they insisted, would balance himself and place himself for a jump much better, if it had been balanced and suppled in early training.

At Fort Riley, Colonel Chamberlin, who had studied both at Tor di Quinto and at Saumur, approved generally of Italian methods and wrote that collection was, in an unskilled hand, 'a razor in the paw of a monkey'. But, rather obscurely, he believed in developing a horse's 'natural collection', his ability to adjust his balance to changes in terrain, without precisely explaining what he meant. He rewrote *The American Manual of Horsemanship and Horsemastership* and had an influence on American riding second only to that of Vladimir Littauer, who set up the 'Boots and Saddles Riding School' in New York in the 1920s. The fruit of their teaching was the success of Americans in international competitions between the wars.

Although universally accepting the logic of the rider conforming to the horse's centre of gravity, instead of vice versa, in jumping, the experts differed on the need for collection, the need to reinforce with leg-aids the forward impulse, and the need to place a horse for a jump and give him the office. The Italians denied all three. But Colonel McTaggart, for instance, one of the few British theorists and an early convert to the forward seat taught that 'we should get the horse so well flexed (by collected

Eddie Arcaro on Assault winning the Butler Handicap

Princess Hamai playing polo

schooling) that even on the approach to the fence he will yield to the slightest touch of the rein'. The rider then decides on the pace, the stride, and the take-off. This was the teaching of Weedon and Saugur.

A typical French view, quoted from Jean Froissard's *Equitation*, is that collected dressage, 'far from harming the schooling over the fences, will make its first steps easier, for successful jumping requires the very same kind of frankness, obedience, and keenness as the other disciplines'. In jumping, 'use your legs energetically, mainly during the last few strides'. Benoist-Gironière, an officer of Spahis and member of the Cadre Noir, taught his horses to flex and insisted that a horse should

In the
Punjabi Hills

The old seat can still be seen in the
hunting field today . . .

jump to his rider's timing, not his own. Henry Wynmaelen, born in Holland but a
M.F.H. in England, equally interested in dressage and in hunting, wrote that 'every
horse, to be really effective for any purpose above the very limited standard of plain
utility, needs at least a modicum of dressage, and some require a good deal'.

    Swedish and German horsemen would emphatically agree. They look back on a
long history and tradition of educated riding based on collection, control, discipline.
The Swedes have, I believe, won more awards in international dressage than any

. . . as well as the new

other nation, and naturally stress the importance of this both as an art in itself and as a necessary preparation for jumping and cross-country work. The Germans, too, characteristically believe that a horse should be above all things obedient, doing what the rider orders when and how the rider commands. All over West Germany are public jumping-rings, with obstacles carefully graded from novice to expert, and young riders and horses are brought on under proper supervision. German books on equitation are superlogical and scientific. Some foreigners – Vladimir Littauer, for example – criticize German equitation for being too machine-like, emphatically a science, not an art. But the results are undeniably impressive, and the Germans are always most formidable competitors in any international event. At a recent Dublin Horse Show it was a matter of common comment that the horses of the German team, which won the highest jumping award, went more kindly than others and seemed to enjoy jumping more. All, I was told, had had a thorough training in dressage. Owing to the presence in Germany of British troops under the NATO alliance, British riders have in recent years learned a good deal from the Germans of the science of equitation.

The partial victory of Caprilli-ism has coincided with an enormous increase in pleasure-riding. Forty years ago it might have been predicted with some confidence

Yang kusi-fu mounting

262

Perfection again – in Ireland

ever growing, the countryside ever shrinking, good hunting country is becoming more and more scarce and more and more crowded. There is still wonderful sport to be had, and I ask for no better fun than a good day with hounds: but with regret I must confess that the next generation of horsemen will probably have to seek their sport in other ways.

Show-jumping, event riding, cross-country riding by a reconnoitred route over specially prepared jumps, following perhaps a drag-line – these are sure eventually to replace hunting as we know it, though I hope they will not do so in my time. Even now the vast majority of riders have their fun, and their jumping which is what they most like, off the hunting-field.

For these people the Italian system is a godsend. It is easily understood and, though not easily practised, is certainly no more difficult than the accurate placing of a horse and 'giving him the office' for a jump.

But ironically the very success of the Italian school has, in recent years, produced a reaction against it. Competition has steadily raised the height of international show-jumps and exaggerated the complexity of the course to a degree which Caprilli never envisaged. In 1912 the biggest jumps in international events were about four foot six inches: now they are up to six foot, and placed in far more tricky combinations. Most top-class show-jumpers believe that it is no longer possible to leave everything to the horse, simply steering him in the right direction, imparting the necessary

Queen Victoria

impulsion, and not interfering while he does the rest. This may suffice for ordinary courses, but international competition requires such prior planning by the rider, who has, of course, carefully reconnoitred the course, that he must accept responsibility for placing the horse, giving him the office – tell him not merely what to do, but how to do it.

Meanwhile, as though Caprilli had never existed, the Spanish Riding School in Vienna continues calmly schooling and riding its beautiful white Lippizaner stallions exactly according to the principle of de la Guerinière. The latter's aim, wrote Alois Podhajsky, most famous and lucid exponent of the School's teaching, 'was to obtain by systematic work a riding-horse that was quiet, supple, and obedient, pleasant in his movements and comfortable for his rider. These are the requirements for any school-horse, hunter or charger, and the methods employed by this famous riding-master have been preserved at the Spanish Riding School.'

266

Queen Maria Luisa on el Marcial

Show jumping – a German competitor at
Hickstead

Training is in three phases: 'riding straight forward' with a natural carriage on straight lines at ordinary paces in free forward movement; 'the campaign school', riding the horse in greater collection with regularity, suppleness, and proficiency, as well as the less ordinary paces; High School and 'airs above the ground'.

The first phase is, of course, common to all schools of equitation. It takes about a year.

In the second phase collection becomes necessary to make the hind-quarters carry a greater proportion of the combined weight of horse and rider (i.e. to bring the horse's centre of gravity back towards the rider's), to improve balance, develop the paces, and establish confidence. It is obtained by 'pushing the hind-quarters towards the reins, which remain applied', by pushing forward, not by pulling back. It is the pushing, not the pulling, which make a horse raise and bend at the poll, but only when the horse has been properly suppled by work in hand, on the longe, in long-reins, and under a rider. The horse is taught to turn and circle on a single track, hind-feet following exactly in the tracks of the forefeet; to describe a *volte* or exact circle of six yards diameter; to change reins within the circle; to start work at a canter. He will then be ready for lateral work – shoulder in, travers head to wall, renvers tail to wall, half pass and full pass, and turning on the haunches.

This second phase, or 'Campaign School' will probably take another year. Only when it has been completed can a horse progress to the High School. Work at a canter becomes more important, including the 'flying change of leading leg' and the counter-canter (centring on a circle with the outer leg leading). The horse is introduced to unusual gaits and turns – pirouettes, *passades*, passages, *piaffes*. Finally, after a third year's training, a few gifted horses graduate with the spectacular 'airs above the ground' – the *ballotade*, *croupade*, and *capriole*.

The rider's is the classical position of de la Guerinière – upright, the small of the back braced, sitting well down in the centre of the saddle with fairly long stirrup-leathers, and lower leg slightly behind the vertical.

Nearly everyone would agree that the preservation of classical equitation, for those who delight in it, is in itself a worthwhile object. No one who has seen a performance of the Spanish Riding School would be likely to dispute that view. Where people disagree is on the relevance of this classical equitation to cross-country riding and jumping.

Littauer, for instance, says it has no relevance whatsoever, but is still worth cultivating for its own sake, as a beautiful and elegant accomplishment. But others argue, like Gervase Markham and Alois Podhajsky, that classical equitation, by making a horse 'quiet, supple, and obedient', produces one that is a delight to ride and apt for any work he may be called upon to do, in the hunting-field, the cross-country test, the show-jumping arena or, for that matter, on the battle-field. Colonel Podhajsky himself hunted and won international jumping competitions on his best Lippizaner High School horse, thereby proving at least that the most advanced High School training is not, as the Caprilli-ists insisted, inconsistent with cross-country and jumping ability: they can be combined, at least by superb horsemen – it being observed that the riders of the Spanish School are full-time professionals with many years' instruction and experience behind them.

The High School riding of the Spanish Riding School and even much of the Campaign School, is of a different standard altogether to dressage tests in Combined Training, but round these, too, the same argument revolves. Some like Littauer say that Combined Training produces a jack-of-all-trades and that in the twentieth century equitation, like everything else, should be more specialized. Others maintain that Combined Training is the best training, and the three-day event the best test, of a horse ever devised.

Nothing is more remarkable in equitation than the extraordinary improvement

Two riders by Renoir

Opposite
Laetitia, Lady Lade,
who in the 1780–90s was
'famous alike for her
horsemanship and her
foul language'

in children's riding over the past forty years. This is due almost entirely to the Pony Club. Before this existed, children could be taught at considerable expense in riding-schools with qualified instructors; but, far more commonly, were never really taught at all, but picked up what they could from parents, grooms, and riding-stable proprietors who were generally quite unqualified to teach. Now they can get, at a very low cost, standardised teaching from instructors who may not all have the technical instructors' qualification, but understand the theory and practice of modern riding and devote an enormous amount of time and trouble to this.

Besides, from an early age children become accustomed to performing in public, at little Pony Club gymkhanas, so that they are not paralyzed by stage-fright at the prospect of show-jumping before a crowd. The gymkhana games, too, bending races,

270

musical poles, 'Chase-me-Charlie' – all accustom children to controlling their ponies at speed, using their legs, not hanging on with their hands.

I am quite certain that, as a result of the Pony Club, teenage children and men and women under forty ride a great deal better, on the average, than their elders, among whom I must regrettably number myself.

9

Women Riders

The earliest women riders must generally have ridden astride, just like men, though for ladies of importance and *embonpoint* the Assyrians seem to have provided a sort of chair in which they sat side-saddle, screened from the sun by a wicker-work hood. As a rule, however, women neither hunted nor rode to war, so did not need to ride very vigorously. An exception may have been the semi-legendary Sauromatians who lived beyond the Black Sea and may have been the Amazons of Greek mythology: their young women are said to have fought alongside the men, and a girl might not marry until she had killed a man in battle. But this is legend, not history, and from legend, too, came the Valkyries, women riders of the far north. Scythian and Sarmatian women did not customarily ride. Greek and Roman ladies sometimes did, and are reproved in the second century A.D. for hunting.

During the Middle Ages the women of Asia without exception rode astride, and even played polo. But in Europe a woman who wanted merely to travel on horseback sat sideways, sometimes by herself and sometimes pillion behind a man. Clearly riding thus she could hardly go out of a walk, so if she wanted, like Joan of Arc, to fight or to go well to hounds, she must ride astride. It seems, however, that few did so: Bertrandon de la Brocquière's observations on the Princess of Constantinople riding cross-saddle suggest that it was a daring feat, not perhaps quite respectable.

However, medieval cross-saddle riders certainly included that hard rider to hounds, Diane de Poitiers, whose spartan habit it was to ride for three hours before dawn and then have a bath before retiring to bed with her current royal lover. In the world of the Renaissance and later the practice, for those women who really wanted to 'go' with hounds, continued. The Spanish Princess Juana, mother of the Emperor Charles V, when she married an Austrian, astounded her in-laws by riding *à la gineta*. Some hard-riding Suffolk ladies were criticized for their 'great vain of wearing breeches' in order to ride astride; and the Duchesse de Mazarin, fleeing from a dull husband to the accommodating arms of Charles II, habitually rode in 'cavalier's' costume. But this was all rather deplorable, and condemned by conventional Europe.

The convention can be attributed to female modesty and female physique. Modesty varies from one generation to the next. Mini-skirts are now conventional but topless dresses are viewed with some disfavour; our ancestresses at various times thought it perfectly proper to display, on formal occasions, generous segments of their breasts, but always concealed their 'understandings'. Moreover, the rounded contours of females were considered inelegant when riding astride: put bluntly, their bottoms were too big.

In days when men rode straight-legged, their weight taken not on the seat but

Women played polo in both ancient China and
Persia

(in Newcastle's word) on the 'twist', for a lady to ride astride might be not merely
indelicate but injurious; even among cavalry-troopers the sugar-tongs seat was
responsible for many a rupture.

It was not thought that women – or, at any rate, ladies – had enough strength in
their thighs to maintain themselves safely in an ordinary man's saddle when a horse
was playing up in any way, jumping or galloping across country.

These considerations, particularly that of delicacy, were taken seriously by the

Nomad chastising his horse

Island Race. John Adams, writing in 1805, noted that 'foreign ladies ride astride like gentlemen, but though their seat may not be sufficiently strong to contend with violent plunging horses, I can assure them it is perfectly secure to ride such horses as are proper to put them on'.

But by the 1830s it was exceptional even abroad for ladies to ride astride. One exception was Marie du Plessis, the 'Lady of the Camellias', who used to be seen in the Forest of Saint-Germain in a very fetching ensemble, with buckskin breeches, a maroon cashmere cape, a golden-knobbed whip and, no doubt, the camellia which was her professional advertisement. She galloped, we are told, at full speed, 'like a Centaurese'. 'Intrepid Amazon!' enthused one of her many admirers. 'How lovely was she, caracoling in the woods! The wind was less light, and less swift the swallow!' One would like to record that her enigmatic compatriot and contemporary, George Sand, did likewise; but perhaps she was too conscious of what Saint-Beuve described as the biggest behind he had ever seen.

Another nineteenth-century female cross-saddle rider was Kate Kelly, whose brother Ned, the 'iron-clad bushranger', used her as a sort of despatch-rider and contact-girl with his agents in the settlements. But these were in a very small minority. In 1893 Alice Hayes, wife of the famous horse-breaker and vet, a noted horsewoman in her own right, put the matter in a nutshell.

'Journalists short of copy and women anxious for notoriety periodically start the notion that ladies should adopt a man's saddle in preference to their own one. Anyone who takes up this idea seriously must be either mad or totally ignorant. In the first place, a woman's appearance in a cross-saddle would be most ungraceful. On this point I need not go into particulars; but may draw attention to the fact that even men who have broad hips never look well in a saddle. Secondly, riding *à califourchon* would be injurious to the health of any ordinary woman who aspired to going out of a walk. . . . Thirdly, the shape of a woman's limbs are unsuited to cross-saddle riding, which requires length from hip to knee, flat muscles, and a slight inclination to bow-legs. . . . I am aware that Oriental women ride astride; but they very rarely (I have never seen any of them voluntarily do so) go out of a walk. Their saddles are made something after the pattern of an easy chair, and their stirrups are very short; so that their seat is altogether different to what it would be in an English hunting-saddle.' So that was that.

The side-saddle – as opposed simply to sitting sideways on a man's saddle or pad – seems to have been invented in the early sixteenth century, reputedly by Catherine de Medici. She discovered that it was safer than sitting sideways, and more seemly than sitting astride, to hook her right knee round the high pommel of a man's saddle. It was an obvious development to move the pommel to a more convenient place – a few inches to the left of the centre-line – and to curve it round so as to hold the rider's leg in a secure and comfortable grip.

This was the side-saddle still in use at the beginning of the nineteenth century, with a single pommel or crutch over which, in the words of John Adams, the rider hooked her right leg 'the knee over the pommel and the leg kept back, with the toe raised'. The left leg 'is nearly, if not wholly, useless; for though a stirrup is placed on

Stallion
chastising
his groom

The Amazons
rode astride . . .

the foot, the only use I know it to be of, is to ease the leg a little, which, for want of practise, might ache by dangling and suspension; and I can assure the ladies the deprivation of that limb will be no detriment to their riding. . . . But where ladies become great proficients in horsemanship, this leg may be employed to aid on the near side, and the whip on the off.'

Ladies could, in such a saddle, ride across country so long as the going was fairly good, and even take occasional small jumps. It was probably used by such hunting women as Queen Elizabeth, and Louis XIV's sister-in-law, 'Madame', who used to hunt for hours a day, pounding along the forest rides 'looking like an enormous blonde policeman'. Pope describes Queen Anne's maids of honour hunting 'over hedges and ditches on borrowed hacks, and coming home in the heat of the day with a fever, and what is a hundred times worse a red mark on the forehead from an uneasy hat. All this may qualify them to make excellent wives for foxhunters and bear abundance of ruddy-complexioned children, but is highly disagreeable to many.'

On some saddles a second crutch was added, to the right of the centre-line. Between these two crutches the right leg was held fairly firmly; but they gave no great help in jumping, and might, in case of a fall, prevent the rider from being thrown clear of the horse. So long as the pace was fairly slow and jumps small and infrequent, this side-saddle served well enough. But by the end of the eighteenth century it was plainly inadequate for hunting over a good country. It was a professional huntsman, Thomas Oldaker, compelled by an injury to ride side-saddle, who made an invention which transformed side-saddle riding – the 'leaping-head'.

The leaping-head is a downward-curving horn fitted to the saddle below the upper crutch: it curls over, and holds in place, the rider's left thigh. In the crudest terms, with no consideration of style or balance, the rider in any crisis can stay in the plate by gripping downwards with her right leg against the upper crutch, and upwards with her left leg against the leaping-head. This gives nervous riders a sense of great safety, though Samuel Wayte, somewhat equivocally warned his fair readers, '*at all times trust to your reins for security in cases of danger*, instead of grasping the pommel of your saddle'. In some American saddles the rider was further secured by the off-side edge of the seat being turned up, like the rim of a saucer. About the mid nineteenth century the third crutch, on the off-side, was discarded.

The trouble with the side-saddle is that it and the rider are fundamentally un-balanced, both crutches and both rider's legs being on the near-side. The cross-saddle rider's weight is automatically on the horse's spine, since one leg hangs down

but the goddesses
. . . side-saddle

on each side: the rider does not need to worry about centring his weight laterally, but concerns himself only with the longitudinal distribution of his weight, fore and aft. But the side-saddle rider must get laterally balanced as well, or her horse will develop a sore back from the leftwards drag of the saddle. Here is the great problem in side-saddle riding, getting and keeping the rider's weight, whether it be forward or back, directly over the horse's spine.

So in order to compensate for the extra weight on the near-side, the rider has consciously to put most of her weight on the right buttock and thigh. In order to keep her centre of gravity directly over the horse's spine at all paces, and when jumping, she must keep her body and shoulders facing square to the front, not facing sideways like women riders in earlier times. The hips, too, should be as square to the front as the rider's build allows. The great aim of the side-saddle rider is to attain a 'square seat'.

Books on the subject, old and new, devote a great deal of attention to this point. 'She should put as much of her weight as she can on her right leg, so as to avoid leaning on the stirrup. By keeping her weight on the right side of the body, she will be able to sit in a nice square position, and her right shoulder will not come unduly forward. The fact of placing the weight on the right leg will also put the weight in the centre of the saddle, and will thus tend to keep both saddle and rider in the proper place. Ladies learning to ride cannot attach too much importance to this point.' So

Queen Christina
arriving in Paris

Watering horses in a moonlit garden

wrote Mrs Hayes in 1893. Mrs Archer Houblon, a modern side-saddle expert, writing under the influence of Caprilli, says, 'The right thigh, on which nearly the whole of the rider's weight is borne, lies along the top of the saddle and should cross the horse's backbone just behind the withers, the point at which it is most comfortable for him to carry weight. . . . Her weight should be borne on the right thigh in such a way that, though it is actually distributed all along the thigh from the seat bone forward, yet she *feels* that the major part is gathered together over the spot where her thigh crosses the horse's backbone. She should draw the weight off her left seat bone forward and to the left until she has the impression that her centre of gravity is over the desired spot.' Mrs Archer Houblon suggests that the beginner will find it helpful to imagine that there is a tintack sticking up on the left side of the seat of the saddle, and that she must avoid sitting down on it.

Victorian hunting women sat well down and back in the saddle, the upper crutch supporting their right thigh just behind the knee, with the lower part of the leg slanting forward along the horse's shoulder, the toe pointing downward lest it make an unsightly bump in the long skirt. The left foot rested in a stirrup, the leather being shortened until the thigh, a few inches behind the knee, was in contact with the underside of the leaping-head, while the lower leg hung slightly behind the vertical.

A 14th-century elopement

To increase the grip, the rider pressed upwards and inwards against the leaping-head with her left thigh, downwards against the upper crutch with her right thigh, at the same time drawing back her right foot.

This gave her a position of great power and security. Captain Hayes, as an exhibition of equestrian skill, often put up his wife on buck-jumpers, and noted that 'if a lady knows how to sit in her side-saddle properly, her seat will be far stronger than that of any man in a hunting saddle'. So a lady was less likely than a man to be thrown; but if her horse were to fall, she was more likely to be rolled upon, not flung clear, which caused many a man to agree with 'The Irish R.M.' that he would rather adhere to the horns of a charging bull than to the crutches of a side-saddle.

French ladies, practising *haute école*, rode rather differently, with a long stirrup-leather, a left leg almost straight, 'not', as Mrs Hayes remarked, 'sitting *down* in the saddle, but merely balancing herself as if by the aid of the stirrup'. The rider could not raise her left leg to grip the leaping-head: or, if she did so, she would lose her stirrup: nor could she 'post' to the trot. The long leather and straight leg was, it seems, required so that the spur could be used in the *airs de manège*. 'It need not be wondered at', wrote Mrs Hayes, 'that these ladies are distinguished neither by their strength of seat, nor by their power of control over "rough" horses. Their grace and skill in the manège on well-trained horses are, however, worthy of all admiration.'

Nor did Mrs Power O'Donoghue think much of the *haute école*. 'Teachers of the *haute école* style of riding may possibly have told you wonders about military horsemanship, and how the movements of an animal may be regulated by certain subtle touches of the thumb or little finger. I must candidly say that I don't believe a word of their efficiency for general purpose riding. . . . Put a girl, for instance, on a high-mettled hunter, loop the reins over the fingers of her left hand only – as fashionable riding-masters do in schools – give her the whip, pointed upwards (another general symptom of defective teaching) in her right hand, and then send her out, not over the smooth grass fields and through the convenient gates of beautiful Leicestershire, where, a few years ago, a whole day's hunting might be had without having to jump a single fence, but away over the rugged plough and trying ridge-and-furrow which take the wind out of our Irish hunters. The high stone walls of Galway's hunting-fields are excellent tests of skill; so are the five-barred gates of Meath and Carlow, and the yawning chasms – sixteen feet wide and twenty deep – at which we in this hapless yet lovely old country have to steady our horses when coming up, and support them when over, or else lie gasping at the bottom, with broken ribs and damaged noses, and dreadful saddle-pommels making havoc of our frames at every struggle of our

A medieval lady of
quality sets out

281

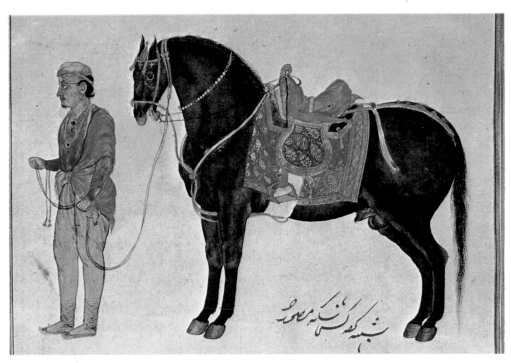

Sais

engulfed and terrified steeds. Send, I say, a *haute école* rider out over Irish hunting-grounds, and see what good she can accomplish with the little finger of the left hand!'

Miss Lucy Quinn, one of the best ladies to hounds in County Tipperary, wrote, 'Over a big Irish country a horse has to be steadied at his banks, but he must make up the lost distance between the fences; for no horse can live with foxhounds unless he is going at fully half racing speed, and is able to maintain that pace. When a lady sets her horse going, she shall place her hands, both of them on the reins well apart and as low as they can go; and she should hold her horse well together. The faster he goes, the more shall she pull him into her at each stride. The left leg should keep up a steady pressure, while the right takes a strong grip of the upper crutch. The horse will then feel that she means going.' A lady, like a man, on coming into a fence should 'sit well into her saddle and bring the upper part of her body to the rear by the play of her hips'.

I may, in the preceding pages, have given the impression that women habitually hunted throughout the nineteenth century. This was not so. Indeed they probably hunted more in earlier days. Apart from Diana, virgin goddess of hunting, several women are known to have hunted their own hounds. There was 'the Reverend and Pious Lady Mary de Boxham', Abbess of Barking, permitted by Henry III to 'have her dogs to chase hares and foxes'. The first authentic female M.F.H. in modern times was the Countess of Salisbury, 'Old Sarum', a formidable figure who hunted

282

Sais

her own pack of foxhounds from 1777 to 1812. But during the Golden Age of fox-hunting, say from 1800 to 1850, hounds ran so fast and bullfinchers were so prevalent that ladies riding in long, flowing habits were generally daunted.

John Adams in 1805 noted that it was no longer considered bold, masculine, and indelicate for ladies to 'enjoy a recreation which invigorates the body, amuses the mind, gratifies the eye, and contributes so much to the felicity of the gentlemen who are honoured with the care and attendance of our fair countrywomen in these salutary exercises'. A few years later Samuel Wayte impressed upon his fair reader 'that the *elegant* and accomplished *equestrian* becomes the *equally graceful* pedestrian, from the improved carriage consequent upon the former accomplishment. . . . We often see the most perfect figure rendered quite commonplace by a bad carriage and a shuffling gait. This can be entirely overcome by attention to the following directions, which apply equally to both accomplishments, walking and riding: Keep the bust and head erect, the shoulders well thrown back, and allow the motive power to proceed *alone* from the hips. Perseverance in these slight directions will soon give the required graceful and healthy carriage.'

So women rode mainly for their health, for their figures, and to give pleasure to gentlemen. In the hunting-field, for the first part of the century, they were not altogether welcome. In Surtees's novels very few women hunt, though he liked to see them at meets where they were as much in their place as out of it 'tearing across country'. The general feeling was that ladies were 'more in their element in the

The trooper's devoted wife who leapt from childbed on to her horse in order to follow her husband's regiment

drawing-room or in Kensington Gardens'. Those who did follow hounds, however, generally had better hands than men.

From the time when hunting took on its modern form up to about 1860, it was unusual for women to do more than appear at a meet. Actually to follow hounds on horseback across country was considered undeniably fast. The only woman who Surtees depicted as really 'going' was Lucy Glitters, 'beautiful and tolerably virtuous'. One of the few women in real life who actually 'went', and well, too, was the enchanting 'Skittles', most attractive of Victorian courtesans, When the Master's wife compelled him reluctantly to send her home, Skittles observed, 'I don't know why Lady Stamford should object to me. She isn't even the head of our profession: Lady Cardigan is.' She was soon out again.

Perhaps what brought women out in the 1860s and 1870s in increasing numbers was the practice of cutting and laying fences, instead of leaving them as face-scratching, habit-tearing bullfinchers. Some hunting women were aristocrats like the Countess of Warwick, the Prince of Wales's 'darling Daisie'. Most were ordinary hard-riding countrywomen such as Miss Lucy Quinn, Mrs Power O'Donoghue, and Mrs Hayes. The Empress of Austria set a good example. 'Remember,' she told her pilot, 'I don't mind the falls, but I will not scratch my face.'

Dressed and delicately nurtured as they were, they showed astonishing fortitude, for the fair equestrienne's pastime was full of hazards unknown to her husband and brothers. Mounting, for instance, in an ankle-length habit, was a major operation. Without help, it was hardly possible unless the horse could be induced to stand absolutely still beside some real or improvised mounting-block. Ideally, two assistants were required, a groom to hold the horse's head and a gentleman to hold the lady's foot. Mrs Power O'Donoghue gives the detail of the drill.

'Take the reins and whip in your right hand, lay the fingers of it firmly upon the top of the up-pommel – grasping it, in fact; then, with your left hand, gather the skirt away from your left foot and place this latter in the hand of your assistant, bending your knee as you do so. When you feel that his palm is firmly supporting the sole of your foot, take your left hand from your habit-skirt and place it on his left shoulder – he being in a slightly stooping position at the time. Then give the signal: any pre-arranged word will do – "Ready!" "Go ahead!" "Now!" or, in short, anything you may choose to fix. As you say the word, straighten your knee and make a slight spring upward, your cavalier at the same time raising himself to an erect position without letting his hand drop in the very smallest degree. By this arrangement you will reach the saddle with comfort and expertness. . . . If your skirt is properly cut, you will have no difficulty in arranging it comfortably over your right knee, when the latter has been placed in position, and you should then lift yourself slightly, and smooth the seat of the skirt from right to left with the left hand.' During this lengthy process

According to *Breviaire d'Amour* at less serious medieval tournaments the ladies of easier virtue would sometimes don the knights' armour and ride round on their horses

Chinese groom catching
his horse

the horse must, of course, stand perfectly still; 'otherwise the consequences may be very disastrous'.

One would have thought that dismounting would be easy enough, but this, too, as Samuel Wayte pointed out, had its perils. 'There is a little tact necessary for a lady in dismounting, in order that she may avoid the inelegance and *exposé* attendant upon (as it were) being lifted from her saddle in a groom's arms – which cannot be done without a liability to accident, and at the same time giving licence to a vulgar class who are sure to offer their *vulgar comments* amongst their associates.'

Ladies were advised by Mrs Power O'Donoghue on no account to 'go out *alone* for the purpose of learning, however high-couraged you may be. Always enlist the services of a suitable companion, or attendant, but remember that if the latter is a servant – even though his service may be of many years' standing – you are not on any account to permit him to give you so much as the very smallest hint on any subject connected with equitation. Coachmen know nothing at all about riding; and grooms, as a rule, very little, a fact that is every day testified by their heavy hands and awkward gait on horseback.'

Many were the sartorial pitfalls in the fair equestrienne's path. Up to about the mid nineteenth century ladies rode in habits six feet long and four yards in width which, like Jane Eyre's, 'almost swept the ground' and added to the hazards of going out of a trot since a galloping horse could easily tread on the trailing hem. Then habits were shortened into 'safety skirts' which, if a lady fell, would come off her so that she could not be dragged. But at least one lady, wearing this 'fig leaf', was cut by the county for 'dressing indecently'. Finally, the habit settled into a rational garment, of heavy Melton cloth, no longer than was necessary to cover the rider's left ankle. 'Safety skirts' were not considered necessary as a well-cut habit would not adhere to the crutches if the wearer was thrown.

Petticoats on horseback were deprecated. Indeed, they were unnecessary, for under her habit the lady wore either breeches and patent leather riding-boots, or riding-trousers fitting over wellingtons. Some lady riders wore long flannel combinations, but they were apt to twist and ruck up uncomfortably. For a moderate rider, three hats were sufficient: 'a silk one, which I prefer low-crowned; a jerry, or

286

melon-shaped; and a soft felt'. (In the tropics, of course, a solar topee or double terai was a necessary precaution against sunstroke.) The corset should fit closely, without being too tight, and must be of the best quality. 'I believe that a great many ladies who are not by any means naturally stout or clumsy are made to appear so by wearing cheap or ill-fitting corsets; while, on the other hand, figures that are inclined to *embonpoint* can, with the assistance of a judicious and capable staymaker, be invested with an appearance of grace and slimness that is not by nature their own. To expect a habit-cutter to fit a bodice over a seven and sixpenny corset, with two long bones, bald and unsoftened, sticking up at the top of the back, and front steels long and obtrusive, is as great a piece of injustice as to expect an artist to paint a picture with broken brushes.'

In mid-century habits were weighted with shot at the hem, to keep them down. By the time Mrs Power O'Donoghue was leaping huge Irish banks and drains twenty foot deep, this had gone out of fashion, but she suggested that for 'fair equestrians who are unduly nervous of exposing even the smallest portion of understanding, a good plan is to have a band of broad elastic affixed to the inside of the skirt, in such a position as to enable the toe of the right foot to be thrust through it, while a similar band does duty for the left'. But a well-tailored habit of heavy material, cut to the rider's measure as she sat in a saddle in the tailor's shop, should not require such devices.

Breeches and riding-trousers should be of stockinet, deerskin, or chamois. 'The

The cob

lady should go to some competent breeches-maker who has a specially trained woman to take the measurements. When trying on, there is no objection to the aid of a man; although it would be quite out of the question to permit him to measure one.' They had, of course, to be cut differently for each leg. Long, close-fitting drawers of tricot or elastic silk might with advantage be worn beneath them.

Between the wars side-saddle riders had to adapt themselves to the forward seat in jumping. This was not altogether easy, for the side-saddle rider tended to sit rather more back than the cross-saddle rider; and, with her left leg pressed under the leaping-head, her right round the upper crutch, it was almost impossible for her to get her centre of gravity forward over the horse's withers.

Singularly enough, the difficulty was overcome by *lengthening* the stirrup-leather.* (Cross-saddle riders, in adopting the forward seat, shortened it.) This brought the rider's left thigh out from the clutches of the leaping-head, enabling her to sit further forward in the saddle and to lean forward, getting her bottom almost off the saddle, to gallop and jump. She could not adopt quite an Italian cross-saddle forward position, but could get pretty near it.

She was now kept in the saddle by factors more subtle than the crude pincer-action of the legs gripping the saddle-horns. First, of course, by balance. But balance was not always enough: it must sometimes be supplemented by grip. On such occasions the left leg (its thigh at an angle of about forty-five degrees, its lower part hanging just behind the vertical with toe up and feet down) pressed not upwards against the leaping-head, but inwards against the saddle-flap. The right leg (resting on the crutch well above the knees, the lower leg vertical) pressed from knee to ankle to the right against the saddle-flap, and with the thigh to the left against the crutch. Finally, for an emergency such as a bucking horse or a mistimed jump, there was what Mrs Archer Houblon called the 'reserve grip' of the left thigh against the leaping-head. This is the side-saddle seat, adapted as much as possible to the ideas introduced by Caprilli.

Another drawback in the side-saddle is that the leg-aids are one-sided. It is perfectly true, that, as the Irishman observed, 'Sure, if one side of a horse goes forward, the other must too.' But there is rather more to it than that. The leg-aids not merely create forward impulsion, but move a horse laterally, and prevent his quarters swinging out in a turn or circle. The side-saddle rider's left leg is there to aid in lateral movements and turns to the right, but what about lateral movements and turns to the left? To some degree a touch of the whip can be used instead of the right leg-aid, but this is not satisfactory for its feel is entirely different. A good side-saddle rider used what is called the 'indirect rein of opposition', applied just behind the withers, to control the movement of the horse's quarters. Thus the right rein drawn back and to the left behind the horse's withers moves his quarters to the left if a passage or half-pass is required, or prevents his quarters from swinging out to the right in a circle or turn to the left.

The use of the 'indirect rein of opposition' is one of the higher flights of cross-

* This is vehemently denied by Major Piero Santini; but the drawings in his own book, compared to the drawings in Mrs Hayes's book, refute him.

saddle riding, used only in dressage because in all other occasions it is easier, if less artistic, to use the leg; but it is of more value to the side-saddle rider who, so to speak, has no right leg. Its use requires considerable skill. In unskilled hands, combined with pressure of the left leg to maintain the forward impulse, it may bring a horse to a perplexed standstill, not knowing where the devil he is supposed to go.

Clearly not every horse, trained to a cross-saddle, would go in a side-saddle: many did not understand the aids, felt uncomfortable and expressed very forcibly their disapprobation of the 'balance-strap', a sort of extra girth, sometimes dispensed with, to keep the rear of the saddle in place. The inevitable leftward drag of the side-saddle made its correct fitting to the horse far more important than with the cross-saddle: side-saddles, my mother tells me, were constantly being sent away to be re-stuffed, lest they rub a sore, generally to the right of the spine behind the withers. They were also, owing to the protruding horns, more liable to breakage than cross-saddles. Furthermore, they had to be fitted to the individual rider: a saddle with crutches placed to suit a woman with short thighs would not fit one with long thighs. The position of the leaping-head could be adjusted with a screw, but most women who rode a lot preferred always to use their own saddles – which might not fit a strange horse.

This caused considerable difficulties in travelling. My mother and grandmother, for instance, who rode for thousands of miles in Mexico, the United States, India, China, and Japan during the early years of this century found that their saddles seldom fitted local horses, who never understood these lop-sided contraptions. So they took to riding astride, the proprieties preserved by ankle-length divided skirts.

She found in Jodhpur, where they took equitation very seriously, that side-saddles were not allowed on any of the Maharajah's horses. At the same time Hanut Singh and his brother, then sixteen- and fifteen-year-old boys but already showing promise of that wonderful horsemanship which was to make them international polo-players, derided her cross-saddle riding, said she knew not the first thing about it, and refused to take her out pig-sticking until she had taken lessons. This was done in the Jodhpur riding-school, at first without reins and without stirrups, like the cavalry recruits. The horse, on a longe, whipped round so quickly that she frequently tumbled off; and, try as she might, she could not obtain early warning, or spot the aids which the instructors gave her horse. Then she was permitted to ride outside, on the polo-ground, galloping down the side-lines, still without stirrups, while the two brothers, one on each side, tried to ride her off the line. After two or three weeks of this, she had a pretty good cross-saddle seat, and was allowed out pig-sticking not carrying a spear herself, but following close behind the heat.

When, however, she came home and started hunting astride, this was considered very eccentric. It was not until after the First World War that cross-saddle riding began to gain popularity with women.

The reason was, undoubtedly, the growing popularity of the forward seat. Not only was it difficult, indeed impossible, to use the true forward seat in a side-saddle, but the shorter leathers introduced by the Italians gave a forward slope to the rider's thighs, which greatly strengthened the seat of the cross-saddle rider. Women who could not develop a strong seat riding long found they could do so riding short.

So the various inconveniences of the side-saddle gradually outweighed its one advantage, the security it gave to a rider who lacked muscular power in the thighs. By mid-century the side-saddle was seldom seen in the hunting-field and, I think (but am open to correction), never in show-jumping or cross-country events. Side-saddle riding is now little more than an elegant and extremely skilful accomplishment, which displays, for instance, Her Majesty the Queen to the best advantage on a ceremonial parade, and for this it is sometimes exploited in the show-ring. Generally it is the older women who use it still; but I know one young woman who always uses a cross-saddle when show-jumping, but prefers a side-saddle when hunting. She goes, and looks, equally well in both.

It is not necessary to write particularly of women riding astride: their technique is exactly the same as that of men. What is of interest, however, is the fact that women on the whole ride better. I am not here writing of top-class international riders, among whom I think a count might show that men predominate; but of the ordinary, run-of-the-mill competitors in local gymkhanas and horse shows, where most of the show-jumpers and cross-country riders, and the best, are women.

In the past the balance was weighted in favour of men by military riding-schools. Women had to pay to be taught, but thousands of young men were positively paid to learn to ride by the very latest methods, whatever these might be, on a great variety of horses. Up to, say, 1939 most of the top-class riders were soldiers. Now that is all over: a few countries maintain military riding establishments, for prestige and competitive purposes, but only a handful of officers and men pass through them, for no one pretends that there is any military value in equitation. Now boys and girls learn on an equal footing, at least in those countries where it is not considered improper for women to take part in sports. In many countries they learn, very cheaply, through the Pony Club, and it is a commonplace that in Pony Club camps girls outnumber boys by three or four to one. Boys, now that the stimulus of the cavalry has been removed, seem to prefer team games or mechanical pursuits. Therefore, far more girls than boys are taught to ride and this is reflected in the hunting-field.

I am inclined to think that another reason for the general superiority of women riders is that women, unable to get their way by physical force, instinctively rely more on patience, or persuasion, on the use of their own and the horse's brain. This pays dividends: women riders are generally, and rightly, believed to have better hands than men.

The only forms of riding in which women do not excel are those which require a good deal of strength, besides skill – polo, for instance, steeplechasing and the rougher rodeo events.

10

The Worship of the Horse

In the minds of men the horse has always held a very special position. This is partly due to the scarcity value of good horses: in Xenophon's time a first-class charger fetched 1,000 drachmae, the equivalent of some £5,000. But there is more to it than price. Cattle, camels, sheep, and goats, even dogs were always the servants, the slaves of man, exploited for what they could do or provide. But the horse was man's comrade, facing equal danger in war; and in peace man's partner – a junior partner, no doubt, but a partner nonetheless, sharing and helping to establish man's mastery over other animals.

This was not always to the horse's advantage, for it made him the most acceptable sacrifice to the gods. White stallions were sacrificed in Greece, Rome, and ancient Persia.

When a Scythian king died, as many as fifty of his best horses were thrown by a rope round their forelegs and pole-axed or strangled by a noose tightened with a stick. They were then buried around him, in places of honour befitting a war-comrade. Sometimes, instead of being buried, they were stuffed and impaled on stakes, mounted in ghastly parade round the tomb by as many young men of the royal bodyguard, similarly strangled. It was a custom singularly extravagant in good horses and young men, but perhaps conducive to diligence in the royal bodyguard who would take a personal interest in their monarch's safety.

The Scythians' art was extraordinarily rich and imaginative, generally based on a horse-motif and lavished particularly on their saddlery. Saddles, saddle-cloths, and bridles were gorgeously dyed and painted, studded, laced, and plated with gold; deeply embossed with fantastic animal-designs – griffons and dragons and lions attacking ibex, deer, and horses, gripping and tearing with tooth, claw, and talon, at victims grotesquely twisted and writhing in fear and pain. Bearded men are shown galloping *ventre à terre* after bulky wild boars, straining at powerful bows to drive their arrows deep into those muscled backs. For life, movement, power, imagination, Scythian art is absolutely astonishing. Chiefs were tattooed with similar designs. All this artistic wealth has been found, preserved by ice, in their tombs.

In their tombs, too, have been found strange objects which can only be described as horses' head-dresses. With a foundation of moulded leather, these fit like a mask over the horse's head and face. Attached to the stiff leather frame are fantastic, towering superstructures of fine chamois-leather and felt, painted and gilded, representing such scenes as a panther springing on a stag, a horned dragon swooping on a griffon which is in turn grappling with a tiger. What was their purpose? No one knows, no one can even now make an informed guess. They could have had no

291

Horse sacrifice in the
Altai

practical use, but those surviving show signs of considerable wear. Perhaps they were
worn in religious or funeral ceremonies.

The practice of sacrificing his favourite horses when a king or great man died
was common also among the X Group people of Nubia. Excavations show that at a
king's burial horses, camels, cattle, sheep, and slaves were all killed so that their souls
could accompany his, and minister to his needs, on his long journey. A sloping passage was dug into the centre of the tomb down which grooms led their horses capari-
soned in the most gorgeous silver-mounted saddles and bridles. When they reached
the end, the grooms were strangled and the horses pole-axed.

The people of northern Europe were not great horsemen in the early years of
the Roman Empire, yet the 'Bog People' of Denmark and the Celtic Cimbri recognized horses as something special. The magnificent silver bowl excavated from a peat-
grave at Gundestrup in Denmark, but probably originating from further east, shows
what seems to be captive enemy foot-soldiers queuing up to be sacrificed and then,
translated into a higher sphere, riding away as cavalrymen.

The Balts in the Dark Ages valued horses far more highly than women. In
Prussia and Lithuania horses were buried upright, saddled and bridled, all ready
to be mounted by the spirits of their owners. Such was the belief in the horse's
resurrection that, in a very poor country, enormous wealth was buried with him –
straps and girths plated with gold and silver, saddle-cloths richly embroidered, even
the bits and stirrup-irons silver-plated. The tails were bound with spiral rings of
bronze. These barbaric rites lasted well into the Middle Ages: in the twelfth century
there were special horse cemeteries in Lithuania; and in the fourteenth century the
Notangians, further south, were often cremated on horseback, or their horses buried
alive, hobbled, blindfold with nosebags full of oats slung round their necks to support
them while their owners rode through the skies to the realm of souls.

Horses were believed to have second sight, enabling them to see ghosts and evil
spirits even in darkness. It is unquestionably true that a horse has good night sight,
and can gallop confidently at night over ground which his rider cannot see; and
many horsemen have had the unnerving experience of a horse suddenly stopping,
looking fixedly into an empty field 'as though he saw a ghost', and absolutely refusing
to move forward until whatever frightened him had moved away. I know an

Australian on whose farm, decades ago, a number of horses had to be slaughtered: no stock-rider can make his horse go quietly past the place of death.

The horse's head, particularly, was believed to have supernatural powers, and was often buried with a Viking in his grave, or hung up near pagan shrines. To put a curse on an enemy, one set up a horse's head on a pole, its muzzle pointing towards him: the baneful affect was enhanced if the mouth was kept open with a stick. (Until well into the fifteenth century poachers in the English Danelaw, having killed a stag in the King's Forests, used to expose its head on a stake, with mouth open, directed towards Westminster.) In the funeral ceremonies of the Crow tribe of American Indians horses' heads and tails were placed on the corner-posts of the burial-platform.

The annual Horse Service on Epsom Downs is generally regarded as simply a device to bring to church people who prefer to go riding on Sunday morning. But perhaps this is a remote, tenuous, atavistic link between all those teenagers quietly sitting their ponies during the service and primitive man who half-worshipped his horse, which was sacrificed as the gift to the gods of his most precious possession, and so that its soul might accompany and support him on the great adventure.

Yet a veneration for the horse has never prevented mankind from exploiting the noble animal. Scythians lived on, with, and by their huge horse herds, eating horse-meat, which they preferred rather 'high', and using dried horse-droppings as fuel on their treeless plains. They drank mares' milk, and to encourage a mare to give it

Man and horse share a grave. Lithuania

down, thrust a bone tube up her vulva and blew vigorously into it – a practice not recommended to the modern owners of nervous and sensitive thoroughbreds. The milk was drunk either fresh, or curdled, or poured into wooden churns which captive slaves, blinded so that they could give no trouble, shook and stirred until the contents fermented and became agreeably intoxicating.

All the nomads of central Asia, the Hun, Mongol, and Tartar hordes, owed their astonishing mobility largely to the fact that they had no bulky grain to carry but lived on, and off, their horses. They pressed raw horse-meat, soaked in brine, under their saddles until the blood had been squeezed out and it was as soft to cut as black bread. This was then kept in a leather bag until needed. De Joinville, on Crusade, came across some Mongol mercenaries and, when these opened their meat-bags, 'had to stop our noses. We could not bear the putrid stench that came out.' The mares' milk, curdled solid, was rolled into little cheesy balls and eaten as an iron-ration.

Probably in the Dark Ages horse-meat was eaten on feast-days over most of western Europe. In Iceland, indeed, where there were herds of semi-wild ponies, it was normal diet until prohibited, along with the exposure of unwanted children, by the Church as a disgusting pagan habit. Thereafter it became a last resort in famine or sieges, consumed only when dogs, cats, rats, and horse-forage were all finished.

But the aversion to horse-meat does not go more than skin-deep: to early settlers on the American Great Plains a juicy mustang steak was as welcome, and much more easily available, than venison or buffalo. Nowadays it is notorious that cheap cuts of meat in continental butcheries are, as often as not, horse.

Horses have always had a special place in the life of the Icelanders, who have their own breed of very sturdy pony. From earliest recorded time the Icelanders have staged stallion-fights, a bloody spectator-sport enlivened by heavy betting and the probability that the owners too would start fighting and a blood-feud thus develop. Each stallion's effort were stimulated by a handler armed with a goad. The stallions tore at one another with their teeth, struck out with forefeet, and sometimes swung round for a full-blooded kick. The most effective coup was to kick out the opponent's teeth, thus leaving him helpless.

Here is a classic description of a stallion fight in *Njal's Saga*.

'The horses were brought together. Gunnar equipped himself for goading as Skarp-Hedin led the horse forward. The horses started fighting, and bit at each other for a long time without needing to be goaded. It was excellent sport. Then Thorgeir and Kol arranged to give their own horse a push when the horses next rushed at each other, to see if Gunnar would be knocked down.

'The horses clashed again, and Thorgeir and Kol threw their weight against their horse's rump; but Gunnar pushed his horse against theirs, and in a flash Thorgeir and Kol were flat on their backs with their horse on top of them. They jumped to their feet and rushed at Gunnar, who side-stepped them and then seized hold of Kol and threw him down so hard that he was knocked senseless. Thorgeir struck Gunnar's horse and one of its eyes came out; Gunnar hit Thorgeir with the goad, and Thorgeir fell senseless.

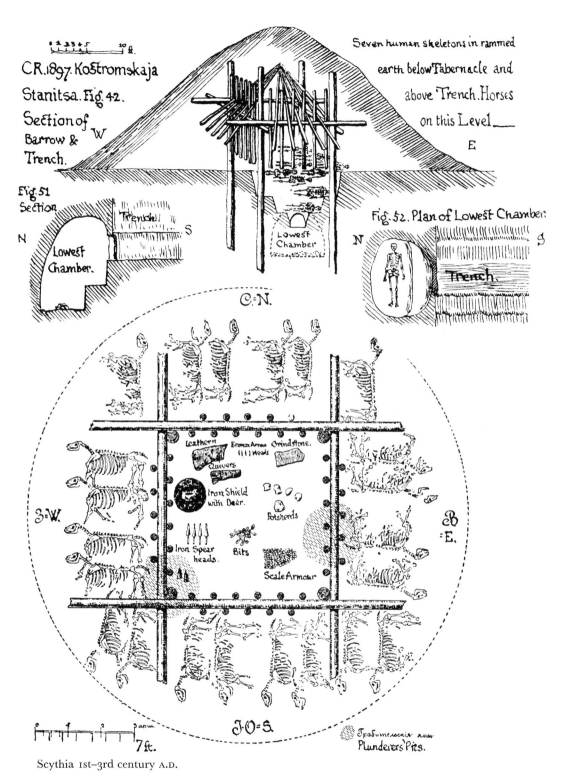

CR.1897. Kostromskaja Stanitsa. Fig. 42. Section of Barrow & Trench.

Seven human skeletons in rammed earth below Tabernacle and above Trench. Horses on this Level ——

W   E

Fig. 51 Section

N

Lowest Chamber.

Trench   S

Lowest Chamber

Fig. 52. Plan of Lowest Chamber.

N   S

Trench.

©.N.

Leathern   Bronze Arrow   Grindstone.
             Heads
Quivers

Iron Shield with Deer.

Potsherds.

Iron Spear heads.   Bits

Scale Armour

З.W.

©Е.

Ю.О.З.

Грабительскіе ямы
Plunderers' Pits.

7 ft.

Scythia 1st–3rd century A.D.

In the Iceland of the Sagas stallions were matched against
each other in a sort of Northern cock-fighting

'Gunnar went over to his stallion. "Kill the horse," he said to Kolskegg. "He shall
not live mutilated."

'Kolskegg killed the horse. At that point Thorgeir got to his feet and seized his
weapons and made for Gunnar: but he was stopped, and people came crowding up.

'Skarp-Hedin said, "I am bored with this scuffling. Men should use proper
weapons to fight each other."'

This fight took place during the eleventh century. The last recorded stallion-
fight was in 1896. Fighting stallions were perfectly quiet to ride and handle, often
being ridden to and from the fight.

In many countries special laws have ensured the safety and well-being of horses.
'A man', said the seventeenth-century statesman, Lord Halifax, 'is not hanged for
stealing horses, but lest horses be stolen.' So horse-thieves were hanged 'lest horses
be stolen' in the American West until less than a century ago; for stealing a man's
horse might be tantamount to murdering him, leaving him in the desert to die.

In the laws of King Athelstane (895–940), and in contemporary Welsh law there
was a fixed scale of compensation for injuries to a borrowed horse – fourpence for a
small rub, eightpence if the 'skin be forced into the flesh', sixteenpence if the 'flesh
be forced to the bone'. Here is a law which might with advantage be revived, due

allowance being made for inflation. It is curious that even people who never ride, and are indeed hostile to equitation, find cruelty to, and neglect of horses peculiarly abhorrent. Athelstane was more horsey than most of our Saxon kings. He received a present of 'running horses' from Hugh Capet, King of France, and thereafter forbade the export of English horses except as royal gifts. Similarly, the Bedouin of the Sahara were forbidden, on pain of death, to sell a well-bred horse, mare, or stallion, to a Christian: if one must let him have an animal, a jade was quite good enough for him.

It is only natural to deck out one's most precious possession, be it wife, mistress, or horse, in the most gorgeous and costly trappings. Scythians, Sarmatians, Cimbri, Balts, and the mysterious people of ancient Nubia devoted a fantastically high proportion of their wealth to horse-furniture. In western Europe, as the tournament grew more spectacular and artificial, the horses were encased in bardings, reaching to the ground, so gorgeous, so heavily embroidered that the horse so encumbered could no more gallop, or even canter, than a lady in hoop-skirts or crinolines. The tournament gave place to the carousel, a sort of pageant in which gentlemen dressed as, say, Turks, or Tritons, or Chinamen paraded and displayed their manège expertise on horses decked out in gold and silver, ostrich-plumes, and heaven only knows what extravagance. It did no harm, except to the family finances, and gave, like amateur theatricals, a lot of pleasure to those who took part. In England there was a reaction against this sort of thing, concurrent with and perhaps influenced by the Puritan revolution: highly decorated horse-furniture came to be regarded as rather vulgar, something to be despised by proper horsemen whose saddlery should be clean, plain, and workmanlike, the leather supple, having a spare, functional beauty but no decoration except, perhaps, for the plume hanging from the cavesson of the cavalry officer's charger. The only occasion in Europe on which modern horses are decked out in plumes and fancy-dress is, significantly, at a funeral.

In general western Europe followed in these matters the English fashion, but in Spain the Puritan influence was minimal, and western American equitation is derived from Spain: so western saddles and bridles are still decorated, silver-mounted, and embossed in a style which has no functional value but looks undeniably handsome, especially in glorious technicolor.

The carousel survives in the 'parade' in western horse shows. A procession of horses, generally Palominos or others of exotic appearance, move round the arena, to appropriate music, at a walk or a prancing, high-stepping, cadenced parade gait. The riders and the horses themselves are decked out in glorious apparel, generally super-western but sometimes, in Arabian horse parades, clad in robes more gorgeous than ever sheikh of the desert wore off the screen. Covering an innocent horse with snake- or zebra-skin trappings, embellishing his bridle with silver, with ribbons, and with flowers, powdering his hooves and quarters with sequins, may seem unrelated to horsemanship, but is fun for those whose tastes lie that way and who can afford it. Singularly enough, the horses seem to enjoy it too.

Long after the horse has ceased to have military value, it is used in many countries, East and West, for ceremonial parades and State occasions in defiance of all considerations of cost, efficiency, and convenience. And rightly!

297

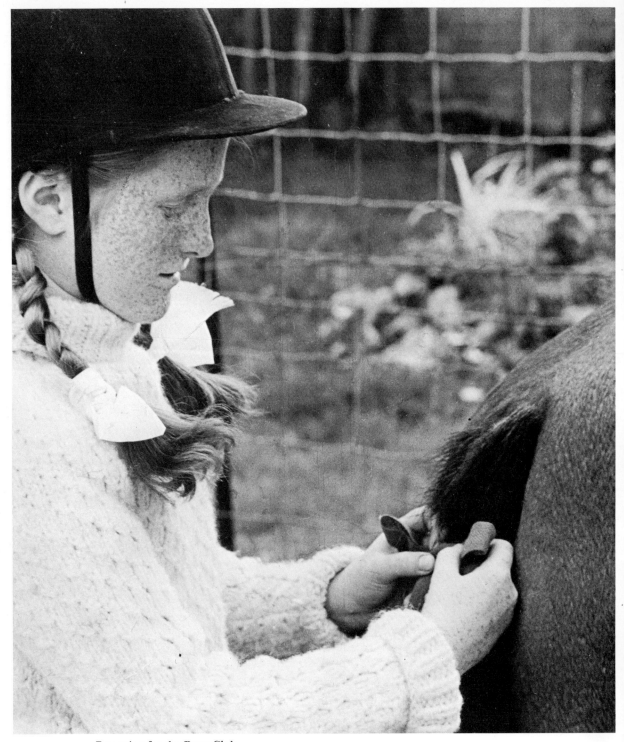

Preparing for the Pony Club

11

Man, the Servant of the Horse

A demigod needs, of course, acolytes to serve him, to see that he is well fed, fit, clean, and beautified, and the horse has never lacked these.

In earliest prehistory we find that in the Atlantis legend horses on the doomed continent enjoyed sweat-baths as part of their grooming.

Very early in the history of riding, an Assyrian bas-relief of 900–800 B.C. shows a cavalry camp with horses feeding, presumably on grain, from mangers, while one is being well strapped, the groom putting plenty of weight behind the brush.

Xenophon had plenty to say about stable management in general and grooming in particular. His groom, like the modern Indian *sais*, used hand-massage (Hindustani *malish*) more than we do. A sort of wooden comb was used for cleaning the coat, and a date-palm fibre rubber for putting a shine on it. Brushes were not used. Much attention was paid to combing and arranging the mane. Persians, also, took great pains over manes, tails, and forelocks. The Greeks attributed to long-maned mares a coquettish vanity which made it necessary to hog their manes before they would consent to be covered by a donkey. Mares were hogged also when the owner was in mourning. Clipping does not seem to have been known to Xenophon, but it was sometimes practised by smart Romans in the days of the Emperor Augustus.

Their horses' feet presented ancients with a very difficult problem. It is perfectly possible to work light horses unshod: I have ridden unshod ponies for thousands of miles on safari in Kenya; but it can only be done in countries where the ground is generally dry and hard, because the dry atmosphere preserves the wall of the hoof and the hard ground wears it down, keeping it to the correct, natural length and shape. In damp countries, on the soft going of north-western Europe, the wall of the hoof softens, and grows too long, especially at the toes where it breaks away and splits: too much strain is placed on the fetlock. It is, therefore, not surprising that, before the invention of the horseshoe, horsemanship and the mounted arm flourished most in the dry countries of the Middle East, North Africa, and central Asia.

So Xenophon, in considering the points of a horse, paid most attention to the feet, 'for just as a house would be useless, even if the upper parts were in excellent condition if the foundations were not properly laid, so too a war-horse, even if his other parts were good, would be valueless if he had bad feet'. What is surprising is that Xenophon totally misunderstood the purpose of the frog. This hard, rubbery pad is designed by nature to absorb the shock of the horse's hoof striking the ground, thus saving it from concussion which can produce inflammation leading to navicular disease and other lamenesses in the foot. Xenophon thought that the frog was simply a weak spot in the sole of the foot, to be preserved so far as possible from contact with the ground. He therefore liked a horse to have 'high' or hollow hooves 'which ring

299

on the ground like a cymbal'. One would expect his horses to suffer a great deal from lamenesses caused by concussion. If they remained sound, it must have been because the hard, stony ground kept the walls of the hoof short and allowed the frog to do its job despite his attempts to prevent this. It was an error that persisted for a very long time: even in the twentieth century conscientious grooms deliberately pared down the frog to keep it off the hard ground.

To harden the feet and keep them in shape, Xenophon floored his 'outer stable' with four or five wagon-loads of smooth, oval stones of about a pound's weight. This seems a good idea. Mucking-out must have been difficult, but with a sufficiency of slaves many difficulties can be overcome.

It is probable, though we do not know for certain, that the Romans had the same ideas about horses' feet.

These served well enough for Mediterranean countries where the summer, season for war and travel, is generally dry. Horses' hooves remain hard, and they can work unshod. But the conquest of Gaul and Britain brought the legions to lands where even in summer the prevailing damp softened hooves. So long as, like ponies in pre-Roman Britain, or wild ponies today, they worked generally on soft ground, that would not much matter, though their feet should be kept in shape by trimming or rasping lest they wear unevenly; but as the Romans covered the country with a net-work of hard metalled roads, the combination of soft hooves and hard roads would soon wear out their horses' feet and bring them to a standstill. So, today, unshod children's ponies work perfectly well on grass, but not on roads.

Greek and Roman horses had for some time been shod for special purposes and short journeys with the 'hipposandal', a sort of boot, iron-soled, laced on to the horse's foot; of which quite a number have been found. It was the height of decadence, extravagance, and ostentation to have hipposandals soled with silver. In the Middle Ages, and indeed right up into modern times, people kept on looking for an alternative to the horseshoe, which requires someone reasonably expert to fit and nail it on. Hipposandals of different kinds were tried right up to 1939, when the French Cavalry School at Saumur tested a version which proved satisfactory except that it had to be removed at least every three days to relieve pressure on the hoof. Their disadvantage was obviously that they were, compared to an ordinary horse-shoe, complicated, expensive, and difficult to fit exactly to an individual horse's hoof. They would wear out just as soon as an ordinary shoe and, as nothing could fix them as firmly as nailed shoes, small stones and gravel would probably work in between the hipposandal and the horse's foot.

We do not know who was the genius who first discovered that iron plates could be fitted red-hot, then nailed when cold, to his hooves without hurting a horse. An astonishing invention! It seems, though one should not be too didactic about this – that the horseshoe was invented in northern Europe; probably the earliest examples yet found are British, dating from the first century A.D. It is right to add that some of the archaeological evidence which dates these early horseshoes from the first century A.D. has been disputed by rival archaeologists who did not discover them. But it does seem undeniable that some horseshoes were found at Camelodunum (Colchester) in a deposit sealed shortly after the Roman Conquest.

Roman hipposandal

There is nothing much wrong with these early shoes; indeed they are very good shoes. The heel is turned to produce calkins which stop a horse slipping, but the calkins are not so long as to throw the horse's weight too much on his toes or take the pressure off his frog. They seem to have worn pretty evenly although, like modern shoes, they have a weakness at the toe causing them, when worn thin, to spread. They do not cover a horse's frog, but allow this to do its proper work.

The early shoe had six nail-holes. They were not fitted with 'clips' to prevent the shoe moving backwards, or sideways, on its seating. Modern shoes generally have clips, but for light horses and ponies they are not really necessary.

It was through grain-feeding in the fertile river valleys and oases of Mesopotamia and Persia that the original tarpan grew into something bigger and stronger. Assyrian cavalry-horses were certainly grain-fed. Scythians saved from their scanty stores of grain, and Chinese emperors imported lucerne-seed, for their best bred horses. From Xenophon himself and from other writers we know that the Greeks fed their horses on oats, barley, hay, clover, and lucerne: these fortunate animals were even given, on special occasions, wine to drink. Xenophon advocated two feeds a day, but the Roman veterinary expert, Vegetius, justly remarked that this was not right, for a horse has a very small stomach for an animal of his size and needs to be fed little and often. 'For horses', wrote Vegetius, 'digest regularly what they receive little by little. But what they have devoured all at once and grossly, they pass out whole and undigested with the dung.'

Excavations from Scythian barrows preserved by ice-caps from decay, and Scythian pictures and carvings show two kinds of horse. The common hacks were rough

Another type of hipposandal

ponies, about 13 hands, ungroomed, shaggy of coat, unkempt of mane and tail. An examination of their stomach contents shows that they were grass-fed and often half-starved in winter. But there are also remains of larger, better bred animals, chiefs' hunters and war-horses, perhaps. These pampered creatures were kept at grass in summer, lassooed when wanted, but in winter they were stabled and fed on their masters' scanty stocks of grain. They were groomed, their manes hogged for smartness and, so as not to interfere with the bow, their tails pulled or knotted. They were clearly a superior breed, coming perhaps from Persia whence the Chinese imported their 'heavenly stallions'. As has already been mentioned, the Scythians preferred riding geldings to mares or stallions. Nineteen hundred years later, among Cossacks of the same region, none but the poorest would ride a stallion. Mares were probably too precious to be ridden, being needed for milk and for breeding.

The Prophet Mohammed had a lot to say, or revealed to him, about feeding horses. 'Thou shalt be for a man a source of happiness and wealth; thy back shall be a seat of honour and thy belly of riches; every grain of barley given thee shall purchase indulgence for the sinner.' And elsewhere in the Koran, 'every grain of barley given to a horse is entered by God in the Register of Good Works'.

Western horsemen who have seen the modern Arab, Bedu or cultivator, as a horseman are not unduly impressed by him or by his horses. But there is no doubt that before he was seduced by the rival attractions of Cadillac convertibles for hunting and travel, the Arab gentleman was an expert horseman and considerate horsemaster.

On his favourite mare he lavished an affection equal at least to that bestowed upon his daughters, even keeping and feeding her in his tent, with the family. To encourage the breeding and care of good horses, the Prophet gave on every expedition an extra share of booty to the man who had the best horse. And Omar, the Prophet's companion, said, 'Love horses, tend them well, for they are worthy of your tenderness. Treat them like your own children, nourish them like friends of the family, clothe them with care. For the love of Allah, do not neglect this, or you will repent of it in this house and in the next.'

Horsemen of the world well know how the Arab horse, by his fire, courage, gentleness, intelligence, and devotion has repaid the love given him for centuries by the dwellers in black goatskin tents.

If Bertrandon de la Brocquière, Knight and First Esquire Carver of the Duke of Burgundy, had not been well versed in fifteenth-century horsemanship, he would never have undertaken his extraordinary ride from Jerusalem. His observations on Moslem horsemanship in Syria and Asia Minor, by then probably an amalgam of Arab and Turkish practices, may be taken as those of an expert.

He noted that the Moslems 'keep their horses very poor (i.e. in light condition), never feeding them but at night and then only given them five or six handfuls of barley and double the quantity of chopped straw, the whole put into a bag which hangs from their ears. At break of day they bridle, clean, and curry them, but never allow them to drink before midday – then in the afternoon every time they find water, and in the evening when they lodge or encamp. The last time they leave them unbridled for an hour like mules, and then, at a fixed moment, each gives his horse provender.' Early in his travels 'at eleven o'clock I gave my horse water, with oats and straw, according to the custom of our countries. This time the Turks said nothing to me; but at six o'clock in the evening, when, having given him his water, I was about fastening the bag that he might eat, they opposed it and took off the bag; for they never suffer their horses to eat but at night, and will not allow one to begin eating before the rest, except when they are at grass.'

Thus one notes that in the Middle Ages both Eastern and Western horsemen watered before feeding, and mixed chopped straw with oats and barley. Known in India as *bhoosa*, it was and still is, part of the ration for cavalry-horses in the Indian Army, to give bulk to the feed and help the horse's digestion. The nosebag seems, by implication, to be an Eastern device. The Moslems fed their ponies less than the Franks, always at a fixed time (a good principle), and kept them in lighter condition; European horsemen adhered to the modern fashion of feeding 'little and often'.

Horses in Europe were shod hot, with a heavy shoe having huge anti-skid calkins, held on by seven nails. Bertrand found that Eastern Shoes are 'light, thin, lengthened towards the heel and thinner there than at the toe, always a weak point. They are not turned up (i.e. they have no clips or calkins) and have but four nail-holes, two on each side. The nails are square, with a thick and heavy head. When a shoe is wanted, and it is necessary to work it to make it fit the hoof, it is done cold without ever putting it in the fire, which can be readily done because it is so thin. To pare the hoof they use a pruning-knife.' Horses difficult to shoe were cast for the operation. So well did a Turk shoe Bertrand's horse that 'on a fifty-day journey I had nothing to do with his feet, excepting that one of the fore ones which was pricked by a nail and made him lame'. This is surprising, one would have thought that in fifty days' travel the shoes would have worn thin and the hooves grown out so that the clenches rose. But the Eastern shoe, which kept the horse's heel down and so made the frog do its proper work, seems to have been better designed than the Western shoe with huge calkins at the heel which throw the horse's weight forward onto the toe, causing more wear at this weak point and preventing the frog from functioning as it ought. One would expect to find medieval European war-horses peculiarly susceptible to navicular disease and sidebone.

It is pleasing to find that 'should you have any business with a rich Turk, and call on him, he will carry you, to speak with you, to his stables which are consequently always kept very cool and very clean'. One is reminded of Bernard Shaw's observation: 'Go anywhere in England where there are natural, wholesome, contented, and really nice English people; and what do you always find? That the stables are the real centre of the household.'

Of the Franks of Outremer, one would expect the Templars, the Hospitallers, and the Teutonic Knights, with their dedication, strict discipline, and long experience of the East, to be the best horsemasters. For feeding, watering, exercising, riding, and clipping horses their Rules are set out in such meticulous detail as to suggest that the average brother-knight or sergeant could no more be trusted to look after his own horses than the average British cavalry-trooper, and required constant supervision.

The farrier sergeant of every 'convent' or castle was, of course, an important personage: on his skill and reliability everything depended . . . 'For want of a nail . . .'. In the Rules of the Templars he was given special privileges, including an extra horse. It seems that the brethren were expected to help him shoe their horses. At all events, from a brother's failure to attend nones and vespers when the bell summoned him, one of the few acceptable excuses was that he was busy in the forge, that the shoe was heating up or he was paring the hoof to receive it. On active service each brother carried a rasp. Did this mean that if his horse cast a shoe he was expected to prepare the hoof and cold-shoe it? Possibly.

All medieval horsemen, of East and West, took particular pains with the care of their best horses. In the words of the medieval Hindu *Asva-Sastra*, horses of the pure breed 'are the invaluable gems to be kept in the front part of kings' palaces'. Kings must obtain horses of the best quality and 'protect them with the great care and kindness that are due to them'. They must be patted daily, grudged no expense or trouble. 'When they turn old and weak in strength, their masters will have to treat them in such a way that they remain ever cheerful. To treat them in the best way, with a good heart, when they are healthy and when ill, is said by sages to be the means of obtaining all kinds of desires.' A European traveller, however, criticized Hindu horsemastership, particularly their feeding horses on rice and mutton curry on which they did not do well.

Gervase Markham certainly practised these precepts. A hunter on being brought up from grass should be fed for two or three days only on wheat-straw and water until his dung has changed from dark green to pale yellow. Then, not before, he shall be curried and rubbed, and his hooves picked out, twice daily, and rigged up at night in a single rug secured by a surcingle well padded with straw.

His exercise can then start, gently at first, followed by mucking-out, more thorough grooming, and a few handfuls of oats. He must be groomed all over with, in succession, a curry-comb, a brush, a wisp of straw, a stable-rubber, and the groom's wet hands until he is spotlessly clean 'with never a loose haze* nor any other filthy thing . . . for it will make his coat shine insomuch that you will almost discern your face therein'. His 'yard' must be taken out and washed, his mane and tail combed. After three weeks of this treatment, and feeding only upon wheat-straw and oats, 'you shall see his belly will be clean taken up and he will be comely and gaunt, his fatness firm and hard'. Now is the time for long, slow road-work, three hours at least, preferably every night.

During the second month he may be given coarse, sweet hay instead of wheat-straw. Besides oats, he can be given a 'bread' compounded of beans, wheat, and rye-flour baked into loaves. 'Some peradventure, that neither love this sport of hunt-ing nor make any care of a good horse, will imagine this bread is too costly, and say that common baker's horse-bread, which is made of nought but bran and wheat-chaff, shall do as much good. But if they did know how many inconveniences are found by this common horse-bread, they would without doubt alter their opinions.' For common baker's horse-bread, said Markham, has no virtue, lies heavy and sad in a horse's stomach, and causes consumption of the lungs, pain in the liver, the yellows, and divers other such-like diseases. He proceeds to describe in detail the particular advantages of beans, wheat, and rye.

The horse is now fit for an easy half-day's hunting, after which he must be rubbed till he is dry, then unsaddled and his back rubbed. After being rugged up, he should be given a feed of oats and hemp-seed, 'the gentlest and easiest scouring for a horse'. At nine o'clock at night he must again be strapped, watered, fed, and mucked-out.

After a longer day's hunting, he may need a more powerful scouring of rosemary and sweet butter, rolled into pellets and pushed down his throat, followed by a warm gruel of oatmeal, malt, and bran.

These scouring of hemp-seed and of rosemary and sweet butter, as they purge the body, 'perfume the head, open the pipes, and make clear passage for wind'. But they 'search nothing of themselves, but only purge away such matter as is before dissolved'. To 'purge the head, break phlegm, and preserve a horse of any disease that cometh of cold', Markham gave his hunters garlic stamped and lapped in rolls of butter. Stronger in effect was butter and saunders mingled together and made into pellets. To purge a fat horse of all gross matter, including his own grease, warm salad-oil and milk was very efficacious. Salad-oil and muscadine 'is of the same virtue that salad-oil and milk is, save that it is somewhat more comfortable. Mustard-seed 'in his provender is very good, for though it cleaneth the stomach little or nothing, yet it purgeth the head'.

'Lastly, and the chiefest scouring of all is this. Take the leaves of bore, and dry them at the fire till you may crush them to pieces, then mingle them with brimstone

* That which issues from the eyes.

beaten to powder, and give it to your horse in his provender, yet very discreetly, as by little and little at once, lest your horse take a loathe at it and so refuse it. This purgeth the head, stomach, and entrails of all manner of filthiness, leaving nothing that is unsound or unclean: it cureth the cold, it killeth the worms, grubs, or bots in a horse, and it never abaseth, but increaseth courage and flesh. Therefore it is to be given either to a foul horse or clean horse, but chiefly to the clean horse, because it shall preserve him from any foulness.'

When 'there comes nothing from your horse but clean excrements, without grease or filthiness, then you may be certain and well assured that your horse is clean within, sound and without any manner of imperfection, either of wind or disease'.

The horse was now ready for a more nourishing form of bread, made of oatmeal, bean-, wheat-, and rye-flour, knoden with new ale and white of eggs, baked in loaves. On this, with oats, 'see that you feed your horse extremely, even so much as he will eat'.

Thus purged and fortified, the horse could be brought into full work, hunted twice a week and on two or three more days exercised by following hounds at a walk or trot. If he was to be entered for a 'match' (race), for the last three days of his training the owner should 'night and day watch' him, making him eat all the meat he eats out of your hand, and when he hath eaten a little, offer him a little dishful of water to drink, and then give him more bread, then offer him more water, and in this manner feed him till he be full. Then let him take his rest and lie down, and always when he riseth do the like, and in this sort feed him till his match day; provided always that you let him have hay in his rack, and then let him be led to the field, bequeathing the rest to God and good fortune.'

Thus Markham dieted and trained his hunters, particularly those which would be entered for a match or wild-goose chase. It will be noted that the responsibility for all this work, for mixing and cooking the bread, for sitting up with the horse and feeding him by hand, Markham lays on the reader of his book, the owner, the hunting-man himself – not on any groom.

The 'bread' and purges of varying strength which he recommends are not un-usual, nor are they in any way veterinary remedies: they are, by implication, part of the diet and training of an ordinary hunter, and a good instance of man's slavish pandering to the supposed whims of his 'servant'. We need not suppose that Mark-ham, writing in the early seventeenth century, invented all this. It is far more likely that he was simply setting down in writing the accumulated lore of English horsemen for two or three centuries.

The diet of racehorses was even more costly and exotic. 'When next morning you find your horse not up, let him rest till he rises, then give him a quart of dried oats which have been washed in ale or beer. After he has eaten them, hold up his head and put a new-laid egg down his throat, squirting some ale or beer into his mouth after it.' In preparation for a race in 1651 the Prince d'Harcourt and the Duc de Joyeuse trained their horses *à l'anglaise*, on bread flavoured with aniseed, and giving them each, on the last two days before the race, 300 fresh eggs. It is a wonder that this did not produce a bilious attack.

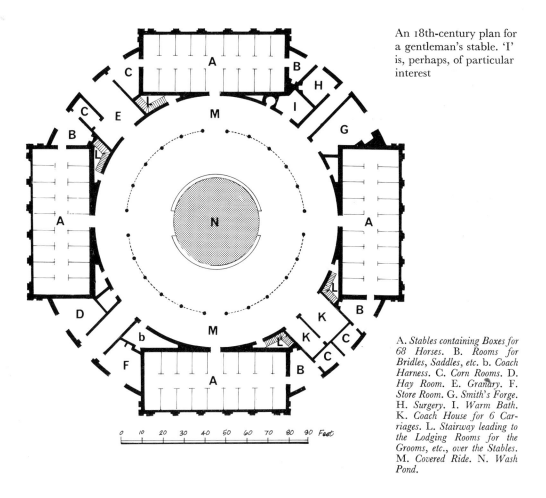

An 18th-century plan for a gentleman's stable. 'I' is, perhaps, of particular interest

A. *Stables containing Boxes for 68 Horses.* B. *Rooms for Bridles, Saddles, etc.* b. *Coach Harness.* C. *Corn Rooms.* D. *Hay Room.* E. *Granary.* F. *Store Room.* G. *Smith's Forge.* H. *Surgery.* I. *Warm Bath.* K. *Coach House for 6 Carriages.* L. *Stairway leading to the Lodging Rooms for the Grooms, etc., over the Stables.* M. *Covered Ride.* N. *Wash Pond.*

As for stallions at stud, their ardour was maintained by the addition to their provender of oysters, always believed a potent aphrodisiac.

Markham was a civilian. How did English soldiers compare with him in the care which he lavished on his horses?

In the words of *The Old Cavalry Soldier* (1800), 'The rider must live only for his horse, which is his legs, his safety, his honour, and his reward.'

Did the average British cavalry-soldier live up to these admirable sentiments? One must record, with regret, that he did not.

Marlborough's troopers seem to have looked after their horses well; but in the wars against the French Revolution and Napoleon, the British trooper's bad horse management was a matter of comment by friend and foe alike.

Wellington, with extreme care for feeding his armies, ensured that British cavalry-horses were fed better than those of the French, though the result was not uniformly happy. 'The French cavalry', said the Duke, 'is often more manageable and useful than the English, because it is always kept in hand and can be stopped at a word of command. This partly results from our horses being kept in a higher condition.' But even his genius could not always produce oats and hay where there are none, and in the Peninsula, except in summer, this was often the case. A few days work in early spring, covering the siege of Ciudad Rodrigo, brought the Heavy Brigade to a standstill: the horses were reduced to pulling up withered grass and eating it complete with roots, earth, and stones.

In such circumstances it was often remarked that the troopers of the King's German Legion looked after their horses much better than the British. 'The German', wrote Captain Mercer, 'would sell everything to feed his horse, while the British dragoon looked upon the animal as a curse and a source of perpetual drudgery to himself.' On one occasion, when forage was particularly short, a King's German Legion trooper was seen feeding his horse with his own beef-ration – a story which recalls the Boran giraffe-hunters feeding their ponies on giraffe-meat.* Sir John Burgoyne remembered that the difference in care bestowed on the horses by the British and German dragoon was so great that the King's German Legion 'could always put a hundred horses in the ranks to our ten'.

Forty years of peace did nothing to improve British cavalry horsemastership. Nor, in the Crimean War, did the attitude to his horses of Lord Cardigan, commanding the Light Brigade. The idea was prevalent that it was 'wather disgwaceful' for a 'cavalwy' officer or 'twooper' ever to be on his feet. Combined with His Lordship's predilection for moving always at a gallop, this resulted in Cardigan's notorious 'Sore Back Reconnaissance' which, without any contact with the enemy, killed 80 and permanently disabled many more of the 196 horses which took part. Mrs Duberly, wife of an officer of the 8th Hussars, saw their return, 'and a piteous sight it was – men on foot driving and goading the wretched, wretched horses . . . a cruel parade of death'.

In the camp above Balaclava there was one handful of grain a day for the horses of the Light Brigade. In the harbour six miles below there was plenty, but no pack-mules to carry it up. Rather than detail his cavalry-horses to the degrading duty of carrying up their own food, Lord Cardigan let them starve by the hundred, let them die of starvation after gnawing leather straps, ropes, and one another's tails to stumps.

Despite the scandals of the Crimea, matters had not improved much by the time of the Egyptian Campaign of 1882. 'A few days campaigning in Egypt saw the cavalry disappear: underfed and overweighted, they melted away like ice in the summer sun. Starved horses were seen standing next to a growing corn crop of which those in authority failed to take advantage, for the reason, it is said, that they did not recognize it was a forage-plant.'

But two years later the 19th Hussars in the Nile Campaign of 1884–5, gave a real insight into what horses and men could do, under severe conditions, provided they were managed with intelligence and imagination. 'The resuscitation of the cavalry arm', wrote Major-General Smith, a distinguished veterinary officer, 'began from that small nucleus of earnest officers and well-trained men; crystallization had begun when the war in South Africa broke out; the crystals were small and imperfect, and readily dissolved on agitation; they soon received this stimulus, and at the hands of the authorities.'

* In the Aleutian Islands ponies were fed upon dried salmon.

Apart from the Royal Artillery, who always looked after their horses well, our mounted troops in South Africa consisted of regular cavalry, irregulars recruited mainly in the colonies, Imperial Yeomanry, and Mounted Infantry. The regular cavalry were not bad horsemasters in peacetime, though their horses, in the opinion of Major-General Smith, were grossly overloaded; the colonial irregulars understood horse management on the cattle and sheep range, where there was always plenty of spare horses available and no animal need be overworked; but neither knew how to keep a single, overloaded, overworked animal fit for weeks on end. The Imperial Yeomanry contained a nucleus of hunting squires and farmers, but of the 1901 contingent it was discovered that three-quarters had never even sat on a horse before passing a 'riding test' on enlistment, and the remainder had ridden very little. As for the Mounted Infantry, for them it was (in Kipling's words) 'three days to "learn equitation" and six months of blooming well trot'. One, quite seriously, asked an officer whether he should feed his horse beef or mutton.

Whether they rode well or badly, none of our mounted troops understood how to look after horses on active service. The cavalry looked upon the horse as a mere conveyance, and considered it dishonourable to be seen on foot. They had never been trained to dismount, off-saddle, water, and graze their horses at every opportunity, and it was remarked that the only men who were 'constantly and eagerly on the look-out for a chance to save their horses and give them a bite of grass or a drink of water were those South African Colonials who rode their own horses'. Officers took no steps to prevent the persistent overloading of horses: 'The produce of a neighbouring farm hung to one side of the saddle causes it to heel over and press

Grooms at work in an Assyrian camp

Greek grooms
at work

on the withers; a chair for firewood hanging from the rear arch, or a farm-door resting on the root of the neck, are not features which can escape observation, and are totally ruinous to horses' backs. . . . There is no part of a mounted soldier's equipment which offers greater temptation to the rider to carry weight than the [saddle] wallets; anything and everything finds its way there, the most tempting souvenir being an unexploded shell.'

In the words of General Brabazon, 'I really believe, although I say it, that I was the only man, certainly the only General Officer, who tried to stop the abuse of horse-flesh. I never saw such a shameful abuse of horse-flesh in the whole course of my life as existed throughout the whole campaign, and not an attempt was made to check it. . . . I was shocked, I was horrified.'

Of all errors made during this error-ridden campaign, perhaps the most disastrous was that of the Commander-in-Chief, Lord Roberts who, with a view to reducing the Army's 'tail', decreed that the daily ration should be only ten pounds of grain per horse *and no hay*. Ten pounds of grain with ample hay is barely enough for a 15 hands horse in full work, quite inadequate for large, heavily laden troop-horses on active service. But there was no hay: the deficiency had to be made up by grazing. Apart from the fact that for much of the year there is very little grass on the high veldt, horses in a campaign do not get the time to graze. It takes a horse about five hours to eat a modest ration of fifteen pounds of hay: if he has, so to speak, to cut and carry his own hay, it may take him twice as long; and even under the best management, troop-horses on active service are not able to spend all that time grazing. (This does not, of course, mean that men should not give them every chance to graze.) So our horses in South Africa were perpetually underfed. Underfed horses feel the cold more, lose condition rapidly, and develop saddle sores or just break down under hard work.*

* Tschiffely, after his famous ride from Buenos Aires to Washington, told a friend of mine that he always kept his horses on short commons, and that British horsemen always overfed theirs. In general, however, experience seems to confirm the British cavalry doctrine that, *so long as a horse is not soft*, the bigger the condition in which he starts a campaign, the better he will stand it. Tschiffely, of course, rode slowly, led a spare horse, and was a very experienced and expert rider and horsemaster.

There were, at the beginning of the war, no spare veterinary stores, so when the issue stocks were exhausted, horses needing treatment just had to do without. There were too few farriers, too few shoes and nails. On one occasion it took seventy-four telegrams to obtain the services of a farrier for a Mounted Infantry regiment.

Finally, no arrangements were made to condition remounts before issuing them to units. They were taken straight off the ship and railed up-country, weak, soft, quite unaccustomed in most cases to hard feed. Those from Europe arrived, often, in October, in 'blackberry condition' – that is to say, soft, their winter coats grown: in South Africa it was then summer, hot by day but very cold by night. At first there was no issue of horse-rugs, so if these unfortunate animals were clipped, they froze at night: if not, they sweated profusely and lost condition by day. The original issue of horses lasted fairly well, but remounts straight off the ship, many of good quality, died like flies, or had to be cast after only a few hours' work.

One regular regiment, which seems to have been unusually careful of its horses and certainly kept careful records, wore out during the campaign one horse for every three and a half miles it marched – in all, 3,281 horses. It was calculated that

Greek youth trying to stop two horses drinking from the wine-bowl

the Imperial forces as a whole lost 7–8 per cent of its horses per month, or 326,000 in all, over three and a half years, out of 494,181 sent to the seat of war.* Only a very small proportion were lost by enemy action.

It is interesting to note that by far the worst horses were from Russia and Hungary: the best, apart from Cape horses, were from Canada and North America, though Walers did very well provided they could get enough food.

* These figures are quite creditable in comparison with the record of the Prussian Army in the Franco-Prussian War of 1870. Operating in a temperate climate and a fertile country, close to their bases and well served by rail communications, they lost over a million horses in eight months, having started the war with about 300,000 and captured many thousands at Sedan.

Man washing a horse by the Japanese artist Hokusai

Major-General Smith, Sir Douglas Haig, and others made stupendous efforts to teach throughout the Army the lessons so cruelly learned in South Africa, with the result that by 1914 the British Army's horsemastership was of a very high standard. For the closing years of its history, the British cavalry-horse was as well looked after as any in the world.

Meanwhile, civilian horsemastership in western Europe followed the high principles established by Markham and de la Guerinière, if not their exact dieting and methods. In France and England – indeed in most European countries and in the United States and British Dominions – there was little difference in the service given by man to the horse. Only one fault did Major-General Smith, never sparing in his criticisms, find in continental stable management.

'It is usual for motives of economy [?] to leave the bedding down in the stables of France, Germany, and Italy for periods of three or four months at a time; meanwhile the dung and urine are covered over daily with fresh straw and well trodden by the horse into a firm, yet elastic, bed which grows. When it has assumed an inconvenient height, it is removed, and the putrid condition of the material and its overpowering stench when the mass is opened up cannot be adequately described. This pernicious system of continental bedding proved popular. The officers like it: the fermentation of the mass kept the stables warm, the saving in bedding gave them a larger ration of hay and corn to work with; the men liked it because it represented a fraction of the usual labour. The veterinary services condemned it as insanitary and destructive to the feet. British stable management had hitherto been regarded as the acme of perfection, the keynote of which was cleanliness. By the adoption of this filthy system in our cavalry stables the hand of the clock of progress was put back. The authorities . . . took no action to abolish the disgusting practice.'

The 'disgusting practice' continues on the Continent, with no very dire effects. In Spain, indeed, the horse-bedding in inns is enriched by chickens and human beings, both of whom use the stables as a lavatory. Shortage of labour and shortage of time have, since the war, led to a revival of the 'filthy system' in England. I am told that it does no harm whatsoever to the horses' feet or general health, and it certainly saves the hard-pressed, do-it-yourself horse-owner a lot of time and trouble. I must admit, however, that I have never had the courage to try it in my own stable.

Nineteenth-century stable management was, of course, markedly facilitated by a profusion of stud-grooms, strappers, and odd-job boys; but if these failed, even a lady owner was expected to know and do her stuff. Mrs Power O'Donoghue had no patience with ladies who were too grand to put their hand to anything in the shape of work. 'I hope, however, I am not writing for any such silly person. You should never be above looking after *everything* connected with your riding-gear. It will not lessen your dignity one whit; on the contrary. . . . One of the most perfectly ladylike women whom I have ever met, on one occasion groomed and fed her own hunter, when the stableman who had charge of him was found tipsy, on her return one wintry evening from a long day with the hounds; and she did it too before ever removing her habit.'

It is my belief that riding-horses are now as well looked after as ever in their long history, either by devoted owners or by stable-girls who, for sheer dedication to the

313

horse, serve in its temples for a pittance, a mere fraction of what they could earn as typists or shop-assistants. That they do so with knowledge and skill is due largely to the Pony Club.

There is no doubt that kindness, and constant handling from an early age, produces quiet, confident horses. People think of stallions as 'difficult', but the white stallions of the Spanish Riding School in Vienna are perfectly quiet. So are the bull-fighting stallions of Portugal, handled kindly but taught obedience from the very start. On stud farms where the bull-fighting horses are bred, the mares are brought in from grass in the evening to a vast stable where they are tied in rows to long mangers. Their colts follow, all very quiet and well behaved, and stay with their mothers until a bell-mare leads them off to another building to their special supper.

The principles of grooming have not changed much since Xenophon's day, nor the grooming-kit since Gervase Markham's. In some stables horses are cleaned by electrically operated brushes which save labour but do not, perhaps, do the necessary job of massaging a horse's muscles, while cleaning it, as well as can be done by hand. The clipping-machine, worked first by a hand-operated wheel, later by electricity, is perhaps the most important development in grooming, greatly easing what in the days of the Knights Hospitaller must have been a long and laborious task. Easier clipping made, in the nineteenth century, a great difference to the performance of hunters, since an unclipped horse, if galloped much, sweats profusely and loses condition.

As in the past, horses are fed basically on hay, on oats when it is easily available, and barley elsewhere, and on bran. Beans, flaked maize, linseed, chopped carrots, apples, mineral salts – any or all of these are added as the owner wishes. Abroad, lucerne (alfalfa) is an excellent feed. Markham's horse-bread, out of use for three centuries, has recently returned in the form of horse-nuts, made up to various recipes and cooked in factories, not in the owner's kitchen. They are an easy way of giving a mixed feed, but perhaps no better than variations on the traditional diet of oats and bran.

LAST THOUGHTS ON THE SUBJECT

Any horseman who gives thought to the matter must from time to time have said to himself, 'We people can't be very bright, to take 4,000 years to discover how a horse likes being ridden. And even now we are not agreed on it.'

There is an element of truth in this, especially when applied to the horsemen of western Europe and of the eastern United States. For at least 500 years after the armoured lancer had been chased off the battle-field, we continued to ride, more or less, in the style developed specifically for him. It did not perhaps much matter for the first 300 years, when cross-country work did not involve jumping obstacles: but for two centuries, during which jumping became more and more the very essence of cross-country riding, we did almost everything ingenuity could suggest to stop a horse jumping or to ensure that he fall. And yet this noble animal continued to leap the most enormous obstacles. We seem, now, to be on the right lines, but of course d'Aure and Fillis thought so too.

Apart from this extraordinary lapse, horsemen of the world seem on the whole to

16th-century man ministering to his horse

have adapted their riding pretty well to the work their horses have to do. The jockey, the cowboy, the stockman, the nomad, the foxhunter, the show-jumper (and until recently the soldier) all ride in different ways because they are all doing different jobs. They *are* all right. There is no such thing as a general-purpose seat to suit all the jobs a horse must do.

But I think we can learn a lot from the way other people ride. Cowboys are now tending to shorten their leathers; foxhunters adopt the forward seat; Nolan strove to impress the British cavalry with the efficacy of Oriental horsemanship. If we had taken more notice of how Tartars and Cossacks rode, the modern cross-country seat might have been developed a century or more earlier. There is no need to suppose it is the last word in equitation.

It is the variety of horse-cultures that gives the subject its interest. I do not in this book pretend to tell anyone how to ride. What I have tried to do is to tell them how various people have ridden in the past and still ride, and why – and leave the reader to draw his own conclusions.

An early
horseshoe

BIBLIOGRAPHY OF CHIEF WORKS CONSULTED

J. Adams, *An Analysis of Horsemanship*, 1799

F. E. Adcock, *The Greek and Macedonian Art of War*, University of California Press, 1961

J. K. Anderson, *Ancient Greek Horsemanship*, University of California Press, 1961

Ruy de Andrade, *Alrededor del Caballo Español*, Lisbon, 1954

Comte d'Aure, *Traité d'Equitation*, 1847

F. Baucher, *Method d'Equitation*, 1874

The Bayeux Tapestry

Haldine Beamish, *Cavaliers of Portugal*, Geoffrey Bles, 1966

T. Bedingfield, *The Art of Riding following Xenophon and Grisone*, 1584

Bertrandon de la Brocquière, travels of, translated by Thomas Johnes, 1807

A. D. H. Bivar, 'The Stirrup and its Origins', *Oriental Art*, N.S., I, no. 2 (1955), 3–7

T. Blundeville, *The Art of Riding*, 1534

T. Blundeville, *The Four Chief Offices of Horsemanship*, 1570

E. W. Bovill, *The England of Nimrod and Surtees*, Oxford University Press, 1959

G. Catlin, *Letters and Notes of the Manners, Customs and Condition of the North American Indians*, 1841

William Cavendish, Duke of Newcastle, *A General System of Horsemanship in all its Branches*, 1657

H. D. Chamberlin, *Riding and Schooling Horses*, Derrydale Press, 1933

J. Curle, *A Roman Frontier Post and its People*, Glasgow, 1911

Henri de Curzon, ed., *La Règle du Temple*, Société de l'Histoire de France, 1886

R. W. Davies, 'Training Grounds of the Roman Cavalry', *Archaeological Journal*, 1968

Edward, Duke of York, *The Master of Game* (1410), New York, 1951

C. D. B. Ellis, *Leicestershire and the Quorn*, 1961

W. Sidney Felton, *Masters of Equitation*, 1962

J. Fillis, *Breaking and Riding*, Hurst & Blackett, 1911

Brian Vesey Fitzgerald, *The Book of the Horse*, Nicholson & Watson, 1946

Marija Gimbutas, *The Balts*, Thames & Hudson, 1963

Federico Grisone, *Gli Ordini di Cavalcare*, 1550

François Robichon de la Guerinière, *École de Cavalerie*, Paris, 1751

Ruth C. Harvey, *Moriz von Craun and the Chivalric World*, Clarendon Press, 1961

Mrs A. M. Hayes, *The Horsewoman*, Thacker, 1893

M. H. Hayes, *The Points of the Horse*, 1893

M. H. Hayes, *Among Horses in South Africa*, 1900

Hemasuri, *Asva Sastra* (The Science of Horses), fourteenth century

Henry Herbert, Earl of Pembroke, *Military Equitation*, 1778

R. Hinde, *The Discipline of the Light Horse*, 1778

J. Hislop, *Steeplechasing*, Hutchinson, 1955

P. K. Hitti, *An Arab-Syrian Gentleman and Warrior* (Usama ibn Munquidh), Cambridge, 1924

Doreen Archer Houblon, *Side Saddle*, Country Life, 1951

R. W. Howard, *The Horse in America*, Follett, 1965

R. W. Hunt, W. A. Pantin and R. W. Southern (eds.), *Studies in Mediaeval History presented to F. M. Powicke*, Clarendon Press, 1948

Comte Jean de Joinville, *Life of St. Louis*, Sheed & Ward, 1935

Kai Kaus ibn Iskander *Qabus Nama, or A Mirror for Princes*, London, The Cresset Press, 1951

H. Lhote, 'Le Cheval et le Chameau dans les Peintures et Gravures Rupestres du Sahara', *Bulletin de l'Institut Français de l'Afrique Noire*, XV, (1953)

Beauvoir de Lisle, *Polo in India*, Thacker, 1907

V. S. Littauer, *Horseman's Progress*. D. Van Nostrand, 1961

Magnus Magnusson and Herman Palsson, *Njal's Saga*, Penguin

G. Markham, *How to Chase, Ride, Train and Diet both Hunting Horses and Running Horses*, 1599

M. F. McTaggart, *Mount and Man*, Country Life, 1935

R. H. Nevill, *The Sport of Kings*, Methuen, 1926

Nimrod, *The Horse and Hound*, 1863

L. E. Nolan, *The Training of Cavalry Remounts*, 1852

Mrs Power O'Donoghue, *Riding for Ladies*, Thacker, 1887

C. Oman, *The Art of War in the Middle Ages*, Blackwell, 1884

A. de Pluvinel, *Maneige Royale*, 1624

R. Pocock, *Horses*, John Murray, 1917

A. Podhajsky, *Equitation*, Country Life, 1938

W. Ridgeway, *The Origin and Influence of the Thoroughbred Horse*, Cambridge University Press, 1905

J. Riley Smith, *The Knights of St. John in Jerusalem and Cyprus, 1050–1310*, Macmillan, 1967

P. Santini, *The Forward Impulse*, Country Life, 1936

Michael Seth-Smith, Peter Willett, Roger Mortimer and John Lawrence, *The History of Steeplechasing*, Michael Joseph, 1967

Michael Seth-Smith, *Bred to the Purple*, Frewin, 1968

Lady Diana Shedden and V. Batthurst, *To Whom the Goddess*, Hutchinson, 1932

F. Smith, *A Veterinary History of the War in South Africa*, 1915

M. A. Storeridge, *A Horse of Your Own*, Doubleday, 1968

R. S. Surtees, *Mr. Sponge's Sporting Tour*, 1853

R. S. Surtees, *Mr. Facey Romford's Hounds*, 1865

T. Talbot-Rice, *The Scythians*, Thames & Hudson, 1957

G. Tylden, *Horse and Saddlery*, 1965

J. B. Ward Perkins, 'The Iron Age Horseshoe', *Antiquaries Journal*, XXI, (1941)

Samuel Wayte, *The Equestrian's Manual*, London, 1850

G. J. Whyte Melville, *Riding Recollections*, 1878

C. Woodham Smith, *The Reason Why*, Constable, 1953

R. Wormser, *The Yellowlegs, The Story of the U.S. Cavalry*, Doubleday, 1966

F. E. Zeuner, *The History of Domesticated Animals*, Hutchinson, 1963

Numerous articles in *Riding, Horse and Hound* and other equestrian papers